Sing the Rage

Sing the Rage

Listening to Anger after Mass Violence

SONALI CHAKRAVARTI

THE UNIVERSITY OF CHICAGO PRESS   CHICAGO AND LONDON

SONALI CHAKRAVARTI is assistant professor of government at Wesleyan University.

The University of Chicago Press, Chicago 60637
The University of Chicago Press, Ltd., London
© 2014 by The University of Chicago
All rights reserved. Published 2014.
Printed in the United States of America
23 22 21 20 19 18 17 16 15 14   1 2 3 4 5

ISBN-13: 978-0-226-11998-4 (cloth)
ISBN-13: 978-0-226-12004-1 (e-book)
DOI: 10.7208/chicago/9780226120041.001.0001 (e-book)

Library of Congress Cataloging-in-Publication Data

Chakravarti, Sonali, author.
    Sing the rage : listening to anger after mass violence / Sonali Chakravarti.
      pages ; cm
    Includes bibliographical references and index.
    ISBN 978-0-226-11998-4 (cloth : alkaline paper) — ISBN 978-0-226-12004-1 (e-book)
    1. Anger—Moral and ethical aspects. 2. Anger—Philosophy. 3. Justice
(Philosophy) 4. Nuremberg War Crime Trials, Nuremberg, Germany, 1946–
1949. 5. Arendt, Hannah, 1906–1975. 6. Eichmann, Adolf, 1906–1962—Trials,
litigation, etc. 7. South Africa. Truth and Reconciliation Commission. I. Title.
    BJ1535.A6C45 2014
    179′.8—dc23

                                                              2013027390

♾ This paper meets the requirements of ANSI/NISO Z39.48-1992 (Permanence of Paper).

TO MY PARENTS,
RUPALI AND PRADIP CHAKRAVARTI,
AND MY BROTHER, DEVJIT

Sing—Goddess—the rage of Achilles, the son of Peleus, that brought countless ills upon the Athenians

HOMER, *The Iliad*

Contents

Acknowledgments

I had the good fortune to be affiliated with several institutions that provided support for this book, including the Ann Plato Fellowship at Trinity College, the Center for Humanities at Wesleyan University, the Centennial Center at the American Political Science Association, and the University Center for Human Values at Princeton University. The book was conceived under the wise and incisive guidance of Seyla Benhabib, whose influence is strong in these pages. Bryan Garsten has been a generous adviser and interlocutor. Many thanks to Ange-Marie Hancock, whose approach to interdisciplinary work continues to inspire, and to John McCormick for his astute counsel. I am grateful to Don Moon, Nancy Schwartz, and Stephen Angle at Wesleyan University for their feedback and warm encouragement. Sharon Krause and Colin Leach provided helpful comments at exactly the right time. I benefited much from exchanges with Ernesto Verdeja, Andrew Schaap, Richard Wilson, Bonnie Honig, and Christina Tarnopolsky.

Yves Winter, Katherine Lemons, and Joshua Chambers-Letson offered camaraderie and freewheeling conversations, scholarly and otherwise. Kushanava Choudhury and Shatema Threadcraft reminded me when to leave academic conventions behind in pursuit of other ideals. Eirene Visvardi helped with the title and with many of the ideas along the way. Neetu Khanna was there to celebrate the small achievements.

Joe Scheier-Dolberg and Sarah Benis Scheier-Dolberg gave me, in so many ways, a home in New York City. I was nurtured by the kindness and intellectual curiosity of Bethany Robertson, Peter Murray, Rachel Mumford, and Jason Mumford. Cecilia Tsu offered many opportunities to pick fruit. For her steadfast care and sisterhood, I thank Reena Vaidya Krishna. While accompanying me on this path, Supriya Kota helped make sense of the solitude. Talks with Miriam Joffe-Block revealed the humor of it all. Many good meals were shared with Maya Dutton-Linn and Stephen Linn. Sanford DeVoe always took the call and responded with affection. My love to James Bonney, a true companion in all things.

For his discerning editorial eye and friendship, I thank Robert Huddleston. Isabella Litke, exemplary research assistant, knows the testimonies as well as I do. My editor, Elizabeth Branch Dyson, was an intrepid trail guide to whom I owe a great debt; I appreciate the hard work of Russ Damian.

This book is dedicated to my parents, Rupali and Pradip Chakravarti, and my brother, Devjit, for all the ways they have nourished me with their love.

*   *   *

Chapter 1 was previously published in *Constellations*, vol. 15, no. 2 (June 2008): 223–235, and I thank them for permission to reprint it here.

Introduction

The proceedings of the South African Truth and Reconciliation Commission (TRC), from 1996 to 1998, were a spectacle worthy of the world's attention. Day after day, individuals took the stand to speak about the violence they had experienced during apartheid. They were mothers, freedom fighters, and policemen, but all had experienced devastation and loss. The goal of "reconciliation" was embedded in the name of the commission, and for many watching the proceedings, the language of forgiveness evoked by Desmond Tutu, the chair of the commission, was striking. Even more of interest were the moments of anger. For the commissioners, the anger expressed by witnesses was both understandable and perpetually surprising, but they seemed uncertain of its value within the process. The anger was too volatile and too violent to celebrate, but it could not be excised.

The words of Godfrey Xolile Yona, who appeared before the TRC in October 1996, exemplify the type of testimony that is the catalyst for my thinking about the significance of anger in testimony after mass violence and its relationship to restorative justice. Detained for his involvement with the anti-apartheid organization the African National Congress (ANC), Yona gave testimony that focused on his experiences while in prison:

> You must remember how it feels if a warder comes to you every time and says you are going to hang and you see those people being hanged and they legitimately hang. I mean how can I trust anybody, I have to trust them, I have to believe in what they say when they say you are going to hang. . . . What I want to tell you there is nobody who has returned from death row who is normal because that thing in death row, even when I sleep at home I dream. I dream

that I am still on death row. . . . We also fought for this country but there is no future for us. We have also fought for this country. We are unemployed. The government, when you look for work, you need qualifications, you must have certain knowledge, you must be trained for that job but my question, my only question is, when we threw stones and petrol bombs, they didn't look for qualifications. They didn't look for knowledge. When I can refer to our President's statement that while he was incarcerated he said keep the country ungovernable and that is exactly what we did but today we, who did those things, we remained behind. There is nothing left for us. If you can see from all the political prisoners, all of those who fought in the liberation struggle, they have been left behind. All the people who sit there and who have food to eat, they have never been part of the liberation struggle.[1]

I define anger as bitter (and potentially violent) feelings that are in reaction to a slight and are directed toward someone or something, and the anger in Yona's testimony is evident when he says, "We also fought for this country." He is upset at being exploited for his labor during the anti-apartheid struggle and then becoming irrelevant within political life. Similarly, the sarcasm of his formulation, "When we threw stones and petrol bombs, they didn't look for qualifications," is a moment that reveals an intensely negative response to ANC leadership and marks an important shift between past and present in his testimony. One of the challenges of listening to anger in the context of victim testimony is such chronological reverberation. Yona's testimony begins with a specific experience but then reveals anger at economic conditions and at what he perceives as the emptiness of citizenship and participation. I suggest that Yona's testimony has value for political life not in spite of its anger but, in part, because of it. He articulated concerns that are central to a society as it rebuilds after mass violence. Prison altered his understanding of interpersonal trust and his ability to feel safe from violence, even after he was released. On one level, his testimony reflected his extreme psychological distress. On another level, however, his testimony had *political*, not just psychological, significance, and the anger he expressed should be seen as necessary for the process of restoring relations of citizenship. His anger is not only connected to the conditions that led to his arrest and his treatment in detention but also to his loss of identity in the present. In the latter part of his testimony, Yona makes a direct appeal for improved socioeconomic opportunities and the recognition of the sacrifices of individuals who were part of the movement to end apart-

heid. The interaction between anger as expressing a desire for reparations and anger for recognition is part of the complexity of its role in the
context of truth commissions.

When Yona says that he had to trust the prison warden who told him
he would be hanged, Yona evinces the difficulty of trusting others under extreme circumstances. The fact that his life was spared was a gift,
but he continues to live in constant fear. This distorted relationship with
authority seems to have also continued after he was released, even if he
does not articulate it. For him to be able to participate as a citizen, there
must be the opportunity to alter this relationship with authority and with
fellow citizens. The language of *trust* in his testimony is not incidental; it
is one of the important ways that the emotions of victim testimony take
on a political dimension. The way trust is tested, strained, and destroyed
during mass violence is the backdrop to its cultivation between speaker
and listener during the process of a truth commission.

In light of this, my book has three goals: the first is to examine the history of victim testimony and the particular case of the TRC; the second
is to analyze the most powerful arguments against the inclusion of anger
in the political sphere; and the third is to offer a model for understanding
its significance. The period of transitional justice may include war crimes
trials, truth commissions, reparations, lustration, and memorials, among
other initiatives, and it is a unique moment in political life because the
social contract is in the process of being redrawn (and because political
obligation is reconsidered); as part of this process the community must
respond to the most serious crimes on a large scale, a task more overwhelming than the work of everyday politics. Truth commissions carry
the potential for rebuilding political life during this singular period both
by defining what justice should mean as well as by fostering interpersonal trust.[2] An engagement with anger is critical to achieving these
ends, and the benefits of anger during the transitional period after mass
violence require looking at three different dimensions of interpretation:
cognitive, confrontational, and kinetic. First, the cognitive-evaluative
dimension leads to insights (difficult to obtain through surveys or other
mechanisms) into what citizens fear and what they need to restore trust
(or to experience it for the first time) in political institutions and each
other.[3] The fears help explain why individuals are unwilling or unable
to participate in political life, while the needs expressed reveal desires
for material reparations, recognition, or reform. Often the witness expressing anger does not see the relationship between the emotion and

larger issues at stake in the process of politics, but a truth commission is the best tool available to make these connections evident. Second, with the confrontational dimension of interpretation, the expression of anger is about the limits of what it is possible to repair in the aftermath of violence. This type of anger is not asking for uptake or recognition but is a way to confront the limitations of the political sphere, including the inadequacy of punishment or repair. Because of its existence on the margins of what is considered political, listening to confrontational anger facilitates the redrawing of the boundaries between the public and private spheres. This reconsideration is necessary because old distinctions no longer hold and new ones can emerge through the agonistic encounter of multiple perspectives at a truth commission. Third, the kinetic significance of anger exists in the sound of the voice and the claim that it makes on the listener to acknowledge the specificity of individual experience and the visceral grasping at survival that is often communicated through anger.

To achieve this engagement with anger, I emphasize the political practice of listening and its relation to judgment. Listening is the praxis which connects anger and justice: without it, anger can only be catharsis or monologue, not constitutive of the process of justice. Listening to anger requires openness to difficult content conveyed in an unsettling tone, and since anger can be quickly dismissed or met with defensiveness about one's culpability, it is one of the most challenging types of communication in political life. To achieve the goal of trust through an acknowledgment of shared risk in the context of a truth commission, citizens and commissioners must develop the skills to listen, respond, and judge. In addition to these two groups of listeners (citizens in the audience and the commissioners), the victims themselves are a third group who are developing new skills as listeners, both in response to what they hear at their own testimonies and those of others. This experience of listening should contribute to the transition from victim to citizen that is one of the primary goals of an engagement with anger.

While informed by an analysis of the transcripts of the TRC, the project is grounded in the history of political thought and debate about the relationship between reason and emotion. The wealth of scholarship on the topic suggests that the argument for divorcing reason from emotion does not have enough life in it even to be a straw man. From Plato to John Rawls, it has been convincingly argued that our ability to reason is, to varying degrees, intrinsically linked to the affective components of the self, including through motivation, cognition, and phenomenological experience. My exploration of the role of anger builds upon the significant work in recent years on these questions in such varied fields as neuroscientific research on the role of emotion, Aristotelian accounts of *thumos*, the impact of shame and disgust on the demos, and the signaling role of the emotions in political psychology.[4] Taken together, these disciplines have much to say about what emotions can be said to reveal and how the capacity to feel and express emotion is critical to the practice of judgment.[5] Within political theory, it is not only Aristotle but also Jean-Jacques Rousseau, David Hume, and Adam Smith whose writings have prompted scholars to suggest that the communication of pain and the response of sympathy is not tangential to the process of politics, but rather at its center.[6] The ability to communicate with fellow citizens in an affective way must necessarily, following this line of thinking, be taught and fostered; it cannot be replaced by the individualistic act of voting or the hostile ambivalence of privacy-seeking strangers.

I make two primary contributions to this literature.[7] First, I am taking on the difficult case of anger while others have often focused on less controversial emotions such as compassion or empathy. Anger is usually seen as a runaway train, impossible to control and likely to wreak havoc, and this, along with the difficulty of distinguishing "helpful" anger from senseless rage, appears to have curtailed work on the topic.[8] I have been influenced by the writings of Jean Hampton and Margaret Urban Walker where they have made the distinction between anger and resentment salient.[9] For example, Hampton has suggested that resentment includes a fear that the offensive action is somehow justified because of a type of inferiority, and Walker ties resentment to particular blameworthy actions. I appreciate the additional content that these definitions of resentment offer, but I want to maintain a broader understanding of anger. A related trend has been the application of rational standards to anger in order to validate its merit in certain situations.[10] If anger is justifiable only when the injustice is easy to confirm, such as the case of righteous anger at racial segregation before the civil rights movement is one example, then rationality becomes the critical filter for legitimacy. An independent determination of the severity of the injustice and not the significance of anger itself becomes the focus. This approach thus parallels the reason/emotion binary it is trying to avoid.[11] My argument about the relationship between the emotions of victim testimony, particularly anger, and the work of justice and democratic inclusion in the aftermath of mass

violence brings back a strong normative framework, an ideal vision beyond what has been realized politically, and it provides a necessary critical distance.[12] By articulating a vision of transitional justice as an exceptional moment in political life with possibilities for the development of
trust not found at other times, I suggest that truth commissions and victim testimony are important institutions for political theorists, not just
for those who work on comparative politics or international law.[13]

Although anger has been defined more recently by its biological function or in relation to aggression, Aristotle's formulation of anger in *Rhetoric* still remains influential in political thought and is, in spite of its limitations, the tradition that grounds this project: "Let anger be desire,
accompanied by distress, for conspicuous retaliation because of an apparent slight that was directed, without justification, against oneself or
those near to one."[14] Anger is thus consistent with the value of emotions
for praxis within Aristotle's broader theory and it has a place in the process of judgment. Emotional responses, including anger, should aid in
the determination of *phronesis* and the practical wisdom required in a
given situation.[15] To put it another way, the virtuous man will experience
anger at the right time, in the right way, for the right reasons. The concept of the slight is particularly important to Aristotle because it indicates that legitimate anger is grounded in the social and political norms
of the time and can be a legitimate response to an infraction.[16] However, if the slight is based on false belief (imagined injuries, false expectations, misunderstandings) on the part of the victim, the anger is no longer legitimate. Aristotle's formulation also attests to the potential that
emerges from anger to remedy the infraction.[17] This concept of anger
as a defensible signal of a challenge to one's status has been the foundation for all attempts to defend the value of anger since then. Lastly, Aristotle's definition captures the pleasure that comes from wanting to see
another person in pain, a complex instinct that many political theorists
find difficult to reconcile with either impartial conceptions of procedural
justice or the cultivation of virtue.[18]

Known for his fiery sermons, Joseph Butler fashioned writings on
anger that continue to be influential, particularly in the distinction he
draws between amoral and moral anger (similar to righteous anger) and
between slow and fast anger. Moral anger, marked by the occurrence of
an injustice, can be fast or slow, but is notable because it is not seeking
immediate and violent revenge. Moral anger takes a considered response
to injustice and pursues accountability. With these distinctions, Butler's

theological voice joins those of Aristotle, Adam Smith, P. F. Strawson, and others who simultaneously warn about the excesses of anger and carve out a space for its singular power in personal and political life.[19]

Anger and Justice in Liberal Democratic Models

Despite the fact that Aristotle's definition of anger has long been part of the debate, the relationship between anger and justice is a tenuous one within the tradition of liberal democracy.[20] This tradition, with its emphasis on deliberation and neutrality, has developed as the best way to ensure retributive justice, and this is an orientation primarily concerned with the punishment of a wrongdoer. In this view, to ensure a fair assessment of the violation of a crime, it is important that anger not be a pervasive sentiment, either in the form of victim involvement or state procedure.[21] Even in the proto-liberalism of Thomas Hobbes, one of the salient points regarding the civil law is that it should not become a conduit for torture or cruelty on the part of the state.[22] Anger embodied by the sovereign cannot be the legitimate basis for punishment. Similarly, for theorists for whom justice is best understood as a procedure with embedded values, particularly John Rawls, the anger of victims does not play a central role.[23] It is epiphenomenal to the process, at times affirming the content and orientation of the procedure and at other moments distorting desirable civility.[24] For those interested in deliberation as central to the formulations of justice, when anger is thought to be useful it may be seen as part of the process of opinion formation, rather than will formation, because of similar concerns about reciprocity and public reason.[25] In Habermasian terms, attending to anger in the process of will formation privileges the volitional basis of validity at the expense of a cognitive one.[26] In this situation, the anger of the victim is justifiably part of the wider societal discussion about justice in the context of civil society, the arts, and other forms of communication. However, with will formation—the process by which decisions (and inevitable tradeoffs between possibilities) are confirmed—anger is not seen to be beneficial. Statements giving public reasons, which can be amended or refuted by others, make up the basis for this stage of conversation.

The legacy of anger's uncertain role in the history of liberal democratic theory can be traced to several recurring concerns. The first, as mentioned above, is the relationship between anger and violence. The most vivid examples of anger in politics, from revolution to assassination, are often those connected to violent and disruptive outcomes. Anger is part of the motivation, it is argued, that leads to a disregard for the law and a willingness to harm other people. Philip Fisher captures the ominous quality of anger in relation to violence when he says, "Anger imagines a future made up of escalating acts that might have taken place if this one had not been protested."[27] Anger, for him, represents a temporary thwarting of the will, which can still later be harnessed with even greater force.[28]

A second concern is the closing of deliberative possibility and the surrender of impartiality. A statement made in anger is feared to be impervious to modification or adjustment, even in the face of conflicting evidence. On this account, anger does not count as an expression of public reason as it ignores universalism and impedes communication. Furthermore, it is not interested in reaching agreement or consensus, but rather looks for validation of its own position, regardless of its legitimacy or accuracy. This concern is related to the idea that when one is angry, holding onto anger and being able to act in an angry way (the authenticity of expression) may be equally as important to the speaker as communicating the emotion verbally (the opportunity for recognition). Another way to express this is the sense that the ultimate value of anger may be expression for its own sake. Anger, as a manifestation of narcissism and self-regard, hears only itself. My exploration of anger in the work of Adam Smith in chapter 4 emerges from these liberal democratic critiques. He shares the two major concerns mentioned above, but he also sees resentment as an important indicator of injustice. Yet, examining his perspective on the legitimate place of resentment reveals the myriad ways in which the liberal democratic tradition reinforces skepticism about anger from many different angles. Thus a full engagement with anger in politics cannot be a mere adjustment to the liberal democratic model but requires a different goal, and it is through Adam Smith that I see the need for a shift to listening rather than seeing in models of judgment.

In contrast to anxieties surrounding anger in liberal democratic thought, it is interesting to consider anger and justice in the Marxist tradition: when justice is defined as a universalization of the ownership of the means of production and the possibility for human emancipation entailed therein, one can imagine anger as providing a necessary spark for revolution.[29] This would be consistent with the intellectual tradition defending righteous anger described below, but there is also a way in which an emphasis on anger can deflect from the action demanded by conditions of injustice. In other words, anger can become a deceptive exercise that appears to heighten consciousness for the purpose of Marxist revolution, but instead siphons collective energy that can then be co-opted by the state. Anger thus only validates the status quo. The angry victim who expresses such intensity of emotion at the injustices she is experiencing may feel momentary satisfaction through recognition, but it is a poor substitute for the change in material conditions necessary for justice.

Within theories of justice that attempt to bulwark vengeance and anger, there is a type of anger that is given a different reception. This is the tradition of "righteous" anger that makes an exception for anger when it is a catalyst for social movements or civil actions against injustice.[30] It is seen to be the communication of the oppressed, often conceived in terms of race or gender. The carefully restrained anger of Martin Luther King Jr. and Nelson Mandela are the paradigmatic cases; the intensity of their anger is a testament to the structural injustices with which they were concerned, but it did not pervade the political practices they advocated. While I do not deny that the inclusion of this type of anger in political life is valuable, it is the easy case. The value of righteous anger at racism, sexism, or authoritarian rule is often either understood only in retrospect or dependent on association with the most blatant forms of injustice. The more incisive question is, "What if the anger shows no signs of being directed to a socially sanctioned movement or a commonly identified type of injustice?" This book begins where theories of righteous anger leave off. During periods of transitional justice after mass violence, the anger that is expressed will not always conform to the sanitized cases in history of righteous anger.[31] It will outlast its welcome as the spark for social movements. Witnesses who express anger may not recognize that substantial efforts are underway to combat injustice and they may be motivated by logistically impossible goals, but there must still be a way to understand the value of anger in political life.[32]

Distinct from liberal assumptions about the value of criminal punishment and retribution, the restorative justice model offers one way of understanding the value of anger. Early experiments in restorative justice began with youth offenders in Canada; these have been taken up in a vigorous way by Mennonite scholars who focus on the repairing of the harm caused to victims and the community by the offender.[33] Restorative justice posits itself as an alternative to a narrow focus on retribution, and it is inherently more open to the possibility of anger within the discussion of justice because at its center is a focus on the relationships affected by the crime and the possibility of the reintegration of the offender into the community.[34] With the youth offender cases for which it is best known, the restorative justice approach arranges for the offender to meet all those who were affected by his actions.[35] The purpose of the conversation is to make clear the varieties of damage that were done and to encourage affective communication but also to provide a path for the offender to become reintegrated into the community. The South African Truth and Reconciliation Commission embraced a similar orientation and self-consciously used the term *restorative justice* in conjunction with *ubuntu*, a word from Bantu meaning individual-community interdependence as the foundation for thinking about justice for an entire society rather than just in terms of individual crimes and rights.

Scholarly interest in the South African Truth and Reconciliation Commission (TRC) has been substantial, particularly in anthropology, literature, and comparative politics. This book complements the work of authors who have investigated the content of the testimonies and their relationship to previous forms of conflict resolution. The first two chapters elucidate the TRC as the inspiration for the project and a potent manifestation of the biggest challenges to confronting anger.[36] The work of Richard Wilson, Fiona Ross, and Catherine Cole has been particularly influential, and all three have looked to the breaks in the narratives of forgiveness to examine how revenge, gender, and performance, respectively, have been overlooked in analyses of the TRC.[37] I find many affinities with Thomas Brudholm's writing about resentment in the context of the TRC and with his lucid reading of Jean Améry and the psychological and moral tensions present in the subject who feels resentment. Reflecting on the moral stature often awarded to victims, Améry writes, "It goes without saying, I believe, that in Auschwitz we did not become better, more human, more humane, and more mature ethically. You do not observe dehumanized man committing his deeds and misdeeds without having your notions of inherent human dignity placed in doubt."[38] Despite his conflicted feelings about victimhood, Améry's writing suggests that the refusal to forgive is a morally demanding position, but it is not without cost. In this interpretation of Améry, Brudholm calls attention, as Lisa Tessman does, to the fact that arguments in support of the expression of resentment or anger must also be cognizant of the moral remainders of regret, remorse, anxiety, and guilt that accompany its expression.[39]

Améry's writing and Brudholm's interpretation of it also point to the simmering hostility that can exist behind the victim's plea to the audience to listen. Améry writes, "You don't want to listen, listen anyhow. You don't want to know where your indifference can lead you and me at any time. I'll tell you."[40] The provocative tone of these lines suggests that listening is far more than a passive activity and does not seamlessly occur because the listening audience, in some vague way, acknowledges that others have suffered. Listening to testimony is a much more demanding task that mandates a consideration of one's own indifference. Yet, feelings of guilt and self-flagellation by audience members are not the desirable responses to this type of listening. How to listen and what to listen for are the themes that guide the normative aspects of this book.

The Limits of Control

Thus far I have provided an overview of the relationship between anger and justice; I now turn to two authors who are explicitly concerned with this question and reveal the secondary issues that underlie this volume. The first is Danielle Allen on the question of anger in ancient Athens, and the other is Seneca, the stoic philosopher, on his deep distrust of anger. Together these two set up the poles of the debate about the political import of anger.[41] Allen argues that in ancient Athens the anger of the victim was a crucial part of the process of justice because victims often served as prosecutors in their own cases, with other citizens participating as jurors and audience members. Using metaphors of illness and disease to discuss anger provided a way for Athenian society to see how entire communities were implicated in crimes and how anger was transmitted between a community's members.[42] The goal in this situation was not to erase anger completely but to understand how it could function as both poison and remedy within a community. Yearly rituals provided opportunities to clarify the conditions that gave rise to crime and to restore the relationships that were affected.[43] My approach to valuing anger is similar to Allen's. For Allen, anger aids in the analytical aspects of understanding justice after mass violence but is also experientially meaningful for the community that must consider its own guilt, acquiescence, and even bloodlust.[44]

Through ritual and the formal prosecutorial role of anger, the Athenian system of justice cultivated the tools for a complex assessment of the validity of anger, and it serves as a model of what could be possible in the context of a truth commission. As in Athens, the validity of anger in this context will not depend on a hard distinction between factual and emotional or ethical assessment. Rather, it should be tied to a more variegated set of factors including *nomos*, "the audience's customary memories and the laws written by the people," and the wider set of cultural and political references that give context to anger in a particular situation.[45] However, the case of Athens also makes salient two aspects of truth commissions that challenge the model: the transitional aspect of society (the fact of new laws and cultural referents) and the shattering of the old status hierarchy that was so central to the circumscription of Athenian anger. Allen shows that anger was controlled in part by limiting who possessed the privilege of expressing it in public. This exclusion, and all that it implies about citizenship and worthiness of dignity, was a necessary part of taming anger so that it could have a place in public life but not be seen as a threat. Without these two critical aspects of constraint, one may doubt that a truth commission would be able to find the appropriate balance between too much and not enough anger, but it is precisely because of its significance as a transitional institution that it is well poised to construct the new ethical and discursive guidelines for anger.

In contrast, Seneca examines the arguments for the efficacy of anger—Aristotle's theory always near in his thoughts—and finds them wanting. Anger, for Seneca, is a burning desire to avenge a wrong. But unlike those who see the benefits of righteous anger or the carefully monitored anger of ancient Athens, Seneca insists the gains are never worth the ancillary costs. It is not that he denies that anger can be directed and perhaps even contained to a certain degree, but this is beside the larger point, which is that anger is always a negative influence on the process of judgment, even when the decision is one about punishment or justice. He does not deny that there are examples where anger has helped lead to a beneficial outcome, and he considers the metaphor of a medically beneficial fever:

> Failings should not be pressed into service on the grounds that they sometimes achieve something. Fevers, too, alleviate some kinds of ill health. But that does not mean that it would not be better to be without them altogether—it is a hateful sort of remedy that leaves one owing one's health to disease. In the same way, anger may sometimes have proved unexpectedly beneficial—like

poison, a fall, or a shipwreck. But that does not make it wholesome. Lives, after all, have often been saved by deadly objects.[46]

Here, in a vivid way, Seneca acknowledges and then decimates any attempt to weigh the benefits of anger against the costs, which can never be accurately assessed. Similarly, in contrast to the militaristic reading of *thumos* in Aristotle and Plato, Seneca denies that anger is a useful impetus for warriors.[47] Those who are brave should be so without anger, and those who are not brave will not benefit from it.[48] All anger can do is lead to a torrent of intense but unsustainable emotion that will not be directed to a narrow or productive task.[49] Even when it is a proportionate and legitimate response (by an agreed-upon standard), it is still vulnerable to being directed by the agent to the wrong ends. The example of anger that is caused by a certain stimulus but is then forcefully directed toward a different one is not the exception but an inevitable quality of anger. Seneca's writing warns that anyone who wants to build a framework for anger in political life will be thwarted by its irrepressible will to inaccuracy and misinterpretation.

Even in the case of an attack on one's family or friends, Seneca is forceful in his prohibition on anger. By engaging with this extreme case, but one that is conceptually close to war crimes, Seneca is exploring what I see as the best-established case for the expression of anger—one connected to the long history of public mourning, potently depicted in *Antigone* and the plethora of scholarship inspired by it.[50] Even in this case, Seneca resolutely maintains that the considerations of duty and judgment should be paramount and are the more refined response. Anyone can become outraged at an attack on a loved one, but "the motivation of such anger is not devotion, but weakness, just as it is with children who bewail the loss of their parents—exactly as they bewail the loss of their toys."[51] Yet with the equivalence he establishes between a child crying for parents and one crying for lost toys, Seneca loses some of the force of the counterargument. The anger expressed in victim testimonies should not be seen as interchangeable with much less serious violations. The fact that some people respond to small and large injustices in similar ways is not significant justification to dismiss the expression of anger altogether. It seems difficult for Seneca to imagine the experience of a violation of the most brutal sort, particularly from the position of a citizen who seeks dignity and recognition that has been withheld; the need for disengagement with anger is much more salient. Still, Seneca's acute perception of the dynamics of anger remains a critical voice. His forceful dismissal of the potential benefits of anger serves as a warning that the benefits of its expression are easily overstated and anger can never be the goal in itself.

My argument about the value of engaging with anger is not a call to reconsider the procedures for testimony at criminal trials, nor do I intend to suggest that war crimes tribunals are unnecessary. Retributive justice, with its expectations of a courtroom free of vengeance and based on neutral and unbiased judgment, has its place. My focus is on the role played by truth commissions during the process of transitional justice. This approach to truth commissions is focused on the political implications of anger in victim testimonies and is located between the skeptical and the therapeutic.[52] I place more emphasis on the political and existential questions present in victim testimony than do scholars (including many political scientists) who are skeptical of the ability of truth commissions to offer anything more than historical documentation.[53] They maintain that the challenge of documentation is difficult and meaningful enough, without asking the state to engage with the psychological experiences of war and conflict.[54] Also, given the sensitivities surrounding emotions such as anger and despair, a skeptic may claim that truth commissions, because of their scale and reliance on state support, are unlikely to be able to respond to the complex needs of witnesses and the audience.[55] I do not agree with this skeptical position; the task of truth commissions is complex, but I maintain that the process of confronting anger should be incorporated and developed in a sophisticated way within political life.

At the same time, I am not arguing for a therapeutic interpretation of victim testimony as the salve that has the ability to ease suffering, prompt reconciliation, or offer catharsis.[56] This volume does not make claims about whether testifying in public is part of the most beneficial course of psychological treatment; I cannot judge this. Rather, my interest is directed toward the political implications of the anger expressed in these testimonies and how it may be incorporated into the strengthening of bonds of trust among citizens. Somewhere between the skeptical and the therapeutic approaches there exists a space where societies, through a politics of listening, can respond to the anger expressed in testimony in ways that are connected to justice and politics but have been overlooked when the focus is solely on criminal guilt and accountability or catharsis and healing. These questions and their potential answers require a willingness to develop new skills of listening and possibilities for the sharing of risk that may lead to trust and greater cooperation among citizens.

From Seeing to Listening

Greek thought, it has been argued, privileges the sensory experience of vision over hearing and listening, particularly as pertains to the communication of the emotions.[57] Grotesque descriptions of eyes dripping with blood and the toxic power of the gaze are manifestations of anger's great power and its ability to undermine the social order. While Greek epics and tragedies were initially heard, Charles Segal argues that their impact is primarily visual, in part to explore (and exploit) the tensions between "surface and depth, between word and deed, between seeming and being," all concepts that lend themselves readily to visual depiction.[58] The value of impartiality gained by appropriate distance from the emotions, as espoused by Adam Smith in his description of the impartial spectator, succinctly captures some of the fears held by thinkers in the liberal tradition.[59] These fears are tentatively resolved—and anxiety about anger temporarily put to rest—through the promise of the right type of vision. I suggest that the metaphor of seeing and the value of distance are obstacles to thinking about the value of anger; a focus on listening better captures the challenges of responding to anger. With listening one cannot be (physically) too far away because the goal is not to prioritize the value of the larger context over the particular emotions but rather to attend to the complexity contained in vocal expression and to respond in a way that clarifies its significance to political life. The idea of listening is also helpful because it allows for a distinction between listening and hearing, that is, the possibility of willful or unconscious refusal to engage with what has been said. Jean-Luc Nancy favors the mandate to listen over hearing because "to listen is to be straining toward a possible meaning, and consequently one that is not immediately accessible."[60] In the case of anger, one can see how the split between merely hearing and the challenge of listening can emerge as a concern. The tone, pitch, and intensity of anger may make it difficult for the audience member to truly listen to what is being said, but this should not negate its distinctive value in political life.[61]

The writings on agonism by Chantal Mouffe, Bonnie Honig, and William Connolly, among others, put forth a critique of liberal democratic approaches because of the constraints, implicit and explicit, on what should be considered political; they advocate both for the creation of new political spaces and new understandings of identity as contingent, relational, and open to upheaval and change.[62] My argument has strong affinities with this tradition, but it also seeks to build a more explicit connection between upheaval and the work of transitional justice. Connolly writes, "Critical responsiveness is critical in that it does not always accede to everything that a new constituency or movement demands. But the catch is this: The criticism is not securely guided by established codes of criteria of interpretive judgment. For some of them turn out to be part of the problem."[63] Critical responsiveness gives a formulation to the process of loosening standards of rationality and consensus but does not abandon the process of evaluation and exchange altogether. The listening skills developed as part of critical responsiveness shift greater responsibility to the listener from the speaker and demand more sustained engagement. I agree with Connolly that the standards by which to evaluate claims that emerge from agonistic encounters require cultivation and negotiation. Truth commissions can serve to encourage this process in the types of questions that may be asked in response to anger, questions that indicate that it is not peripheral to the function of the institution and that the insights of testimony will inform the political practices that emerge after the work of transitional justice has been completed. The patterns that emerge through anger, as well as the significance of engaging with the testimonies, should be the subject of negotiation.

The connection between upheaval and the work of justice also depends on the transformation that occurs on two levels during a political exchange: the first level is a change in the conception of self as citizen, and the second is in the way the possibilities of political practice are envisioned, what James Tully calls "the rules of the game."[64] Tully emphasizes that during the practice of the "game," citizens reevaluate and change their actions in light of the dynamic process transpiring around them. Something similar is possible with anger: as the commission is able to see the various meanings of anger and as witnesses come to trust that the commissioners and audience are not made anxious by such expression, the political community itself undergoes a transformation. It has enacted a new type of citizenship and set a precedent for future relations based on dignity and shared concern.

Ressentiment and Victimization

A critic may say that conceding that anger is prone to misjudgment is an understatement; it is a force so hungry for expression that it is uniquely vulnerable to being directed at the wrong target, for the wrong reasons and to the wrong degree. A related concern is that anger is indelibly tarnished by its identity as a weapon of the weak. Friedrich Nietzsche famously argued in the morality tale of the lambs and the birds of prey that anger stemming from one's inferiority is never a sign of strength but a desperate measure to assert a hollow moral superiority.[65] Frustration stemming from weakness can easily be transformed into *ressentiment*, a particular variant of resentment that blames others for one's own failings and uses the language of justice or goodness to do so. Nietzsche's searing insight is that anger, in the form of *ressentiment*, is a poor substitute for the agonistic contestation of politics. More broadly, the point is that anger emerging from one's own status as a victim will never allow one to achieve either power or dignity. Instead, it merely highlights how little one is able to participate in the agonistic struggle of the political sphere as an equal among equals.[66] Arendt shares this concern; it is evident in her description of the distortionary influence of suffering on action in the public sphere and the threat of intimate concerns masquerading as political ones in the rise of the Social.[67] This fear about the glorification of victimhood and the pathetic clinging to "wounded attachments" is the critique that haunts my argument and I grapple with it in chapter 3.[68] While I do not agree with the bright line she draws between public and private, Arendt's fears prompt me to foreground the forward-looking aspects of testimony and its implications for citizenship. I maintain that through responding to the expression of anger, both the victim and the listener will be agents in the construction of restorative justice, and it is this dynamic model of listening and responsiveness that will resist the reification of prior roles.[69]

Debates over the interpretation of Antigone parallel the issues that arise when thinking about how to respond to victim testimony at a truth commission as they turn on the value of mourning as political action in itself. Can we see her desire to mourn her brother (despite an order from King Creon) as a political act in itself or only as a precursor to one? While Judith Butler has argued that the politics of mourning reveal the exclusionary practices of the demos, Honig points out that expanding the scope of "grievability" cannot become a substitute for the recognition of new types of sovereignty or political practice.[70] This perspective illuminates my desire to engage with the political claims and desires found in the testimonies beyond the acts of grief and mourning. While mourning is a component of truth commissions, and the frequency of witnesses asking for a proper burial for loved ones testifies to this, the engagement with anger I am suggesting is distinct from the politicization of mourning.

Chapter Overview

Chapter 1 traces the use of testimony at three key moments of transitional justice, the Nuremberg trials, the Eichmann trial, and the South African Truth and Reconciliation Commission, to show the recent genealogy of the relationship between testimony and justice. Robert Jackson, the American Supreme Court justice who was the chief prosecutor at Nuremberg, considered using oral testimony to make the case against the Nazi officers but decided against this strategy because of his sensitivity to being charged with offering victors' justice, a show trial that was meant to humiliate the losing side in the war. The Eichmann trial, in contrast, invited to the stand witnesses who had been detained in the concentration camps in order to demonstrate Eichmann's guilt and render legitimacy to the Israeli state. The Eichmann trial can be seen as a pivotal moment challenging the relationship between testimony and justice and a precursor to the work of truth commissions. This approach was met with criticism about the miscarriage of justice and the instrumental use of the suffering of others, perspectives that continue into the present. Hannah Arendt and Judith Shklar act as interlocutors for thinking about the experiences of the Nuremberg trials and the Eichmann trial, and their reactions to the trials reveal why liberal political theorists may be inclined to underestimate the potential significance of victim testimony.[71] The third historical moment in the chapter, the South African TRC, did not include criminal trials and was thus free to consider the value of testimony apart from expectations of legal procedure. Over two thousand people testified in public, and twenty thousand submitted written testimonies; the stated goals of these testimonies included catharsis, national "healing," and greater historical accuracy.[72] Yet the role of anger in testimony and its impact on the collective process of transitional justice and future political life was ill-defined and misunderstood.

In chapter 2 I engage in a discourse analysis of the transcripts of the TRC and find moments where witnesses at the Human Rights Violations Committee hearings expressed anger. These instances were some of the most compelling moments of the testimonies, but they were often stifled. I analyze how the commissioners *failed to engage* with anger and the obstacles and tensions that accompanied the presence of anger as part of the process of transitional justice. The transcripts reveal that the commissioners had certain types of response to anger that kept recurring, and these included an emphasis on forgiveness, the prioritization of material evidence, and a tendency to see certain emotions solely as indicators of mental health issues. The chapter concludes that although there were many aspects of the TRC that allowed for a confrontation with anger, the failure to listen and respond stymied the possibility of connecting anger to justice.

In the second part of the book, I use the questions that arise from the transcripts of the TRC to direct my excavation of the works of Hannah Arendt and Adam Smith, the theorists who represent the most powerful skeptics of the argument. In chapter 3 I adjudicate the tension between the value Hannah Arendt places on narrative in public life and her disdain for expressions of pain and suffering in the same sphere. Were she to have written on the subject, I suggest that Arendt would initially have considered institutions of transitional justice to be full of political possibility.[73] The very act of gathering so many people together in a public space could encourage action, not just reflection on the pain and suffering of the past. Yet her response to victim testimony in the Eichmann trial showed that she was uncomfortable with the level of emotional expression that was displayed by the witnesses in a criminal trial, and this would likely carry over to institutions like truth commissions. Instead of celebrating the potential for new action in victim testimony, Arendt would have found victim testimony in the context of truth commissions to be a *near miss*: a gesture that came close to initiating a new process in politics but was thwarted by the content of the testimonies and the behavior of the witnesses. Examining her reasons for the "near miss" exposes what is at stake in the project and what I consider to be the most important counterargument to the engagement with anger in public life.

Adam Smith's *The Theory of Moral Sentiments* is valuable for my

project in two ways: first because his attention to the affective bonds between strangers connects emotional expression to the work of citizenship.[74] The second reason is for the value he attributes to the expression
of resentment as an important marker of injustice. Both reasons are addressed in chapter 4. In Smith's view resentment can be a legitimate and
valuable part of political life and should not be excised for the sake of
creating liberal judicial institutions. Resentment is, however, prone to
be exaggerated, distorted, and directed to the wrong ends. While Smith
sees resentment as only helpful for initiating an investigation of the injustice and then distancing oneself from the emotion, the argument here
is for a sustained engagement with anger. It can be the impetus for an investigation, but it can also provide insights that other approaches would
miss. Thus, unlike in Smith's writings, the argument for citizens to engage with anger is both instrumental and intrinsic. Anger is important
for what it tells us in addition to what it "does" when it is vocalized in
front of others.

Smith's critique about the volatility of anger, reminiscent of Seneca's
concern about anger, is best mitigated, he says, through the judgment of
an impartial spectator who can be called upon to arbitrate the merit of
the injustice. The concept of the impartial spectator is held as the ideal
of ethical virtue and is manifested in an individual who is able to respond in a proportional and rational way to the sufferings of others.
Moreover, the person who embodies the essence of the impartial spectator is able to distance himself from his *own* experiences of suffering and
act in an emotionally detached way. Thus the centrality given to the impartial spectator overrides both the need for sympathy in response to the
pain of others and openness to the value of resentment when it does not
fit narrow expectations. Yet, the moments that do not fit Smith's model
of impartiality, when the intensity of resentment appears to disrupt communication, are fruitful places to develop a new model of listening to
anger.

In the fifth chapter, I build on work in political philosophy that has
been sympathetic to anger in order to develop a three-part normative
model for understanding its political value. Each of the three dimensions,
the cognitive-evaluative, confrontational, and kinetic, can contribute to
justice and the cultivation of trust. The cognitive-evaluative dimension
builds upon the Stoic and Aristotelian traditions that have taken a more
integrated approach to the relationship between reason and emotion,
as well as second-wave feminist critiques. They have built on the con-

cept that emotions contain evaluative judgments about what individuals consider to be most important; anger, in particular, can provide insights about what citizens need and fear in the aftermath of mass violence that would not be revealed though other political mechanisms. These are insights about how individuals' perceptions of the state have changed over the course of mass violence, how they understand their role in the political community, and what may be preventing them from fully participating as citizens. The cognitive-evaluative dimension of interpretation also allows for the sharing of risk, including the risk of being ignored, rejected, and forgotten, as well as the risk that one will always be disadvantaged in political negotiation.[75] The way this risk is shared by the commissioners and the listeners becomes a basis for future trust.[76]

However, it is limiting to think about anger only through a cognitive-evaluative lens, and I see this as conceding too much to a rationalist language of what should be valuable in the public sphere; the confrontational and kinetic dimensions of anger do not fall neatly into the language of instrumentally valuable knowledge. The confrontational dimension of anger exists even when anger does not demand uptake or recognition, oft-cited outcomes of the cognitive-evaluative approach.[77] Anger should be interpreted along the confrontational dimension when it expresses the contradictions and limitations at what the public sphere and institutions such as truth commissions can provide. Acknowledging the confrontational significance of anger reveals the ways in which previous hierarchies continue to exist and the burden of having anger as one of the few tools of social impact for marginalized groups. Listening for the confrontational dimension also allows the audience to experience, in a mimetic way, what it means to distance oneself (through anger), while also being drawn to public life through a desire to be recognized and included in the community. The final value of anger comes from the experience of its expression and is not dependent on content or recognition. Buddhist thought offers a way to think about it as an incandescent, raw energy that has no correlate, and I import this as a useful political concept.[78] In addition, Adriana Cavarero's work on voice and the Greek idea of *phônê* testifies to the uniquely human act of speaking.[79] It is through the act of vocalizing that we assert our identity in the public sphere, and such a focus corresponds to the praxis of listening rather than seeing.

Understanding the ways in which anger is beneficial for public life provides a critical link between its expression and the development of trust, the ultimate goal of this work and the theme I take up in chapter 6. Intuitively, the expression of anger seems to go against any audience predisposition to trust the witness. Precisely for this reason, the decision to trust the witness at the outset of testimony establishes a different affective landscape for the communication that makes up testimony. An attitude of trusting the witness is only the beginning, however, of a process that is grounded in the expression of anger and the response to it as a model for the work of citizenship. Ultimately, the goal of an engagement with anger is to facilitate the expectations of shared risk and recognized sacrifice that I take to be the basis for civic trust. Responding to each of the dimensions of anger described above expands the array of communicative possibilities open to citizens that indicate shared risk. Engaging in responsive listening is a difficult task, one that potentially prompts unease in the listener but should be seen as a transferable skill to political life after transitional institutions have ended. The confrontational interpretation of anger reveals the limitations of politics and thus suggests a type of recognition that is usually not included in formal democratic practices. Lastly, attention to the kinetic dimension of anger is, in part, a countering of the pain and viscerality of violence with the viscerality of voice.

For the witness to express each of the dimensions of anger is a risk and a way of placing something that is of value to the individual in the hands of the commission and the collective. Returning to the testimony at the beginning, when Yona spoke about his experiences of torture, he was angry, in part, because of the way the experiences constrained his life in the present. The commissioners had the opportunity to engage with his anger and his references to a type of citizenship denied, but they were uncertain about how to proceed. The practice of holding the anger of another in one's care is a skill unto itself, one that must be consistently nurtured in a political institution if it is to take hold in the democratic polity. Engaging with anger presents a risk for the listener in that it demands energy and the possibility of rebuke, yet this risk is shared with others through the process in a way that can be productive. The difficult nature of an engagement with anger in the process of victim testimony is what makes it a singular case for the cultivation of trust; the process of expressed anger, active listening, and a response allows for a transformation for all involved. Setting aside the defensiveness that is often a response to anger, listeners can see themselves and their interests in the background with attention to the testimony as the point of interest in the foreground. Their task then becomes not to pity or offer sympathy to the victim, but rather to discover and acknowledge the causes of anger and the humanity it conveys. Most importantly, listening to anger ushers in a transformation from victim to citizen. A victim is seen to be stuck in the past, condemned to suffer and able to make claims only based on that suffering. A citizen is one who is an equal participant in political life and not always asked to be the bearer of sacrifice. A citizen can expect to influence and experience the rewards of political negotiation, at least some of the time. The communication of anger provides an opportunity for citizen relationships to emerge and set a precedent that will outlast the truth commission.

The energy and experience of anger in the public sphere is undeniable. It finds a way to influence politics whether or not it is sanctioned, and it is the consistent remainder of liberal democratic action. A political life continually beset by angry exchanges would be paralyzed, but in the period after mass violence, the expression of anger provides a path from the reality of violence to the renegotiation of citizenship roles, now marked by greater dignity and interpersonal trust. Truth commissions provide the rare opportunity to engage with anger politically. What is required now is a willingness to take it up.

More than Cheap Sentimentality

Victim Testimony at the Nuremberg Trials, the Eichmann Trial, and the South African Truth and Reconciliation Commission

Antjie Krog, an Afrikaner journalist who covered the South African Truth and Reconciliation Commission, described her time at the hearings as follows:

> Week after week; voice after voice; account after account. . . . It is not so much the deaths, and the names of the dead, but the web of infinite sorrow woven around them. It keeps on coming and coming. A wide, barren, disconsolate landscape where the horizon keeps on dropping away.[1]

Her words capture what was felt by many in the audience, along with those who were following the proceedings through the media—emotional exhaustion and uncertainty. The phenomenon of hundreds of public testimonies prompted several questions: How does one make sense of the countless testimonies of grief, suffering, and loss? What purposes do they serve? Are the testimonies of victims connected to justice?

Gathering the testimony of war victims, in contrast to that of a victim or a family member during an individual criminal trial, is an overwhelming endeavor because of the number of people involved and the often complete physical and psychological devastation they have faced. Asking victims to testify may seem like a foray into "infinite sorrow,"[2] yet this practice has become a central element of truth commissions, temporary institutions set up by heads of state or the United Nations to investigate the violence of a previous period.[3] The South African Truth and Reconciliation Commission, the most well-known of the more than thirty truth commissions that have been created since the late 1970s, made victim testimony central to its mission and solicited it on an unprecedented scale, inviting over two thousand people to testify at public hearings and collecting written statements from thousands more.[4]

The concept of victim testimony as a part of the transitional justice process was foreshadowed by experiences of criminal justice and oral history in the aftermath of World War II. The trial of Adolf Eichmann marked a watershed moment in the relationship between the experiences of victims, their impact on society, and the demands of justice in the aftermath of war and mass atrocity. Whereas prosecutors at the Nuremberg trials aimed to convict Nazi officials solely on the basis of documentary evidence, the chief prosecutor during the Eichmann trial, Gideon Hausner, made the oral testimony of victims central to his case against Eichmann and to a larger argument about the relationship of the Holocaust to the legitimacy of the state of Israel. This approach to victim testimony, although in many ways flawed and potentially undermining to the ultimate goal of the prosecution, sparked a discussion about the significance of victim testimony that continues to the present.

Not everyone agreed with the inclusion of victim testimony in the proceedings of criminal justice. Hannah Arendt, the person largely responsible for documenting the Eichmann trial for the international media, and the trial's most famous interlocutor, was suspicious of the ability of testimony to provoke emotions in the audience and highly critical of the prosecution's strategy of using witnesses who could not provide direct evidence about the defendant. For Arendt, the ideal witness in a criminal proceeding should testify for the purpose of providing greater facts about the case and should be able to do so without the complicating factors of emotional expression.[5]

Despite Arendt's criticisms of victim testimony in the Eichmann case, it represents a pivotal moment for transitional justice. The trial of Adolph Eichmann was the most prominent case of a war crimes trial that considered the emotions of victims as central to the practice of justice. By doing so, it challenged previous distinctions between reason and emotion and between the public and private spheres. The Eichmann trial, although not without serious shortcomings in procedure, laid the foundation for a new, still-unrealized type of transitional justice that has the potential to engage with anger in a way that encourages trust. As a way of situating the Eichmann trial between the conventional perspective of criminal justice after war and new frameworks for understanding justice, I place it on a theoretical continuum between the Nuremberg trials and the South African Truth and Reconciliation Commission. Over the course of these cases, there has been a move toward a more integrated conception of reason and emotion, a renegotiation of the public-private boundary, and a greater acceptance of the significance of unsocial emotions—Adam Smith's term for the emotions that are difficult to sympathize with—including anger after mass violence.[6]

The Nuremberg Trials

The Nuremberg trials were the most influential of the twentieth-century tribunals addressing postwar justice.[7] Conducted in 1945–48, they established the precedent for prosecuting war criminals that would later be used to form the International Criminal Court. They gave an institutional framework to the principle that crimes committed during war fall under an international jurisdiction and that the perpetrators of war crimes, such as the torture of detainees, and of larger "crimes against humanity" can be held accountable. The architects of the trials at Nuremberg were concerned with being charged with offering "victors' justice" through proceedings that, while invoking principled moral and legal justifications, would be merely a façade that allowed the winners of the Second World War to impose punishment and retribution on their defeated enemies. Instead, the Allied forces in charge of drafting the charter to set up the International Military Tribunal at Nuremberg wanted to be seen as offering a new model for international justice, one based on international law and the impartial application of prohibitions against aggression and war crimes, not victors' justice.[8] The lessons learned in hindsight about the debilitating impact of the Treaty of Versailles on German political and cultural life informed this orientation, and the language used by the judges at Nuremberg was meant to mute the centrality of vengeance and retribution in the rhetoric of the trial in order to focus on narrower concerns of criminal responsibility.[9] The actions of the International Military Tribunal would show in word, as well as legal procedure, that it was part of a more just political structure than the one of Nazi Germany. To protect against the perception of a miscarriage of justice, the judges and prosecution at the tribunal emphasized the rationality of the charges, rules of evidence, and protections for the defendant.[10]

Robert Jackson, the American Supreme Court justice who served as the chief prosecutor at Nuremberg, most clearly embodied this vision of an impartial and rationalistic approach to transitional justice after war. In his opening statement, Jackson articulated that an American was best suited to lead a dispassionate inquiry into the war because his country did not experience the physical devastation of the European allies. Moreover, he suggested that he, in particular, was an appropriate candidate for the job of chief prosecutor because he was able to separate his personal feelings about the defendants from his legal obligations.[11] Both of these justifications for the legitimacy of American leadership in the prosecution stemmed from the belief that an emotional predisposition to anger or vengeance had no place in a criminal trial and that the separation of rationality from emotion was the mark of a just and legitimate trial. This philosophy carried over into the strategy for providing evidence that would show the individual accountability of the twenty-four Nazi officials on trial, including Hermann Göring, the commander of the Luftwaffe; Albert Speer, an architect who served as minister of armaments; and Hans Frank, ruler of the central government of occupied Poland. They were charged with the following crimes under international law:

1. Participation in a conspiracy to commit crimes, including crimes against the peace
2. Planning, initiating, and waging wars of aggression
3. War crimes
4. Crimes against humanity[12]

Of these charges, the ones related to wars of aggression and crimes against humanity were the most contested. Critics argued that waging a war of aggression was an inadequate legal charge because it would be interpreted as a way to blame the losing side for its defeat. Defining the proximate cause of war is always difficult, and the lack of specificity as to the definition of "aggression" further obfuscated the precision of this charge.

The trials at Nuremberg were the first to prosecute individuals on the charge of *crimes against humanity*, a term that first appeared in 1915 in a joint declaration by France, Great Britain, and Russia directed toward the Ottoman Empire with respect to the genocide of Armenian Ottomans. It came into popular use after its inclusion in the London charter for the formation of the International Military Tribunal in 1945.[13] The charter, signed by representatives from the United Kingdom, France, and Russia, defined *crimes against humanity* as "[m]urder, extermination, enslavement, deportation, and other inhumane acts committed against any civilian population, before or during the war; or persecutions on political, racial, or religious grounds in execution of or in connection with any crime within the jurisdiction of the Tribunal, whether or not in violation of domestic law of the country where perpetrated."[14] Two of the notable aspects of this definition were the attention given to the political, racial, or religious motivation for murder and the transcendent jurisdiction of the International Military Tribunal over domestic law.

The defense that was mounted against these charges, although tailored to the situation of each defendant, was based on the claim that the defendant either did not know the extent of the crimes that were committed in the name of the Third Reich or was simply following orders within a regime.[15] Such orders did not allow those commanded the individual autonomy to decide whether or not to carry them out. For example, in his testimony under cross-examination, the defendant Hermann Göring stated, "So far as opposition is concerned in any form, the opposition of each individual person was not tolerated unless it was a matter of unimportance."[16]

The prosecution, under Jackson's leadership, considered using the testimony of victims to establish the extent of the crimes and the direct complicity of the defendants because they thought this approach would be sufficiently dramatic to hold the attention of the international media while also portraying the Allies as empathetic toward the experiences of victims and survivors.[17] In the end, however, the prosecution decided not to use victim testimony and relied only on documentary evidence in the form of invoices, letter communication, and photographs to provide a straightforward paper trail of the case, one not susceptible to the type of criticism that could be directed toward the credibility of the witnesses. By excluding victim testimony from their strategy, the prosecution was able to further emphasize the idea that the Nuremberg trials were meant not to manipulate the public or international media through a rhetoric of suffering but, rather to present a detailed account of the specific crimes of Nazi officials during and leading up to the Second World War. In his opening statement, after outlining the systematic anti-Semitic practices of the Nazi party and the structures that were put into place for the elimination of the Jews, Jackson said, "I shall not take the time to detail the ghastly proceedings in these concentration camps. Beatings, starvings, tortures, and killings were routine—so routine that the tormentors became blasé and careless."[18] This statement encapsulates Jackson's orientation to the particular experiences of victims during the trial: they were central to the case because their experiences showed the extent of the crimes committed, but there was no need to spend time and effort detailing the particularities of suffering. Far more important was to convey how the "tormentors became blasé and careless" and thus create a psychological profile of the defendants.

In contrast to the Eichmann trial that would take place fifteen years later, the prosecutors at Nuremberg did not consider the education of the public about the Nazis' crimes to be a primary goal. Such education would happen as a by-product, insofar as the evidence would reveal Nazi activity with which many would not be familiar, but it would not be an ongoing concern. Even though the judges and lawyers who participated in the trial knew that they were involved in a historic event in the nascent field of international justice, they did not consider themselves to be historians of the Holocaust or the collectors of oral testimony; the legal aims of criminal prosecution and punishment were focus enough. The court also did not see itself as offering a model for catharsis or reconciliation. Thus, Nuremberg is the paradigmatic case of a conventional postwar criminal trial, one that represents a rationalistic idea of justice through its language of "staying the hand of vengeance," its dismissal of oral testimony, and its narrow scope for the purposes of pursuing criminal justice rather than education or social transformation.[19]

I agree with scholars Gary Bass, Lawrence Douglas, and Martha Minow that Nuremberg was largely successful at achieving its goals of setting a precedent for trying war crimes and crimes against humanity in an international court.[20] The highly rationalistic discourse that shunned the language of vengeance and the potential volatility of victim testimony is understandable given the context of the Allied victory and the general perception of the Nazis as "evil," an image that was perpetuated by the popular media. To avoid publicizing the trials at Nuremberg as yet another battle that could be celebrated as an Allied victory, the prosecution needed to distance itself from the self-righteous language of war and the corresponding demand for retribution that had been part of Al-

lied wartime propaganda. However, while the Nuremberg trials offered a
solid foundation for the establishment of international courts to try war
crimes, they relied on a schism between reason and emotion that is limiting when considering the broader needs for justice and the psychological
restoration of a society in the aftermath of war. The needs of perpetrators, victims, and bystanders to judge the actions of the past and participate in the reconstruction of society are not met by a criminal trial and
could not even be articulated during the Nuremberg tribunal given the
limitations of what was considered relevant testimony. Emotions, particularly anger, despair, and resentment, could not play a prominent role in
Nuremberg because of the constraints of legal procedure. Nonetheless,
they cannot be ignored as part of the collective needs of postwar justice;
to include them as part of the process of transitional justice would force
a reconsideration of the boundary between the legitimacy of reason and
emotion in public—a confrontation that is necessary in the wake of mass
violence.

Shklar's Legalism

The trials at Nuremberg served as a case study for Judith Shklar in *Legalism* (1964), her book about political trials and the theory of law. Although the contemporaneous nature of *Legalism* and *Eichmann in Jerusalem* prevented Shklar and Arendt from directly responding to each
other, they engaged with the same topics, at the same point in history,
with certain similar orientations toward the project of liberalism. Both
considered the liberal paradigm to be dependent on individual autonomy and were skeptical of ambitious state endeavors that interfered with
such autonomy. Shklar and Arendt differed, however, when it came to
the legal ideology that permeated liberalism, an ideology Shklar called
"legalism" and described as "the ethical attitude that holds moral conduct to be a matter of rule following, and moral relationships to consist
of duties and rights determined by rules."[21] She noted that this approach
had so distanced itself from questions of history, politics, and ethics that
it fell into a solipsistic trap, making it stagnant as a theory of law. In addition to the commitment to rules, legalism was marked by "the dislike
of vague generalities, the preference for case-by-case treatment of all social issues, the structuring of all possible human relations into the form
of claims and counterclaims under established rules."[22] Instead of these

characteristics, Shklar advocated an approach to law "as an historical phenomenon," and she wanted to "replace the sterile game of defining law, morals, and politics in order to separate them as concepts both 'pure' and empty, divorced from each other and from their common historical past and contemporary setting."[23] Legalism was an ideology, a set of beliefs held by a group of people, and Shklar was particularly critical of those who tried to present it as a natural extension of logical, deductive thought rather than acknowledging the force it gained through ideological affiliation.

With her critique of legalism in mind, Shklar turned her attention to the Nuremberg trials and suggested that they may be the paradigmatic case of the flaws of legalism. By constructing a framework for international law and charges such as "crimes against humanity," the legal community of the Allied countries assumed that its work would lead to the creation of a new set of norms independent of historical and political context. She was critical of the lack of institutional infrastructure that would help establish the legality of international law, but she did not think such institutions could ever be entirely effective. Such institutions, she believed, may actually distort incentives for taking other actions that could promote the ends of justice. Shklar stated, "The liberalism of yesterday is the conservatism of today. The idea that all international problems will dissolve with the establishment of an international court with compulsory jurisdiction is an invitation to political indolence. It allows one to make no alterations in domestic political action and thought, to change no attitudes, to try no new approaches and yet appear to be working for peace."[24] Although her assessment seems dramatically pessimistic, her statement reveals the extent to which she was skeptical of depending on the law and legal institutions to solve political and social rifts.

Despite these criticisms, Shklar was in favor of the Nuremberg trials because the context of a devastated German bureaucratic and legal structure meant that Germany could take the trial as a precedent for its reconstruction. She supported this narrow pedagogic function of the trials (that of aiding Germany in rebuilding its legal structure) and the type of rationality they highlighted. Despite her critiques of legalism, she did not challenge the fundamental assumption that emotions would be disruptive to rule following and, hence, to justice. This was a dichotomy between rationality and emotion that I take to be untenable given the anger that exists after war and that permeates all aspects of transitional justice. Shklar wanted to see more scholarship examining formal legal rules, which legalism purports to live by, and the political realities that allow those rules to be enforced. On these matters, she was in agreement with the legal realists who were gaining influence in American law schools during the 1950s with their view that the law must take into account the realities of power and practice and not just concern itself with ideal jurisprudence. Shklar's perspective, along with that of the legal realists, advocated a new approach to rationality that was more inductive and emergent from the facts at hand but did not question the exclusion of emotions from either the deductive rationality of legalism or the inductive rationality that comes from paying attention to history and politics.[25]

Shklar did not directly address the question of victim testimony. It was not significant in Nuremberg and, as mentioned above, she did not comment directly on the trial of Adolf Eichmann. At first glance, her silence about the potential for victim testimony to aid in the process of justice may seem to indicate that she dismissed it as theoretically insignificant. This approach would be consistent with her commitment to neutrality and objectivity as the tenets of justice, with no mention of emotion. Nevertheless, I argue that Shklar's critique of legalism cleared a theoretical space for the testimony of victims, perpetrators, and spectators and for the expression of emotion. Such a space was suggested by her rejection of formalistic procedure and her attention to the historical and political realities that provide the context for justice. The establishment of legal norms and institutions is one aspect of the process of reconstruction after war—the most important part, according to Shklar—but it is undermined if anger and despair still permeate citizen perceptions of government and politics in general. The suffering and anger of victims, along with their calls for justice, cannot be avoided, and moral considerations require far more than the vague sense of duty "determined by rules" which she already rejected as part of legalism.[26] Shklar's suggested response to the purity of legalist ideology included being cognizant of the historical particularities of societies after war and of the specific needs of justice in a given situation. This approach would demand attention to the experiences of victims. Her argument does not tell us why victim testimony is socially important, but her critique of the legalist approach paved the way for incorporating it into systems of postwar justice.

Shklar argued that legalism played an important role in establishing the legitimacy and respectability of the trials at Nuremberg, since the tribunal, through "addressing itself to the political and legal elite, gave that elite a demonstration of the meaning and value of legalistic politics, not only by offering a decent model of a trial, a great legalistic drama, but by presenting evidence in a way that the political elite could not shrug off. It could and did illustrate what happens when Nazi ideology replaces legalism."[27] Although she emphasized the pedagogic quality of the Nuremberg trials' procedures and gestured toward the larger social goals of the trials, her optimism about the precedent that could be set at Nuremberg was always measured. Shklar was also critical of Robert Jackson's ambition and his tendency to overstate the potential of the trials to influence military and political decisions in the future. "No trial," she cautioned, "not even a spectacular one such as the Nuremberg Trial, can achieve such enormous consequences by itself."[28]

Shklar's endorsement of Nuremberg, offered begrudgingly at times, was part of a larger dialogue with her American colleagues about anti-Communism in domestic political trials, such as those of Alger Hiss and the Rosenbergs, that took place in the early 1950s. Such trials were premised on the elimination of political enemies and were not beholden to the standards of evidence and procedure that the constitutionally based American legal system would require. The method of using courts to achieve political ends was consistent with the logic of political order orchestrated from above that characterizes totalitarian regimes, but, Shklar adamantly asserted, these trials were highly destructive for democracy in a liberal regime. Thus, her positive position on Nuremberg evolved out of a comparison to what it could have been: an international version of a political witch hunt, one that could undermine future attempts at international justice. She applauded the fact that the trials at Nuremberg did not collapse into such a spectacle.

Given the anti-Communist fervor that was still in force when Shklar was writing, there is another reason why she avoided considering the question of victim testimony: such testimony and the emotions it elicited could easily have been used to garner support for the prosecution in a show trial.[29] Without a framework for understanding how victim testimony could be helpful either to victims or to society more generally, Shklar could only conceive of the misuse of testimony for political ends. Shklar's perspective on the Nuremberg trials is evidence of how fears about "show trials" and spectacles may prevent democratic theorists from fully considering the potential value of victim testimony in specific institutional contexts.[30] Anxiety about the volatility of emotions and their role in the manipulation of justice for political ends is deeply embedded within liberal democratic theory and had, as Shklar's views on Nuremberg indicate, shaped perceptions about victim testimony even before such testimony emerged as a possible response to mass atrocity.[31]

It is interesting to note that, much later in her career, Shklar came to explicitly consider the relevance of victim perspectives in understandings of justice. Her book *The Faces of Injustice* challenges the distinction between misfortune and injustice as politically constructed in order to argue for the need for a social response to injustice in its many forms. To classify an event as a misfortune rather than an injustice is often to be passively complacent to the misery of others, and she rejects arguments about public/private and objective/subjective that are used to bolster this distinction.[32] She writes, "If we include the victim's version, not least her sense of injustice, in our understanding of injustice, we might get a far more complete account of its social character. We might find it more difficult to tell an injustice from a misfortune but we might also be less ready to ignore the implications of passive injustice as a part of the full career of human injustice."[33] Here Shklar suggested a more expansive scope for the work of justice than she provided in her analysis of the Nuremberg trials. Furthermore, I would suggest that the *social* character of injustice that she identifies might include the emotional legacy of injustice, in the form of anger and its impact on politics.

Eichmann on Trial

The trial of Adolf Eichmann remains the subject of scholarly and popular inquiry largely because of Hannah Arendt's evocative reportage. She covered the trial, which took place in Jerusalem in 1961–62, as a correspondent for the *New Yorker*. Her articles were later published as a book, *Eichmann in Jerusalem: A Report on the Banality of Evil*, a title that includes her most notorious phrase. Arendt's portrayal of Eichmann's apparent lack of malicious intent, his tendency to speak in cliché, and his utter ordinariness as a man, mediocre in almost every way, gave rise to a new stereotype, that of the bureaucratic war criminal. She described his orientation toward the crimes that he committed—not the crimes themselves—as banal, and, according to Seyla Benhabib, "Eichmann becomes for her a paradigm case for analyzing how neither partic-

ularly evil nor particularly intelligent people could get caught in the ma-
chinery of evil and commit the deeds they did."[34]

Adolf Eichmann was apprehended in May 1960 by Israeli agents in
a suburb of Buenos Aires, his home in exile after he fled Germany and
used the underground network of SS officers to make his way to Argentina. He lived there under a false name and worked in various towns, always anxious about being identified and captured since he was aware
of his status as one of Israel's most wanted men. His wife and children
joined him in Argentina and were active in the community of former
Nazi officials and their families, a community that by then numbered in
the hundreds. After receiving a tip, relayed through Simon Wiesenthal,
about Eichmann's location, the Israeli military captured and brought
Eichmann back to Israel without following the protocol for legal extradi-
tion, an omission that led Argentina to bring a case against Israel before
the United Nations. Those charges were eventually dropped, and Israel
continued with its plan to try Eichmann in a domestic court.

Eichmann was one of the most wanted Nazi fugitives not because of
his high rank but because of his unique status as the only Nazi official
specifically concerned with the deportation of the Jewish people in Austria and elsewhere.[35] Eichmann took great pride in the fact that he had
read and advocated the theory of Zionism found in Theodor Herzl's *Der
Judenstaat*, and he took it upon himself to convince other SS officers of
the benefits of Zionism. In 1938, his zealous belief that Jews should be
forced out of Europe led to a position as the officer in charge of admin-
istering the "forced emigration" of Jews in Austria, the Czech Republic,
and elsewhere.

During the trial, Eichmann was represented by Robert Servatius, a
German lawyer, and faced fifteen charges including multiple counts of
"crimes against the Jewish people," crimes against humanity, and war
crimes. The indictment under the first count of "crimes against the Jewish people" read, "The Accused caused the deaths of approximately half
a million of the Jews of Hungary by means of their mass deportation to
the extermination camp at Auschwitz and other places during the period between 19 March 1944 and 24 December 1944 when he was serving as Head of the Eichmann Special Commando Unit (Sondereinsatz-
Kommando Eichmann) in Budapest."[36] Other parts of the indictment
were more specific, such as his role in forced abortions for all women
who lived in the Kovno Ghetto, but the prosecution did not refrain from

broadly implicating him in the deaths of six million Jews who died in the Holocaust. Eichmann's formal plea on each charge was, "Not guilty in the sense of the indictment."[37]

In contrast to the Nuremberg prosecutors, Gideon Hausner, the chief prosecutor in the Eichmann case, decided to make the testimony of Holocaust victims central to the trial. One reason for this decision was the relationship he wanted to establish between the trial and the legitimacy of the state of Israel.[38] The justification for trying Eichmann in Jerusalem and not in front of an international tribunal, as Arendt would have preferred, stemmed from the specific claim made by the prosecution that Israel was the nation best suited to speak in the name of the Jewish people and that their suffering needed to be remembered by the new generation in Israel and around the world who had come of age after the war. Indeed, as a counter to charges of retroactive justice, Hausner argued that every Jew, including every unborn child who died as a result of Eichmann's administration, was a potential citizen of Israel, and thus each murder could be taken as violation of the Israeli body politic. In his opening statement, Hausner evoked the names of all those who died to show that his responsibility to prosecute Eichmann came directly from them. He further stated, "When I stand before you, judges of Israel, in this court, to accuse Adolf Eichmann, I do not stand alone. Here with me at the moment stand six million prosecutors. But alas, they cannot rise to level the finger of accusation in the direction of the glass dock and cry out *J'accuse* against the man who sits there."[39]

The memory of the dead was the justification for the trial, and the prosecution, on behalf of the state of Israel, positioned itself as carrying out the wishes of the murdered victims and also of all those who survived and who deserved recompense and justice. The focus on the testimony of survivors, many of whom lived in Israel, highlighted the triangular relationship between Eichmann's responsibility for the Holocaust, the ongoing suffering of the Jewish people, and the legitimacy of the state of Israel. The trial thus became a central piece in the Zionist project of nation building. The decision to bring victims to court as witnesses against Eichmann served the interests of the Israeli government in constructing a narrative about the relationship between Jewish suffering and the Zionist *raison d'état*.

Arendt saw this logic as responsible for the imposition of an all-encompassing narrative of Jewish victimhood onto the testimony of the witnesses, with the occasional story of Zionist heroism. What was missing from such a univocal and homogeneous narrative was acknowledgment of the complicity of the Jewish leadership, particularly the *Judenräte* (Jewish councils that administered activity in the Jewish communities of Germany, Poland, and elsewhere), in the Nazi deportations.[40] Arendt questioned why so many members of the Jewish councils were willing to comply with Nazi demands to give up the names and residences of members of their communities when they were aware that this information would be used for the purposes of deportation and later execution: "The whole truth was that there existed Jewish community organizations and Jewish party and welfare organizations on both the local and international level. Wherever Jews lived, there were recognized Jewish leaders, and this leadership, almost without exception, cooperated in one way or another, for one reason or another with the Nazis."[41] The role of the Jewish leadership in Europe during Nazi rule was a story that emerged only in small pieces throughout the trial, and Arendt's emphasis on and condemnation of the cooperation of the *Judenräte* was one of the most striking aspects of her writings on Eichmann.[42]

Arendt's most vehement criticism of the Jewish councils dealt with their policy of brokering exceptions to the rules of deportation and forced labor for the most prominent members of their communities.[43] The power of controlling the exceptions allowed Jewish leaders to save themselves and ensure the death of all nonspecial cases. Furthermore, the willingness of the councils to enter into such agreements with Nazi officials gave Nazi policy an illusion of legitimacy. During the trial, the prosecutor, Gideon Hausner, tried to neutralize this argument with a counterclaim: although Jewish resistance was extremely dangerous and nearly impossible given the available options, when it did occur in the camps, it was led by those who would become the Zionist leadership. Arendt, however, described the complicity of the Jewish leadership as "morally disastrous" and used it to question the monolithic victim narrative that was permeating interpretations of the Holocaust, even beyond the scope of the Eichmann trial.[44] Arendt's position distanced her from Jewish communities in the United States and effectively marked the end of her intellectual relationship with Zionism.[45]

Arendt's frustration with the framing of witness testimony to bolster one narrative of Jewish suffering and its connection to the Israeli state was part of her larger concern that the trial of Eichmann verged on becoming a show trial, a term reminiscent of the trials in the Soviet Union in which guilt was predetermined and credible evidence was optional.[46]

Just as Judith Shklar could not help but judge the success of the Nuremberg trials in relation to the anti-Communist trials in the United States,
Arendt was continually haunted by the specter of show trials in authoritarian regimes. She begins *Eichmann in Jerusalem* by highlighting the
theatrical spatial orientation of the courtroom and the showmanship of
Gideon Hausner, but it was the inclusion of victim testimony in the Eichmann trial that, for her, most closely resembled the distasteful aspects
of show trials. She feared that, in such trials, states could manipulate
emotions to create spectacles to bolster their authority—a critique that
would later be used against the implementation of state-sponsored truth
commissions.

On a fundamental level Arendt did not want to conflate the suffering of victims, particularly those victims who had never interacted with
Eichmann (almost all of them), with the establishment of his guilt. She
wrote, "Justice demands that the accused be prosecuted, defended, and
judged, and that all the other questions of seemingly greater import—of
'How could it happen?' and 'Why did it happen?,' of 'Why the Jews?' and
'Why the Germans?' . . . be left in abeyance."[47] This was an indictment
of the pedagogic use of the Eichmann trial, another point of divergence
from the strategy at Nuremberg. Intertwined with the prosecutors' desire to connect Jewish suffering with the legitimacy of the Jewish state
was their intention to teach the world about the events of the Holocaust,
a goal that Arendt considered redundant given the number of Jews in the
audience who, like her, were survivors of the period.

Arendt described the testimonies heard at the trial in the following
way: "As witness followed witness and horror was piled upon horror,
they sat there and listened in public to stories they would hardly have
been able to endure in private." That description captured one of the
most controversial aspects of the inclusion of emotion in the legal process—the renegotiation of public and private.[48] By the *public*, I am referring to the political realm—a realm of citizenship, rights, and equality under law—whereas the *private* connotes the more intimate spheres
of family and household concerns, including the realities of pain and suffering.[49] In her coverage of the Eichmann trial, Arendt did not indicate
that she saw value in renegotiating the boundary between public and private within the scope of a legal proceeding, especially not in the context of victim testimony. However, I posit that this is one of the tasks of
political institutions in periods of transitional justice. With war, and the
suffering that accompanies it, one can no longer pretend that one's pri-

vate world is protected from the intervention of the public world and the state. Not only are traditionally private concerns, such as those relating to the body, sexuality, and family, disrupted by war, but also one's very right to life has been threatened by public concerns directed by the state. Allowing victims to testify about their private lives, including their experiences of suffering—possibly the most private of private concerns—is one way to acknowledge the collapse of the public/private distinction in the wake of mass violence and the need to rebuild the political world in light of this reality.

The eliciting and public airing of information that was previously considered private was one of the two main reasons for Arendt's dissatisfaction with victim testimonies; the tone and emotional tenor of the testimonies was the other. For Arendt, the invitation to victims to testify for the prosecution gave the trial the air of a "mass meeting," a term that, for her, connotes even more emotional manipulation than "show trial." She wrote, "The atmosphere, not of a show trial but of a mass meeting, at which speaker after speaker does his best to arouse the audience was especially notable when the prosecution called witness after witness to testify to the rising in the Warsaw ghetto and to the similar attempts in Vilna and Kovno—matters that had no connection whatever with the crimes of the accused."[50] The phrase "arouse the audience" indicates Arendt's discomfort with the display of any emotion during the course of victim testimony. By calling the trial a "mass meeting," Arendt was suggesting that there was an expected performance of feverish emotion, as would be found in a political rally. The testimony of witnesses did not just happen to cause shock, grief, and physical weakness (several audience members fainted), but was precisely meant to evoke such intense feelings. From Arendt's point of view, this undermined the integrity of the trial and the prosecution's case against Eichmann.

In contrast to the witnesses Arendt believed were placed on the stand to rile up emotions, she preferred the type of testimony delivered by Zivia Lubetkin Zuckerman: "The purest and clearest account came from Zivia Lubetkin Zuckerman, today a woman of perhaps forty, still very beautiful, completely free of sentimentality or self-indulgence, her facts well organized, and always quite sure of the point she wished to make."[51]

Arendt's description of Zuckerman's testimony sets up the dichotomy between well-organized facts and a coherent presentation on the one hand and sentimentality and self-indulgence on the other. Because

Arendt equated the contributions of rationality and facts with the workings of justice in the trial, bridging the divide between sentiment, in
the form of emotions, and reason was not a possibility; such a perspective would have allowed her to appreciate the political significance of
testimonies that included an expression of emotions such as anger and
despair. The tone of Arendt's description also intimates that the view
that Zuckerman's ability to be "free of sentimentality" despite being a
woman made her even more worthy of praise. Throughout *Eichmann
in Jerusalem*, Arendt appears to be critical of both the stereotype of the
overly emotional woman and the public acts of suffering themselves.
Arendt saw herself as a Jewish woman and a political theorist who could
set aside the biases of her background to objectively cover the Eichmann
trial; she would have liked others to do the same. Her observations about
the witnesses at the Eichmann trial revealed that Arendt's preferences
end up aligning with the preferences of Robert Jackson and others who
had wanted a separation of the rational, factual documentary evidence
from the volatility of emotion in the Nuremberg trials.

Arendt's observation about the banality of Eichmann's attitude toward the crimes he committed, along with her distaste for the inclusion
of emotions in the trial, leads to a paradox within her writings concerning the authenticity of emotions displayed in public, particularly those
of the perpetrator. Eichmann's defense was based on his commitment
to following orders that he felt bound to administer. As such, he framed
his attitude toward the goals of the Third Reich in terms of a duty to
be undertaken without passion; detached indifference was his overriding
tone throughout the trial. Arendt, noticing this, was somewhat shocked
by his utter lack of creativity, personality, and ability to see things from
another's point of view, yet she also indicated that she would not have
been more convinced by words of contrition and hopes for forgiveness.
This is a paradox that may be intrinsic to the inclusion of emotions in
criminal trials or the proceedings of truth commissions: when a defendant displays the emotions that are expected by the court or the audience, that action is interpreted as an insincere ploy to manipulate others; when the defendant refrains from displaying such emotions—or any
emotions other than detachment—she is criticized for being indifferent
and lacking any human affect.

Witness testimony during the Eichmann trial was meant to teach a
new generation of Jews and the rest of the world about the devastation

of the Holocaust, but the act of communication was largely in one direction: the victims spoke to the rest of the world, but there was no response. Neither the judges nor the attorneys could spend significant time responding to the variety of individual experiences, especially those that deviated from the metanarrative of survival and persistence that the prosecution intended to be part of each victim's testimony. The emphasis during the trial was on (1) connecting the individual victims' testimonies to the massive atrocities that happened to millions who suffered similarly at the hands of the Nazis and (2) reasserting the legitimacy of Israel as the Jewish homeland. Neither of these goals allowed for a complete articulation of individual experiences, including anger, to be connected to the process of transitional justice, as could be the case with victim testimony in the context of a truth commission.

No Space for Despair

Whereas Jackson and Arendt were skeptics about the place of emotional testimony in the courtroom, the prosecutor in the Eichmann trial, Gideon Hausner, had a very clear vision of how the testimony of victims could (1) help convince the judges and the audience to accept the harshest punishment for Eichmann, (2) serve as a way to educate people about the Holocaust, and (3) highlight the resiliency and strength of the Jewish people. The testimony of the victims was a chance for Hausner to articulate a vision of Jewish identity that superseded individual, personal characteristics and thus affirmed the necessity of the state of Israel and the logic of laws that put Jews in a privileged position, such as the right of return for all Jews of the Diaspora. In Hausner's strategy, the court's acknowledgment of the suffering of victims would highlight by contrast the cold, calculating demeanor Eichmann displayed in the courtroom, as well as put forth a model of overcoming suffering with dignity.

The testimony of Holocaust survivor Leon Wells is an example of the prosecution's preferred narrative.[52] Wells testified that while in the concentration camp he was so malnourished and maltreated that he began to hallucinate and imagined that he was forced to drink his own blood. On the day that he was taken with other prisoners to a field to be executed, he was able to escape by faking his own death.[53] Yet after escaping from the camp, he was unable to begin a new life: he attempted suicide and was recaptured by the Germans and again forced to work in a labor camp. In the dramatic climax of his testimony at the Eichmann trial, Wells recalled that he was forced to dig up the grave that would have contained his own body. After Wells concluded recounting his Holocaust experiences, Hausner shifted to questioning him about his life at present. He asked Wells whether it was true that he had recently received an award for excellence in engineering. Wells answered affirmatively. As Douglas notes, this was Hausner's preferred way of concluding witness testimony: he would end with an anecdote or fact that reflected the witness's triumph over a dark period in his or her past, a heroic moment that showed strength and resiliency.[54]

Hausner's tendency to conclude victim testimony on a triumphant note reveals how someone can see the experiences of victims as central to justice after war but still not be comfortable with all the emotions of these experiences, particularly the emotions of intense anger and despair. By ending in this way, Hausner attempted to mitigate the most unsettling parts of the testimony: the psychological pain and existential questions that emerge from experiences during war.

The allaying of the most difficult emotions that emerged from victim testimony was not merely a strategic choice on the part of Gideon Hausner but reflected some of the intrinsic tensions when victim testimony is included as part of criminal trials. For instance, for the sake of legal procedure, only certain aspects of the testimony are considered relevant for the trial. The judges allowed Wells's testimony over the defense counsel's objection that it, like the testimonies of other victims, was irrelevant because Eichmann had no contact with Wells or any direct impact on his experiences.[55] Although Wells was allowed to talk about his experiences during the war, his testimony had to conform to certain expectations of length and content that prohibited him from fully articulating the emotional and psychological impact of his time in the camps, including his views of what justice might entail in the context of Israel after the Holocaust. There was no time for Wells to reflect on how his experiences continued to shape his perception of politics and the idea of progress. These questions are important to the rebuilding of society after war; they cannot be automatically deduced from formal documents or material evidence.

As victim testimony during the Eichmann trial indicates, people who live through a war may want to testify about how the violence of the past affects their life in the present and to reflect on how violent experiences shaped their core beliefs about politics and existence. The limitations, apparent at the Eichmann trial, on expressing these types of concern demonstrate that criminal trials could never allow for the full range of emotions that may emerge as part of victim testimony because these emotions would diverge too far from the primary task of establishing guilt or innocence. Nevertheless, other institutions, such as truth commissions, have drawn upon the legacy of testimony in the Eichmann trial and used it for different ends. The experiences of the Eichmann and Nuremberg trials revealed the importance, but also the inadequacies, of a criminal and legalistic response to the atrocities of war.

The second tension that became evident during the testimonies at the Eichmann trial was the question of who deserves sympathy. Although the prosecution wanted to include both the psychological and physical suffering of the victims as part of its larger strategy of attributing to Eichmann accountability for the mass murder of Jews and arguing for legitimacy of the state of Israel, there was a fine line between the emotions that were worthy of sympathy and those that were either self-indulgent or too difficult to understand. The Oxford English Dictionary defines *sympathy* as "a (real or supposed) affinity between certain things, by virtue of which they are similarly or correspondingly affected by the same influence, affect or influence one another, or attract or tend toward each other."[56] One's ability to identify with a victim or see similarities between the victim and oneself is a prerequisite for sympathy, and the potential for such similarities between victim and spectator decreases not only with the horror of the experience but also with the way in which it is expressed.[57] The shedding of tears, while indicative of vulnerability and human fragility—and thus a reason for human solidarity—may appear to others as unnecessarily dramatic and difficult to comprehend in the context of a trial. The witness who appears to have triumphed over the difficult experiences of his or her past through career success or having raised a family makes for a worthy object of sympathy.

The testimonies of victims often become a mirror of the way in which society more generally is recovering from war and mass violence. If spectators are confronted with feelings of bitterness instead of triumph, it becomes much more difficult for them to listen to this testimony in a sympathetic way. Hausner was aware of this, and Douglas notes that the structure of Hausner's questions "had the consequence of conventionalizing [the testimony], in so doing, containing its deeper, bleaker aspects."[58] The despair of a witness on the stand, such as the feeling that politics or life itself is ultimately meaningless, leaves the judges, attorneys, and audience in a difficult position. It is not clear how others in the courtroom should interpret this position. Given the extreme sentiments expressed, is this witness credible? Should the defendant be blamed for the victim's response? If not, how is it relevant to the trial? This type of emotional testimony during the Eichmann trial may have decreased the credibility of a witness and thus undermined both of Hausner's goals for the trial: it would be harder for the judge to hold Eichmann directly responsible for the emotional state of the witness, and the victims' expressions of pain and despair would not have bolstered the legitimacy of Israel. In the context of a criminal trial, the emotions of anger and despair can be voiced only in a moderate way. For victims to be truly allowed the freedom to express the contradictory, often unsettling emotions they are experiencing or have experienced in the past, there needs to be a different type of institution for transitional justice, one that can have a broader scope than that of criminal prosecution.[59] Truth commissions provide one such model.

Although I am critical of the limitations placed on witness testimony during the Eichmann trial, I am calling for neither a radical revision of criminal legal procedure nor the end of emotional restraint in courts of law: criminal prosecution through strictly enforced legal procedure, especially as part of justice after war, is important and *cannot* be replaced by victim-centered approaches alone. I do not intend the type of institution for which I am advocating—one that is more focused on the emotional aspects of testimony —to be a substitute for criminal trials, but rather to act as a supplement to them. As the field of transitional justice expands, I see the need for future scholarship that is concerned with how truth commissions and trials can work in a coordinated way to address a greater range of a nation's postwar social, political, and legal needs than either institution can address by itself. The obstacles to and limitations of victim testimony in the Eichmann trial are understandable given the primary goal of holding Adolf Eichmann accountable for crimes against humanity. Similarly, criminal trials should continue to have strict guidelines for procedure in order to ensure protections for the defendant and impartial judgment. However, criminal trials should not be the only manifestation of justice in the aftermath of war. By studying the points of tension between victim testimony and the legal goals of the Eichmann trial, an alternative framework emerges for understanding such testimony in the context of transitional justice.

Arendt contra Shklar

Arendt did not take as critical a stance toward the limitations of legalism as Shklar did; to the contrary, it often seemed that Arendt wished the Eichmann trial were more legalistic in Shklar's sense of the term. Shklar did not comment directly on Eichmann in her text, so it is not certain that her feelings about Nuremberg would automatically apply to this very different case. Yet the question remains: Would Shklar have wanted a more legalistic approach for the Eichmann trial? Arendt, largely because of the central role of oral testimony in the Eichmann case, advocated consistently for the type of justice premised on strict categorization of crimes and the impartial application of rules. Trying Eichmann on the basis of applying the ideas of "crimes against the Jewish people" and the illegality of waging an aggressive war was not troubling to her; neither was the charge of crimes against humanity, an allegation that Shklar found spurious because it lacked precedent. Arendt was also less committed to the pedagogical function of the trial. Nowhere does she say that Israel needed the trial to reinvigorate its own legal system or provide a prototype for specific cases in the future. Rather, the connection between the trial and nation building *writ large* was a source of concern for Arendt. She was not troubled by the fact that adherence to legalism would demand a singular focus on the actions of the accused and a rejection of pedagogic and nation-building goals of the trial; rather, she thought that this might actually be the most desirable approach to postwar justice.

Arendt's preference for a more legalistic orientation to the trial and her skepticism about the role of victims as witnesses closely parallels her expectations of journalistic writing. While covering the trial for the *New Yorker* she had the liberty of writing editorial pieces, but throughout her coverage it is evident that she wanted to situate herself as a rational and detached observer who was less motivated by vengeance and retribution than were other members of the audience and the Israeli prosecution. Arendt knew that she would be offering her own analysis of the political and psychological logic of the trial and considered her philosophical background and journalistic expertise, not her status as a Jewish émigré, to be the source of her authority to make such claims. However, although she attempted to approach the trial as a detached observer, it was much more difficult for her to shed her emotional preconceptions and biases in this context than in the context of any other of her works.

Seyla Benhabib argues that, compared to the rest of Arendt's oeuvre, *Eichmann in Jerusalem* is her least objective work, in which she "exhibited at times, an astonishing lack of perspective, balance of judgment, and judicious expression."[60] Here Benhabib is referring, in part, to the way Arendt spoke about Gideon Hausner and about the "oriental mob" outside the courtroom in Jerusalem.[61] Similarly, in the section where Arendt describes the actions of the *Judenräten*, her tone shifts from one of detachment to one of frustration and shame.[62] This alteration in emotional tone that accompanied Arendt's reporting on the actions of the Jewish councils, coupled with her willingness to challenge the master narrative of Jewish victimhood that underwrote the trial, reveals the impossibility of separating fact from emotion in her own understandings of the trial. Her identity as a Jew, her complex feelings about having survived the Holocaust but having to leave Europe as the cost of survival, and her status as an intellectual all influenced her reportage, especially her recounting of the facts of the Jewish councils. Had she engaged with this, it may have been fruitful for valuing the emotional expression of testimony in a different way.[63] Arendt's writing also reveals the complexity of the position of the spectator who is witnessing victim testimony—it is an experience that often prompts reflection on one's own complicity, guilt, and fear.

Lessons from Arendt's Book on Eichmann

Arendt's concern that victim testimony was elicited in a way that primarily served Zionist needs for legitimization and made it more difficult to determine Eichmann's responsibility leads her to dismiss the value of that testimony altogether. Moreover, her contempt for Hausner's strategy extended to contempt for all emotional expression by the victims during the course of the trial. She was too preoccupied with the distortions of what she perceived to be the most important questions of the trial—the ones relating to Eichmann's guilt—and thus could not see the potential for victim testimony to influence political life. She did not understand how such testimony could be the source of meaningful insights about the psychological legacy of war, nor did she consider the significance of expressions of anger and despair for Israeli political life that would exist long after the Eichmann trial. Whereas she dismissed all expressions of grief and despair as part of Hausner's opportunism and strategy to foment nationalism and a sense of victimization, I see the experience of victim testimony during the Eichmann trial as the beginning of a new role for such testimony in transitional justice and the precedent for truth commissions in contemporary politics.

Nonetheless, although Arendt's critique of the use of victim testimony in the trial of Adolf Eichmann denies its potential, she brought up issues that will continue to shape understandings of victim testimony in the context of truth commissions. These issues include the danger of imposing a singular narrative onto all the testimonies, whether for an instrumental purpose, such as the legitimization of a regime, or as the result of cultural or religious assumptions about the nature of suffering and redemption. Arendt's critique of Hausner's strategy also demonstrated the necessity of separating the different needs of transitional justice, including punishment, and the danger of conflating methods and goals without thoroughly understanding their implications. When individuals are made vulnerable by having to disclose traumatic experiences in the context of victim testimony, there is an even greater need to be vigilant about how their testimonies will be used by the state.

Trauma on Trial

In her book *The Juridical Unconscious*, Shoshana Felman looks at examples of trials in the twentieth century, including the trials of Eichmann and O. J. Simpson, and shows how the experiences of trauma, particularly the traumas of racial and sexual violence, are enacted in the courtroom.[64] According to Felman, even when the traumatic experiences of victims are explicitly addressed, as was the case in the Eichmann trial, the legal process must always aim for closure and documentation, while the experience of trauma consistently resists both these goals. Testimony about trauma resists the idea that language can adequately represent the violence that the witness has experienced. Thus, just as the law tries to incorporate the idea of trauma into the trial, testimony about trauma evades and eludes the functional role that it should serve in a trial. Felman's argument supports the theory that there is always an uneasy rela-

tionship between testimony and the criminal trial and that arrangements
to include victim testimony often leave multiple parties unsatisfied. However, despite these tensions, Felman thinks that victim testimony is still
necessary within criminal trials.

The testimony of K-Zetnik, a Holocaust survivor and author who testified during the Eichmann trial, is a good example of the complex relationship between trauma and trial procedure that Felman describes.[65]
K-Zetnik was called to testify that he had seen Eichmann at Auschwitz,
a key piece of evidence that would help prove that Eichmann was fully
aware of the extent of the killings taking place in the name of the Third
Reich. K-Zetnik was not the witness's real name; it was an alias referring
to the colloquial term for the identification numbers that the Nazis tat-
tooed on the arms of all concentration camp inmates. Yehiel Dinoor took
this pseudonym when he began chronicling the experiences of those who
had perished in the death camps. Dinoor viewed his role as an author to
be that of serving as a means of communication between the living and
the dead—a liminal role that Felman argues he continued to occupy during the trial. Dinoor/K-Zetnik had just begun his substantive testimony
during the Eichmann trial when he suddenly collapsed beside the witness stand. He was carried out of the courtroom by policemen and spent
the next two weeks in a hospital as part of his recovery from a paralytic
shock. Felman asserts that K-Zetnik's collapse represented a moment of
rupture in the trajectory of the trial that made bare the essence and limitations of witness testimony. His physical collapse was the most dramatic
example of the centrality of the human body, in all its fragility and weakness, to the trial, and it showed that the documentation of trauma could
not easily be translated into words and could not rely on the disembodied
intellect. Furthermore, the fact that K-Zetnik could not offer testimony
in the way that Hausner wanted him to makes apparent the difficulty of
using testimony about trauma as part of a linear narrative about suffering and guilt within the context of a criminal trial. For Felman, this will
always be a practice fraught with contradiction, even as such testimonies
provide rich moments of insight into the unconscious pain and hopes of
individuals and communities. Felman celebrates the significance of the
dramatic moments in the Eichmann trial and the unpredictable nature
of the testimonies about traumatic experiences.[66] More broadly, Felman
argues that "the trial is, primarily and centrally, a legal process of translation of thousands of private, secret traumas into one collective, public
and communally acknowledged one," and the constraints of a criminal

trial are a small price to pay for such acknowledgment.[67] Although Felman sees the value of incorporating testimonies about trauma into criminal trials, they may be better suited for victim testimony in the context of truth commissions. In the period after war, truth commissions should be seen as complementary institutions to criminal trials that have fewer constraints on the format of victim testimony than would be found in a criminal trial and, thus, provide greater opportunities for engaging with traumatic experiences in a politically significant way.[68]

The Eichmann Trial as the Gateway to Emotions in Transitional Justice

Victim testimony occupied a very uneasy role in the war crimes trials that followed World War II. By examining the discussion that surrounded the use of such testimony at the Nuremberg trials and the trial of Adolf Eichmann, I have shown how victim testimony was viewed during Nuremberg as separate from questions of justice but it became part of the prosecutorial strategy during the Eichmann trial. Those debates and controversies surrounding victim testimony are representative of the larger debate in political philosophy about the separation of rationality and emotional expression in discussions of justice, but the line between what can be considered "rational" and what is "emotional" can never be definitively decided. The boundary is malleable largely because of the experiences of war themselves—experiences that cannot be easily recorded as objective facts nor translated into purely rational language, nor are they experiences that exist only within individual psychology and do not influence the larger society or politics after war. Understanding the events of war and their ongoing effect on political life requires attention to the factual and emotional aspects of testimony, both of which are parts of a rational understanding of the legacy of war.

The emphasis on victim testimony during the Eichmann trial laid the foundation for new approaches to considering justice in the period after World War II and has made an impact far beyond the scope of the Holocaust. Truth commissions are part of the legacy of Eichmann and they have been premised on the idea that the testimony of victims can serve as a way to educate the public about the experiences of war and also provide a place for victims and perpetrators to renegotiate their reentry into society. Since the late 1970s, there have been over thirty truth commissions set up by states as temporary bodies to investigate violence during a particular period in history; they often complete their work with the submission of a report.[69] Truth commissions, by virtue of operating outside set legal codes and not being primarily concerned with the prosecution of individuals, have much more freedom than normal criminal trials in constructing the role of victim testimony.[70]

In his reflections on the Eichmann trial, German philosopher Karl Jaspers advocated for the idea of a commission solely in charge of gathering facts about war crimes. In a letter to Hannah Arendt, his former doctoral student and close friend, he wrote, "I have already stated my view that this trial is wrongly conceived at its very root. Now I have this foolishly simplistic idea: It would be wonderful to do without the trial altogether and make it instead into a process of examination and clarification. The goal would be the best possible objectification of the historical facts. The end result would not be the judges' sentence, but certainty about the facts, to the extent such certainty can be attained."[71] Jaspers hoped that such a commission would be more objective than a trial, unhindered by the constraints on discovery and disclosure that exist within criminal procedure, but he was not particularly concerned with victim testimony. Jaspers would prefer more "facts," while I would argue for greater attention to the psychological consequences of war as seen through the emotion of anger, but we are both motivated by the need for a more comprehensive picture of war and its ongoing significance within political life.

Since it does not have the burden of remaining relevant to conventional legal proceedings or the actions of a defendant, the type of testimony that is admissible in a truth commission is much broader than would be the case in a trial.[72] Specifically, there is much more room for emotional reflections on past actions and the psychological legacy of trauma. Although they allow more room for emotions in addition to the factual communication of events, truth commissions may be vulnerable to the same problems of institutional manipulation and a coercive, univocal narrative that Arendt saw at play in the Eichmann trial. Depending on their format and the predispositions of the commissioners, truth commissions may also be limited by their inability to fully acknowledge the complexity of anger. Because of its unsettling and confrontational nature, anger occupies a tenuous position in truth commissions, just as it did in war crimes trials, and although I advocate for an engagement with anger, I do not deny that truth commissions are vulnerable to manipulation and misuse. Questions of historical and cultural context, along with administrative competence, shape the possibilities of victim testimony in substantial ways. Experience has shown that although truth commissions have the potential to be more focused on the needs of victims in terms of judgment and response, the framers of truth commissions are often unsure about what to with this responsibility.[73] Still, the great significance of truth commissions lies in their potential to achieve two important goals of transitional justice: (1) they can allow victims, perpetrators, and bystanders to fully communicate their emotions, particularly anger, and (2) they can lay a foundation for the trust that is necessary for civic participation.[74]

The South African Truth and Reconciliation Commission

The South African Truth and Reconciliation Commission (TRC) is a paradigmatic case of the centrality of victim testimony in the context of a truth commission. From 1996 to 1998, thousands of South Africans testified in the hearings held by the Human Rights Violations (HRV) Committee of the TRC about their experiences under apartheid. They came from many different backgrounds and included activists, security guards, and students. They spoke about the deaths of loved ones and the feeling of living in constant fear of violence. Many wanted to find out the details about how a family member had died so there could be a proper burial.[75] Those seeking amnesty for political crimes committed during the apartheid era took part in a separate process since the HRV Committee hearings were not connected to any criminal charges or investigations. The hearings were covered daily on national television and also received significant international coverage. A weekly television program, hosted by journalist Max Du Preez, covering the events of the TRC that week became the most watched television series in South African history.[76] By all accounts, the testimony of victims at the TRC was the center of a national drama and one of the strongest images of the transition from apartheid to the new democratic republic of South Africa.[77]

The leadership of Archbishop Desmond Tutu was crucial to the public image of the TRC because of the widespread respect he had earned across different religious communities within and outside South Africa. He often made the final comment that would conclude an individual's testimony, and this acted as a type of symbolic response from the commission. He thanked the witnesses for telling the commission what happened, commended them for their courage, and shared personal observations about their testimony. As opposed to acting as an attorney who elicits testimony for the sake of establishing guilt, or as a judge who must maintain the rule of order and impartiality, Tutu was able to have the authority of a judge while serving as an empathetic ally of those who took the stand. Each witness was also provided with an advocate familiar with the process who sat next to him or her during the testimony and facilitated the debriefing process afterward. Witnesses were thus given attention beyond their brief moment of testimony because the act of testifying was seen as a thing-in-itself, not just, as in a criminal trial, another part of the case against the perpetrators.

When Archbishop Tutu was interviewed at the end of the HRV Committee hearings, he focused on the three functions of the testimonies that he considered to be the most important.[78] First, the hearings gave victims an opportunity to restore their dignity: they were allowed to be treated as respected members of the community who had something useful to offer, and Tutu saw his role as helping to restore the human and civil integrity of each person. Second, they made the experiences of those who had been marginalized in the past the center of the new official history of South Africa. Third, they provided what could be seen as part of an individual therapeutic process. Each of the functions described by Tutu is plausible and potentially important enough to warrant such a type of public institution. Still, none focus on the potential impact this type of testimony may have on broader society, which is a motivating question of the present project.

One of the most notable features of the TRC was the language of forgiveness that surrounded it. In his book *No Future with Forgiveness*, Desmond Tutu writes: "Social harmony is for us the *summum bonum*— the greatest good. Anything that subverts, that undermines this sought-after good, is to be avoided like the plague. Anger, resentment, lust for revenge, even success through aggressive competitiveness, are corrosive of this good. To forgive is not just to be altruistic. It is the best form of self-interest."[79] Although his theological use of the concept of forgiveness set an idealistic tone for the commission, it served to limit the commission's ability to respond to the emotions of anger and despair within the context of victim testimony.[80]

Some critics have argued that the coercive narrative of forgiveness and redemption became a form of state control over South Africans and an invasive tool of hegemonic power.[81] On the influence of the language of forgiveness, Richard Wilson writes, "This discourse, in providing new meaning for suffering and death, created heroes and martyrs in a new mythology of the state. Being memorialized was the victim's recompense for suffering, vitiating the need for retaliation or retribution."[82] I find Wilson's claim that the TRC acted as a conduit to strengthen the legitimacy and coercive power of the state, with or without forgiveness as the central concept, to be a persuasive argument against the political significance of truth commissions. His critique of the legitimacy of the TRC may appear to make unsalvageable any argument for the political significance of victim testimony, but this is not the only option.[83] There is a type of narrative openness—one that includes anger—that has the potential to act as a counterpoint to coercive narratives put forward by the state. Moreover, the expectation of a response by the political community to the particular needs and fears voiced through the process of victim testimony would also act to prevent a truth commission from becoming a tool for predetermined self-legitimating action by the state.

Although Archbishop Tutu and the TRC were criticized for harboring biases against the expression of anger and despair that were similar to those seen during the Eichmann trial,[84] there were moments in the hearings that allowed these emotions to be expressed candidly, exemplifying the narrative openness mentioned above. The following excerpt is taken from the testimony of Sepati Mlangeni. She testified about her husband, an attorney and activist with the African National Congress, who was killed after opening a letter bomb sent by Eugene de Kock, the head of foreign counter-terrorist operations for the South African Defense Force and a notorious figure within the TRC because of his ill-treatment of political activists. When a TRC commissioner asked Mlangeni what she would like from the commission, she began by saying that she had heard that de Kock had applied for amnesty:

Other issues that I have been getting from newspapers is that Eugene de Kock says he's going to ask amnesty from you. I contest this. Eugene, when he did what he did, he knew that somebody would die. Today I'm a widow, I'm an outcast in our society because I'm a widow. In our community and our society you are associated with all sorts of things when you are a widow because of a person who didn't think through when they were doing this, so that when this person comes to you to ask for amnesty, how do you forgive such a person? If I can find an answer to this question, how do you go about forgiving this person who is a cruel murderer, who killed a defenseless person who'd never killed anyone, to a person who'd never raped anyone, a person who never committed any crime, who was just fighting for peoples' rights but without carrying a gun? I would love the Commission to assist me there.[85]

Mlangeni did not want to forgive and did not want the TRC to accept de Kock's plea for amnesty. Her anger at de Kock and her frustration with the commission was palpable, as was her dissatisfaction at her current place in society: "I am an outcast" she said; it is clear that she felt that her life has been defined by the death of her husband and that neither telling the truth about what happened nor punishing de Kock could change this. Her testimony was one of anger and despair, and the commissioners realized that there was nothing they could or should do to mitigate it. When Archbishop Tutu responded, "We do not have words to console you but as you saw, it was as if there was nobody inside this house as because they were listening [*sic*]," he was acknowledging the difficulty of expressing these emotions and the fact that they cannot easily be turned into hopes for perseverance and triumph or a renewed faith in justice.[86] The testimony, including the silence of the audience that occurred in response, had a value apart from its instrumental use in contributing to a more accurate record of the violence that occurred: it provided information about what would be needed to incorporate Mlangeni into the political community. The uncertainty that the commissioners, the audience, and perhaps even Sepati Mlangeni felt regarding what could come out of this testimony was an unavoidable part of the process, and the fact that the commission allowed difficult experiences of anger and despair to be voiced despite that uncertainty demonstrated the great potential of the Truth and Reconciliation Commission. Sepati Mlangeni's testimony contributed to a more accurate record of historical events but also articulated the ongoing impact of her loss and described an aspect of the psychological legacy of apartheid that was not to be erased just because political structures had changed. The way she was treated as a widow influenced how she understands her self-worth and her role in the political community, and these topics should be as important for a commission and the public to consider as the factual details of the violence.

The testimony of Mlangeni is representative of what can be achieved through victim testimony in public after mass violence. Through testify-

ing, individuals have the chance to contribute to the collective historical record and to reflect on the psychological and material legacies of the
violence in their lives, including the presence of anger. Political and institutional changes after war will not lead to a thriving civil and political culture unless these underlying emotions are acknowledged. This acknowledgment entails a reconsideration of the strict boundary between
rational truth and emotion. In the context of postwar justice, the boundary between what can be considered "rational" and what is "emotional"
is inherently malleable because the experiences of war cannot easily be
recorded as objective facts or translated into purely rational language.
A cognitive-evaluative approach to emotions does not claim that rational deductions and the insights gained from emotions are interchangeable; they are not and cannot be verified in the same way. But emotions
can still provide important insights into what individuals consider to be
significant and urgent in their lives and suggest what is needed to foster a
sense of trust and legitimacy in politics. A cognitive-ealuative reading of
them is not the only way that trust will be fostered; the confrontational
and kinetic dimensions of anger are also important. In addition, testimonies also reveal why individuals may choose to refrain from participating
in politics. These insights are not necessarily articulated clearly by individual testimonies, but they become apparent through repeated themes
and concerns that emerge over the course of a truth commission. The
anger and despair of victims permeate citizen relationships and perceptions of government after mass violence, and this is revealed through the
process of victim testimony in a way that would not be possible through
other political channels.

The Nuremberg trials were a remarkable attempt to create a legal
arena for crimes and criminals who transcended any one nation. The unprecedented nature of the crimes and the charges (i.e., crimes against
humanity) meant that attention to legal procedure was important to provide the trials with legitimacy. Yet, in contrast to the emphasis on documentary evidence at the Nuremburg tribunal, victim testimony was at
the center of the case against Adolf Eichmann, the Nazi officer in charge
of the deportation of Jews. The narratives of victims were important
both to the criminal proceedings and to a collective awareness about the
events of the Holocaust. Most importantly, the Eichmann trial, through
its willingness to let victims take the stand, initiated a new trajectory in
transitional justice. This trajectory posited justice as a concept that went

beyond accountability and punishment and included the emotions of the victims and the legacy of suffering that affects entire societies—not only perpetrators and victims—after mass violence. The concept of victim testimony, which suggests the potential of individual narratives to reveal, document, and hold others accountable, was born of the Eichmann trial and is now a central part of truth commissions.

CHAPTER TWO

Confronting Anger

Where the South African TRC Fell Short

In its ambitious reckoning with the violence of the apartheid era, the South African Truth and Reconciliation Commission (TRC) included testimonies that revealed emotions that would have been considered beyond the appropriate scope of testimony in most criminal trials. Yet, although formally included, the moments when victims expressed anger were either ignored altogether or met with ambivalence and confusion about their significance and the appropriate response. This chapter analyzes moments of anger that I found in the written transcripts from the Human Rights Violations hearings—these include direct references to anger, sentence structures that suggest anger, and a quick succession of issues that implies that the speaker may be conveying anger. Without video footage, I had to make sense of moments of anger from what was on the page and was often found in moments of disruption—that is, moments when the question-and-response structure was suspended for other types of comments from the judges. An examination of the transcripts revealed the many ways that an engagement with anger was eclipsed by other concerns and by uncertainty regarding its purpose.

The TRC began each witness's testimony with an open-ended question about the key event of violence such as "What happened to your cousin?" or "What happened on June 16, 1976?"[1] These types of questions allowed the witnesses to have some freedom in constructing a narrative around the event and also provided a space for expressing the emotions that were connected with the human-rights violation at the center of the commission's inquiry. The open-ended nature of the initial question was followed by a specific question about the details of the event,

often details that would be useful in a further investigation of the violence.[2] At this time the commission asked, for example, "Where were
the other people in the house?" or "Did you know the names of the people that were assaulting you?" These types of question allowed the commissioners to add information to the historical record and also to piece
together evidence that emerged during the course of different testimonies. The questions represented for the commissioners a clear path to a
more inclusive record and fulfilled the goal of documentation that scholars such as Priscilla Hayner and Michael Ignatieff think is central to
the aims of truth commissions. In his introduction to Jillian Edelstein's
Truth and Lies, a photographic essay about witnesses who testified before the TRC, Ignatieff wrote, "One could say that the whole process
had one irrefutable result. It narrowed the range of impermissable lies
that one could tell in public. . . . It is sometimes essential that former regimes are shamed into unalterable moral disgrace: that their inner moral
essence is named and defined for all times by an objective process of
fact-finding."[3]

During the witness testimonies at the Human Rights Violations hearings the commissioners consistently asked two other types of question:
the first was a question about the impact of an incident on the witness's
health. When a commissioner asked, "And how is your health now?" this
was an invitation for the witness to address both her physical and emotional well-being. In response, some witnesses talked about their ongoing need for medical care or their desire for psychiatric counseling:
mothers who had lost sons talked about what it was like to grieve the
loss of a child, and men who were unable to father children because of
the torture they experienced talked about their humiliation and frustration. When asked about the legacy of violence in their lives, witnesses
had an opportunity to respond in a way that confronted grief, anger, and
despair in a direct way. However, witnesses often gave terse answers,
and it appeared that they were not prepared to elaborate on this question. They seemed to think that the commission did not want to hear a
broad interpretation of the events through the lens of their psychological health. Moreover, the commission often did not recognize expressions of anger with questions that would have encouraged witnesses to
go into greater detail about these issues. The reluctance to engage with
anger at this time was unfortunate because this was precisely the place
where information could have emerged about what aspects of the vio-

lence continued to trouble witnesses and the extent to which this shaped their ability to trust the current police system or state.[4]

Finally, the commissioners would ask a witness, "What would you like the Commission to do for you?" This question was one of the clearest indicators of how the orientation of a truth commission is different from that of a criminal trial because it suggests that the commission had a direct relationship with the victims and a responsibility to be open to their requests. Many witnesses responded to this question with a request for some type of material reparations, such as medical coverage, a house, or a pension.[5] Other witnesses asked for a memorial to remember those who had died. In addition to giving witnesses a chance to address the specific issue of reparations, the question gave individuals a chance to express disappointment and doubt with the commission itself, a foundational experience that is necessary for the reestablishment of political values after mass violence. The consistency of the questions that witnesses were asked at the Human Rights Violations hearings served as a way to standardize the breadth of individual testimonies and was meant to structure the balance between a material and a psychological focus. Still, the commission was ultimately not able to fully explore the expressions of anger both because of an interest in other goals and because of an uncertainty about the value of such an endeavor. I suggest that the commission constrained the expression of anger in four main ways: (1) through its inability to resolve the conflict between an investigation of material evidence and the psychological legacy of war; (2) its emphasis on forgiveness; (3) its tendency to consider anger as an individual psychological problem rather than political commentary; and (4) its usage of the language of getting back to "normal."

The consistency of requests for material reparations heard during the testimonies at the TRC further confirms the idea that victim testimony is not effective in isolation: it should be accompanied by criminal trials and reparations as part of the process of transitional justice. Each element in the triadic structure bolsters the other two in the process of justice after war; all are necessary to nurture the elusive goal of political trust.[6] I agree with Ernesto Verdeja's claim that reparations play an important role in transitional justice, although I attribute to victim testimony greater power for political transformation than reparations have.[7] In his writings, Verdeja makes the argument that reparations are morally significant and should not be dismissed as instrumental efforts by the

state to "buy off" victims.[8] He situates reparations within a larger process of transitional justice in which the main purpose is to seek a critical
engagement with the past. However, while Verdeja places his emphasis
on reparations, the process of victim testimony is more capable of doing
the symbolic and moral work of transitional justice and being oriented to
future action, although I concur that reparations strengthen trust in public institutions in a way that victim testimony by itself cannot.[9]

Tension between Material Evidence and the Needs of Victims

A truth commission is often described as containing aspects of both
criminal justice and restorative justice. One implication of this hybrid
model is a more open orientation toward the types of testimony that
will be admissible on the witness stand; whereas in a criminal court, a
witness is limited to providing evidence that is directly relevant to the
case, the testimony during a truth commission is not limited by these
constraints. This two-pronged orientation toward justice was evident in
the origins of the South African TRC, and the charter of the commission described its purpose in the following way: "to provide for the investigation and the establishment of as complete a picture as possible of
the nature, causes and extent of gross violations of human rights" and to
afford "victims an opportunity to relate the violations they suffered."[10]
Thus, from its inception two goals were equally important for the TRC:
The first was to collect material evidence, and the second was to allow
witnesses to speak more broadly about the violations they suffered. Although both goals were important, an examination of the transcripts of
the testimony shows that at many points during the TRC the commissioners privileged the investigative function of gathering material evidence and thus lessened the opportunity to address the psychological aspects of victim testimony.

The investigative emphasis on recounting the specific facts of an event
served the needs of certain witnesses as well as those of the commissioners. For many witnesses the details of the day a loved one died were still
very vivid in their memories, and the transcripts of the testimonies reveal that they appreciated the opportunity to share these details with
the commission. The chance to recount the day a family member disap-
peared was also a chance to reflect on the emotions that one felt at that
time, including the frustration and sadness that stemmed from not hav-

ing information about what happened. However, certain commissioners seemed to particularly emphasize their investigative role and were
driven by the opportunity to aid in future criminal investigations, and
some spoke as if this were the biggest contribution that the TRC could
make to South African history.[11] From their vantage point, the TRC was
most useful when it played the role of lawyers in the discovery phase of a
trial, synthesizing details and amassing factual testimony. This tendency
reflects the tension within all truth commissions between the need to
remember those who died and the need to focus on the experiences of
those who are providing testimony. The commission was never able to
reconcile these two functions and wavered between wanting to uncover
the details pertaining to the investigation of a disappearance or killing
and focusing on the impact on the survivor.[12] On a fundamental level, the
commissioners seemed unsure as to how exploring the emotional legacy
of violence could be as fruitful as exploring the details of the crime and
thus ended up promulgating a more conventional view of what emotions
were appropriate for political life.

In his influential book Richard Wilson expresses a concern with how
the discourse of human rights and reconciliation worked in the practice of the commission, and not just in the theory that surrounded it. His
overall position is one of skepticism about the goals of the TRC, which
he sees as an institution meant to legitimate and foment the power of
the state in a specious way.[13] He argues that the "TRC's account of the
past was constrained by its excessive legalism and positivist methodology, which obstructed the writing of a coherent socio-political history
of apartheid."[14] Wilson's understanding of "excessive legalism and positivist methodology" refers to the TRC's desire to act as an investigative
body whose main purpose was to disclose facts, and the positivist methodology was one that relied on statements that could be verified with
other types of evidence. Wilson is skeptical of the emphasis on reconciliation, especially in its co-option of the indigenous concept of *ubuntu*
as the basis for restorative justice, and of the metaphor of the nation as a
wounded body in need of healing. His research shows the entrenchment
of the language of revenge within institutions of local justice and suggests that such feelings could also have facilitated just outcomes as promoted by the TRC.[15] Instead, the discourse of reconciliation and healing
acted as a way for the state to consolidate control over the lives of citizens
and to assign an overarching narrative to South African history. Wilson
writes, "Nations do not have collective psyches which can be healed and

to assert otherwise is to psychologize an abstract entity which exists primarily in the minds of nation-building politicians."[16] Wilson takes a critical approach to the concept of a collective psyche and the psychological language that permeated the TRC, and although I take his point about the dangers of assigning a psychological identity to the nation to be quite valid, I am more sympathetic than he is to the possibilities of exploring the presence of anger within a truth commission.

In contrast to Wilson, Drucilla Cornell finds the inclusion of *ubuntu* to be one of the strengths of the Truth and Reconciliation Commission and one of the most promising concepts in the new South African legal framework.[17] She writes:

> *Ubuntu*, in a profound sense, and whatever else it may be, implies an interactive ethic, or an ontic orientation in which who and how we can be as human beings is always being shaped in our interaction with each other. This ethic is not then a simple form of communalism or communitarianism, if one means by those terms the privileging of the community over the individual. For what is at stake here is the process of becoming a person or, more strongly put, how one is given the chance to become a person at all.[18]

Critics have charged *ubuntu* as being defined too expansively in order to catch a wide variety of concepts and, as such, have claimed that it is not precise enough to be a useful legal term. Cornell's interest in *ubuntu* is both philosophical and anthropological and points to alternative conceptions of justice that exist within established traditions. If the commissioners had asked questions that probed how an individual considered their experiences with violence in relation to understandings of justice, particularly culturally situated understandings such as *ubuntu*, it would have allowed for a more expansive conversation about what was necessary for transitional justice.

Wilson's text also addresses how the process of taking written statements changed over the course of the commission, namely how it started as an open-ended interview, but then changed to a narrow questionnaire that precluded discussions about the ongoing emotional impact of past violence. All witnesses who testified in public were first interviewed by a trained TRC staff member and then submitted written statements. In an interview with Wilson, Themba Kubheka, chief data processor in charge of the TRC testimonies, describes how the process evolved: "When we started it was a narrative. We let people tell their story. By the end of

1997, it was a short questionnaire to direct the interview instead of letting people talk about themselves. . . . The questionnaire distorted the whole story altogether . . . it destroyed the meaning."[19]

Kubheka's observations indicate that the tendency to focus on the investigative rather than the psychological aspects of witness testimony began with the methodology of the interview that occurred even before the witnesses took the stand. Preliminary interactions with the commission already communicated that the most valuable parts of the testimony were those that could add to the official record of human-rights violations, and the evolution of the written statements taken from witnesses over the course of the TRC reflected the larger trend of the commission: a retreat from the goal of a direct engagement with the psychological aspects of the apartheid era in order to emphasize verifiable facts.

The following is an example of how the investigative benefit of the testimony was seen as more important than the psychological legacy of the event. In the excerpt below, the witness, Mabotha Nurster Madisha, testified about the death of her son, a black anti-apartheid activist who died while in the custody of the state. After he was killed she found several notes in her son's jacket that contained information relevant to his disappearance, and she brings this up in her testimony. The commissioners did not ask her how she responded when she read the notes or how they have shaped the memory of her son, but they were interested in obtaining the notes as evidence:

MRS MADISHA: I didn't know why he was arrested but they suspected that there were bullets. And I went to his bedroom, I found some dry cleaning which I didn't know to whom it belonged. They just told me that he had hanged himself with his shirt.

CHAIRPERSON: You've got those notes that your son kept and wrote down?

MRS MADISHA: I still have some at home, because *I told myself that I'm going to give them to his son, the one that his mother was expecting at that time.* So I kept them to give to my grandchild.

CHAIRPERSON: Is it possible for you to let us have copies of that so that we can also try and piece together what happened?

MRS MADISHA: Some of those notes were taken by the inquest people but I still have some and I can bring them to you. [20]

Although Madisha spoke about wanting to give the notes to her grandchild, the commission moved directly to a consideration of the notes as key pieces of evidence. This moment again revealed the potential for conflict when there is responsibility to gather evidence, juxtaposed with the responsibility to respond to the particular emotions of the witness. For Madisha, the opportunity to talk about the significance of the disappearance and death of her son could have included how she made sense of the information she received (including what was in the notes) and how this changed the way she thought about her role in the political community. The opportunity to talk about this was closed off with the commissioners' focus on the evidence. The transcript reveals how easy it might be to subordinate the emotional expression of the victim to other goals because it is only a small part of the testimony. I suggest that the systematic overlooking of a certain line of questioning regarding emotional expression limited the transformation from victim to citizen that was possible within the truth commission. When the commission thought of its role as primarily legalistic, it missed the opportunity to adequately explore the psychological perspective, including the anger, of witnesses who were providing oral testimony.

The tension between the mandate to gather material evidence and the need to be attuned to the psychological legacy of violence was intrinsic to the hybrid structure of the TRC and of truth commissions more generally. This conflict between the two goals can be mitigated by clear guidelines for the mission of such a commission and for the division of labor between amnesty hearings, criminal courts, and victim testimony. In reality, even when these guidelines were quite clearly defined, as in the case of the TRC, the individual predispositions of commissioners resulted in a more investigative tone. The model of privileging investigation is connected to an idea of reason rather than to a cognitive-evaluative or confrontational reading of the emotions as providing insights necessary for restorative justice. Another way to describe this predisposition to material investigation is the notion that in a morass of interpretations and counter-interpretations of the same event, the most durable work an institution can do is to record as many facts as possible. This factual approach is consistent with the ideology that pervaded the Nuremberg trials and their focus on retributive justice. I do not set up this idea of a justice based on positivistic methods only as a foil; on the contrary, it is one of the most persuasive perspectives within scholarship on transitional justice and generates important standards of impartiality for war crimes trials. Yet, the decision to default to a narrower understanding

of justice during victim testimony, one that can be deduced from verifiable facts, is to turn away from the possibility of a new type of justice
that acknowledges the benefits of an engagement with anger for both the
speaker and the listening audience.

The Emphasis on Forgiveness

The overlapping nature of the private and the public spheres is a salient
feature of the content of testimony at truth commissions. The role of
statements of faith and spirituality at the TRC is part of this interaction
of public and private, and in the period after mass violence questions of
ultimate commitments cannot be separated from politics in the way that
is often articulated within liberal democratic theory. The rebuilding of
the world in the wake of devastation is an existential project, along with
a political and legal one, and may use religious language and concepts.[21]
This is not something that should be feared or avoided; yet, at the same
time, it is a difficult proposition within the context of a democratic public institution.

In the South African case, Desmond Tutu set the tone for thinking
about the commission in terms of forgiveness and redemption.[22] When
speaking at the Johannesburg hearings, he said, "Almost all who have
testified thus far have amazed us, have amazed the world with their willingness to forgive. They want not to revenge themselves against perpetrators. They are not looking for retribution, but quite remarkably they
do want to forgive."[23] While this was an exaggeration of the sentiments
of "almost all," it reflected Tutu's vision for the commission: he professed
that the act of testimony would prompt individuals who took the stand to
consider forgiveness, rather than anger or bitterness, and that this would
inspire other individuals to do the same.[24] All aspects of forgiveness in
one's personal life also took on a collective significance; forgiveness was
necessary for the future of a democratic South Africa. The act of forgiveness was the pivot upon which the transition to a more peaceful future rested, and each individual act of forgiveness was seen as a sacrifice
necessary for the success of the nation.

In his response to the testimony of Gregory Beck, a policeman, we
see a further elaboration of Bishop Tutu's hopes for the narrative of
forgiveness:

Now the Commission is in fact being charged with telling this story, not so that we should be masochists who enjoy pain, our pain, the pain of others, that we should in fact then, as the Act says, transcend, rise above the conflicts of the past and ultimately, if we are going to have the change then it is clear that forgiveness, reconciliation, are quite central to that process. . . . We pray that the process will be accelerated and that we, all of us, because all of us need to change, *all of us are wounded people, all of us are traumatized people, all of us are people who need to forgive and who also need to be forgiven.* And for all of us then to move together into what is a wonderful prospect that God places before us.[25]

South Africa is a nation where the vast majority of citizens identify as Christians and at the inception of the TRC it was recognized that the commission, because of the leadership of Desmond Tutu, could incorporate terms that drew their significance from a Christian theological context.[26] The passage excerpted above includes several of the most prominent features of Tutu's narrative of forgiveness as it is connected to goals of restorative justice for the TRC. First, the goal of forgiveness created a clear purpose for the exploration of the emotional affects of past violence. The invitation to discuss the physical and psychological pain of the past would not be vulnerable to charges of merely "opening old wounds," because the questions were meant to do more than just relive past feelings. The goal of forgiveness was a worthwhile end that would justify the discomfort and uncertainty that came out of expressions of anger and despair. In theory, with forgiveness as the telos, there was a justification for an exploration of the unsocial emotions, and this should have allowed for an exploration of anger and despair. In practice, however the goal of forgiveness was ultimately very constraining and prevented a full engagement with anger.[27] Heidi Grunebaum and Yazir Henri come to a similar conclusion about the effect of a metanarrative of nation building on individual testimonies; they write, "It is precisely this type of remembering—the unheroic, the anti-linear, the fragmented memories and their haunting afterlife—which is displaced by the nation-building discourse that mediates much of the TRC testimonies."[28] While their focus is on exploring the "fragmented" and "anti-linear" ways that testimonies about trauma take shape (and this is an approach that is consistent with the work of Shoshana Felman and others who approach testimony from a psychoanalytic standpoint), I am more interested in how the narrative of nation building constrained anger and its significance within political life. In the transitional period individuals and political groups should demonstrate greater openness toward the questions and responses present in victim testimonies because of the potential to see patterns in what citizens need in order to participate in political life.

In addition to the logic of forgiveness as the highest ideal, the discourse of forgiveness evoked by Tutu had the result of universalizing the experience of suffering. By saying that all people in South Africa, regardless of race, had done things for which they should ask forgiveness, many different kinds of crimes became aggregated. For example, Mahmood Mamdani argues that the TRC had an individualized conception of victimization and was thus blind to the ways in which the apartheid regime systematically oppressed entire communities of people and did so in both formal and customary ways. An individualized approach to experiences of human-rights violations, while distorting the way violence could be discussed and focusing on elite perpetrators and victims, also served to highlight the commission's reluctance to emphatically declare that apartheid was a "crime against humanity."[29] In a manner analogous to the TRC's distortionary emphasis on individual victims in Mamdani's formulation, Tutu's theological conception of forgiveness served to obfuscate different types of crimes and the variety of emotional responses they engendered.[30]

The third way in which the language of forgiveness affected the proceedings of the TRC was in its equation of forgiveness with evidence of healing. There was a way in which the emphasis Tutu placed on the speech-acts of forgiveness made it seem as though reconciliation between perpetrators and victims was a plausible goal for the commission. However, as time went on, the media coverage indicated that national and international observers were becoming disillusioned with the idea of reconciliation within the context of the commission. Priscilla Hayner writes that by mid-1998, "the commission had long since realized that its initial claims of achieving full reconciliation had been unrealistic. Archbishop Tutu began to articulate that a more reasonable goal for the commission was to 'promote' reconciliation, rather than to achieve it, as indicated in the name of the Promotion of National Unity and Reconciliation Act that created the Commission."[31]

Individual Psychological Problems rather than
Political Commentary

When the commission asked the question, "How do you feel now?" it attempted to connect the violence of the apartheid past to the present moment and shift attention to the current experiences of witnesses. The question suggested that the psychological and physical legacy of the violence was, on a formal level, important and worth articulating, and at times these emotions were able to emerge in startling ways. In a vivid example, Hester Grobelaar talked about the psychological effects that followed the death of her son, an Afrikaaner member of the extreme right who died under mysterious circumstances:

> I would like to know who was responsible for this, who can be so sick to blast away a dead person's face? The effect of this whole incident on our family cannot be described. In about two years I spent almost three months in psychiatric hospitals, *I have tried to commit suicide, I couldn't work, my husband had no wife, my child had no mother*, my husband had to remain strong throughout all of this and I think that ultimately he suffered most. He sat with the body, he saw how it was maimed but he had to keep going through it all.[32]

In Grobelaar's testimony the commission allowed for the expression of suicidal thoughts and an overarching feeling of despair; they did not curtail her desire to talk about her psychological difficulties. The commission did not press her to talk about how her suicidal thoughts may have affected her political worldviews. Similarly, her statements referring to her identity as a wife and mother, "My husband had no wife, my child had no mother," have influenced her perception of self-worth and revealed a desire for greater inclusion in interpersonal relationships and are thus central for understanding her identity as a citizen. Hester Grobelaar was able to talk about the psychological legacy of the death of her son in a courageous way, but the TRC did not push her to explore the implications of her feelings for her life now. Thus, by leaving the political implications of her testimony unexplored, the commission missed the opportunity to engage with anger and despair in a way that could have highlighted their political significance.[33]

The case of Grobelaar was representative of a pattern within the

TRC: a witness would express anger but the commission would immediately move onto other questions, such as requests for facts or a clarification about family status. It is as if the commission invited a reflection on the question of the psychological legacy of pain but could not be attuned to the subtleties of the answers that it received. If after the initial question about the witness's feelings at present, the commission had asked *another* question relating to the specific emotions that had been revealed, this would have encouraged the witnesses to speak, for example, about the causes of anger and how this had changed their worldviews. By failing to ask a follow-up question, the commission could not initiate the necessary step for an active confrontation with anger. It also revealed a lack of understanding about what types of skills for listening could be developed in this situation. This was a lost opportunity to cultivate the skills of listening that would be beneficial for citizenship in the future.[34]

The testimony of Zimasile Bota in Grahamstown was another example of how a potentially revealing response from a witness was not fully explored by the commissioners. In the following excerpt, Bota has just testified about his experiences of torture at the hands of the police.

MS MAYA: Do you have a request to the Commission?

MR BOTA: My request is that it is very painful to me, because the Government is telling us, saying that we must forgive the perpetrators. It is very difficult to forgive someone who was an enemy, who is still an enemy even today. *We cannot forgive them because they are still our enemy.*

MS MAYA: Thank you. Do you have any other requests to add?

MR BOTA: One of my requests is that the perpetrators, the Government must bring them forward. We cannot work together with the police. We know that the police are protecting us, but we cannot work with the police who have blood in their hands. *We are still Comrades, they are still dirty, they are doing dirty jobs. My request is that the police must come forward and the Government must see what to do about the police.* I will be satisfied if they come forward, although I was not killed, but others were killed.[35]

Bota communicated his feeling that the current police force is tainted by their complicity in the violence of a previous era and he does not want to forgive. His comments about the police and the integrity of the enforcement of law in the new South Africa were relevant to his larger views about politics and citizenship, but he did not get the opportunity to

make this connection evident. For example Bota's anger and resentment toward the people who inflicted torture on him have shaped the way he understands his identity as a citizen and his ability to trust the state and state institutions. This sentiment is important to consider when thinking about why people may choose not to participate in politics, and it is particularly important when it concerns those who had been very politically active before. In the context of transitional justice, Bota's testimony raises a question about what actions should be taken to increase the level of trust that citizens like him have toward law enforcement. Commissioner Maya did not dissuade him from communicating his feelings about the guilt of the police, but she also did not ask him to speak about how his anger has influenced his political worldview and ability to participate in civic life. Some may argue that this is too much to ask of the commission, which does not have the time or the expertise to probe traumatic events. I agree that witness testimony is not the equivalent of a therapeutic relationship, but there was the possibility of a type of engagement between the commissioners and the witness that could have included a fuller exploration than what was encouraged at the TRC.

Bota's comments could have been the beginning of critical commentary about the police and security in the apartheid state and in the present. He pointed to a disparity between the ideals of police protection and the rule of law and the reality of its implementation. By challenging the most basic assumptions about the police and security in South Africa, Bota's testimony suggested that the values of the new democratic South Africa could not merely be asserted by the state or the commissioners but rather needed to be earned by taking into account the hypocrisy and inadequacy that were connected to these same values. These are some of the steps that can contribute to shared risk and the foundations of trust discussed in the final chapter.

If the commissioners had asked witnesses to talk more about the emotions they continued to experience as a result of the violence and to connect these emotions to politics, this might have led to insights about what was necessary for transitional justice in practice. Their responses might have included content that revealed what social services were most urgent in their communities. These were insights that did not emerge from a direct line of questioning, but were embedded within testimony, where a different expectation of both speakers and listeners was required.

Instead of the model of an active confrontation with anger and despair, the South African TRC model fits within a cathartic approach to understanding truth commissions. The cathartic assumption begins with the commissioner asking the witness a question that could elicit a strong emotional response, such as "How do you feel now?" and the question presumably included the unsocial emotions. However, the commissioners were not attuned to the nuances of the emotions that were revealed and they did not explore the political ramifications of these emotions. After this experience of catharsis, individuals were expected to proceed with less anxiety and should have been able to better moderate their extreme feelings. The outcome of this process would be a return to a more stable emotional position. I do not view the process of victim testimony in truth commissions primarily as opportunities for catharsis and maintain that this should not be the primary goal for either the witness or the audience.[36] Applying the idea of catharsis to victim testimony attributes too much significance to one moment of emotional expression rather than to the larger process of political transformation. To understand victim testimony as a type of Aristotelian catharsis for the witness would be to assume that the anger that arises in the context of testimony should be expressed and then moderated. This notion of catharsis denies the possibility that individuals may be profoundly changed by anger, which cannot be moderated by "discharging" it. Because the confrontation with anger that emerges from the expression of emotion has the potential to lead to changes in worldview, the idea that a cathartic moment will allow individuals and societies to return to a more "healthy" status quo does not make sense. Better is a model that values a confrontation with anger because of the political information it contains and the human connection it evokes in the listener.

Emotions as Indicators of Individual Mental Health Concerns

I have suggested that a consequence of the lack of uptake in response to anger was a missed opportunity to explore how the emotions connected to violence and suffering may connect to larger views on politics. Without making these connections, expressions of anger were more readily viewed as individual mental health problems, including symptoms of depression.[37] It was acknowledged that these emotions would have serious ramifications for individual flourishing and for the well-being of one's family, but there was no place within the commission to think of this result alongside implications for politics and progress on a larger scale.

Solely viewing these emotions in light of individual mental health issues also meant that the rest of society could choose to see itself as unaffected by the anger that was expressed during the testimonies at the TRC. By implicitly categorizing the most extreme expressions of anger and despair as mental health problems, the commission also set boundaries on what was considered appropriate for public expression.

When the commission did not explore how anger represented a type of political critique, it closed off the opportunity to be responsive to the needs that were embedded in the emotional expression of the witnesses. For example, when Sepati Mlangeni (in chap. 1) referred to herself as a widow and recounted the prejudices she faced, she was referring to individual frustration as well as to a larger frustration with the political community for not responding to the prejudice against widows.[38] Again, the possibility to be seen as a citizen, rather than just a victim, was lost. Similarly, there may be connections between individual thoughts of anger and transformations in perspectives on politics, including new priorities for public services, new ways of assessing the costs of war, and new ways of thinking about the solidaristic bonds between citizens.

The argument is not that witnesses should have been encouraged to see the similarities between their anguish and the pain of others. This would have been unfair to the witnesses who came forward to share their *particular* stories: As Susan Sontag notes, "It is intolerable to have one's own sufferings twinned with anybody else's."[39] The specificities of each narrative deserve attention on their own and not just as part of an aggregated commentary on political ideals. The critique then is not that the particular stories should have been aggregated to highlight similarities, but rather for the commissioners to have considered exploring how expressions of anger in testimonies could have implications for an understanding of politics and progress. Once the connections to a larger system of politics and ethics become objects of analysis, there is an opportunity to question the failure of these ideals during periods of mass violence (e.g., sacrifice for the sake of justice). The hypocrisy of the actions undertaken in the name of political and ethical virtues is part of a genealogy of values and a necessary part of the transition to a new (or newly affirmed) set of values in the aftermath of war. By allowing anger to be interpreted as an individual mental health concern rather than as politically significant criticism, the commission denied its systemic causes.

If a more active confrontation had been encouraged by the commissioners at the TRC we would have seen more of an exploration of how the *content* of anger, such as experienced by men who were still enduring the physical effects of torture, could have led to specific changes in the structure of political community. The testimony of Moganedi Ntoampe Stephen, who spoke about his experiences of torture while being detained by the police, serves as a telling example:

> I cannot produce children with the woman that I stay with. I've been married to her for twelve years and I don't have a child. Even today when I sleep with her, there is nothing I can do. . . . I request the Truth Commission to investigate this with a very sharp eye because the woman that I'm staying with now wants to hear everything and she wants to understand what's really happening with me. Now I'm not living happily with my family because of the child that I cannot produce.[40]

The testimony of Moganedi Ntoampe Stephen resonates with the testimonies of other men who spoke about the humiliation and hopelessness they feel about their inability to have children. Many described how they had sacrificed so much in the struggle against apartheid but now felt that the younger generation did not value their efforts. They were even more saddened by the fact that they will not have children of their own who could enjoy the rights for which they had given so much. Through these testimonies members of the commission, the audience, and the larger public became increasingly aware of how this was an issue that affected many people in a profound way. Like Moganedi Ntoampe Stephen, many of these men were activists during the anti-apartheid movement but no longer saw a place for themselves in political life.[41]

"Getting Back to Normal"

The period of war and its aftermath are not only anomalous experiences that are outside of "normal" political life; they are intricately connected to political life that occurs before and after. The testimony of victims in public has the power to alter what will be considered the normal politics of the future. This could lead to negative outcomes (such as societal comfort with levels of violence that were previously considered extreme), but it also has the opportunity to lead to a more inclusive and honest discussion about political ideals and the costs of mass violence.

Yet the opportunity for this transformation is premised on integrating the experiences and reflections on violence into a larger political world-view, not isolating them as separate and anomalous events. In the South African case, the TRC was clearly part of a transition to a new democratic order, one informed by the injustices of apartheid. The following excerpt from the testimony of Andries Koto, an apartheid activist with the United Democratic Front (UDF), shows how the commission took violence and the confrontation with death as an extraordinary event that should be "gotten over" rather than incorporated into understandings of individual and political life.

> MR MANTHATA (Commissioner): I would like to know whether you have any injuries or pains in your body which you can tell the Commission about.
>
> MR KOTO (witness): Yes, I'm having pains with this operation and my right hand is not functioning well. Even the temporary jobs I'm trying to find I can't really achieve them because I work only for a few days and then I have to quit . . .
>
> MS SEROKE (Commissioner): Since yesterday, we see that the pattern of torture conducted by the policemen involved electric shocks, being applied to the private parts of other people, and also it shows this place Lang Boom where people were taken to for torture. We thank you for your coming and we trust and hope that you'll get some help and you will be able *to get back to normal.*[42]

In this excerpt the first commissioner asked a question about physical pain and Koto responded with testimony about the pain in his hand that was the result of the violence he experienced while in detention. However, the commission did not continue the conversation about what would be needed for full physical recovery and did not explore the psychological consequences of this injury.[43] The commission responded to his description of pain by looking at how Koto's experience fits with other experiences of torture. Again, further questioning could have revealed the ways that Koto's pain affected how he understood his role as a citizen and his ability to participate in civic life, but the commission closed off this conversation by not asking follow-up questions and by assuming he should be "getting back to normal."

On one level, the tendency to focus on "getting back to normal" is understandable. The commissioners saw that a witness was experiencing pain, often both physical and psychological, and wanted to wish him comfort and an end to this pain. However, they are preventing the chance to explore how this event may have changed the way an individual thinks about his own disability and the impact of this perspective on political life. The violence of war changes individual and political narratives in substantial ways, and the possibility of "getting back to normal" after mass violence is a futile goal. Victim testimony is one of the only spaces within political life where this relationship can be explored and become part of the process of transitional justice.

The language of "getting back to normal" works in opposition to the confrontation with anger I suggest precisely because of assumptions concerning what is normal. If truth commissions saw their mission as part of the process of questioning old values and the beginning of a conversation about new political values, then the emphasis would shift away from hoping that individuals will be able to get back to "normal" and toward accepting that they have had experiences that have changed the way they think about politics. This is the crux of the transition to a new set of values. There is no returning to normal but only a reconsideration of previously held beliefs in light of the reality of pain and anger.[44]

The TRC's decision not to allow a full expression of anger can be seen as both a conscious and unconscious one on the part of the architects and members of the commission. On a conscious level, there was the sense that a dual emphasis on investigation and testimony about the emotional legacy of war would simultaneously satisfy needs for evidentiary disclosure and catharsis. Desmond Tutu's religious stature and his ability to speak in an inspirational way about forgiveness allowed abstract psychological concepts, like forgiveness, to be a part of the language of the TRC but it also set forgiveness as the goal of individual testimonies and the TRC. On a subconscious level, the commissioners at the TRC took a more skeptical position than I am taking about the potential for a truth commission to grapple with the needs of justice after the commission has ended. In significant ways, the commission saw individual expressions of anger and despair only as mental health problems to be gotten over, and this reveals a pattern of discomfort on the part of the commission that is premised on the intensity of these emotions and an uncertainty about their value. It seems that their task may have appeared to be so enormous and the implications so uncertain that an active confrontation with anger was not a possibility.

While the overriding narrative of the TRC worked to minimize the open confrontation with anger, there were two instances that offered an alternative approach. The first instance occurred during the TRC hearing about the Guguletu Seven, the case of the murders of seven agents of the military wing of the ANC in 1986. The TRC subpoenaed the police officers alleged to be responsible for the killings and mandated their presence at the hearing. While a video containing footage of torture and the dead bodies was shown, one of the mothers took off her shoe and threw it at the police officers. Two were hit by the shoe and the transcripts show that chaos erupted and the police officers quickly left the room. The media heavily covered the incident, and critics saw it as a sign of the lack of order in the proceeding. For others, it was an important reminder of the anger that existed just below the surface of the TRC and the dramatic sacrifices demanded of family members who had to hear details of death and torture without the possibility of punishment for those crimes.

The shoe-throwing incident during the hearing for the Guguletu Seven captures the fears that many have regarding the expression of anger in public life and what might happen if it is given too much attention during a truth commission. While I agree with Catherine Cole's reading about the power of the incident to disrupt narratives of the truth commission, I would not suggest that it should be seen as evidence for my argument as such.[45] The thrown shoe is a testament to the presence of anger but cannot be easily transposed into a model for the greater *formal* inclusion of anger that I will describe in the next chapter. The model I suggest is one in which there is a formal place to express frustration and resentment in the context of the testimony itself, but this requires a willingness on the part of the speaker to articulate the anger in a verbal way and take ownership of it. By ownership I mean a willingness to be identified with the testimony, in person and as part of the official record. Because of this, the act of anger should not be just a one-off moment, remembered only as a spectacle. The significance of anger within testimony is not just the sudden anger of outrage, but the durable anger of injustice, frustration, and the irreducibility of complex feelings about past violence and present opportunities.

Another example of anger breaking through the dominant narrative of the TRC is the case of Yazir Henry, a young man who testified about his torture by security police at the Human Rights Violations hearings in Cape Town. His anger is acute during the testimony, particularly in relation to how he was used as a pawn in a larger plot to capture one of his comrades, and he sharply corrects the translator who tries to neutralize his language.[46] His anger becomes even more strident in his own writing after the TRC. He is motivated to write about his experiences as a witness in part because of his frustration at how his testimony had been edited and evoked by others.[47] In her critically lauded memoir *Country of My Skull*, Antjie Krog wrote about Yazir Henry's appearance at the TRC in connection with the theme of betrayal.[48] This identity as a traitor to the cause, he says, has led to threats on his life and many other types of hardship. Henry's anger is directed not only at Krog for her misrepresentation, but also at the TRC for its responsibility in the aftermath of the Human Rights Violations hearings. He wants the evidence surrounding the accusations of betrayal to be consolidated and assessed. This is not part of the scope of the TRC report and may, in fact, be inconsistent with the evidence collected. Henry's anger in relation to this claim is an example of the problem of unreasonable responses, even if there had been greater room for the communication of anger. Although his anger was palpable during his testimony at the TRC and he had the opportunity to express his anger in a direct way several years later, he was still upset at the interpretation and the unanswered claims about what the TRC failed to provide. A greater engagement with anger in the way I am suggesting will not solve all of these concerns. In later chapters, I will discuss three approaches to understanding the significance of anger at truth commissions, but Henry's experience should be remembered as a cautionary note about the complexity of anger.

The experiences of the South African Truth and Reconciliation Commission generated the questions about the significance of anger in public life that motivated this book, and the TRC's failures speak to the difficulty of this proposition. Still, the transcripts show missed opportunities that can be analyzed in hindsight. Anger should not be eclipsed by expectations of forgiveness, just as it should not be seen as an individual mental health issue or a necessary experience of catharsis. These types of response deny an engagement with what is most powerful about its expression. More importantly, an investigation into the patterns of response shows how even well-meaning attempts to make the witness feel comfortable or express empathy can end up preventing an engagement with anger. The tendency to want to affirm the goal of social harmony was so strong at the TRC, especially with a large number of commissioners who were trying to coordinate responses with each other, that documenting material evidence and admiring the most heroic aspects of the testimony were arguably the best uses of limited time. The case of Yazir

Henry shows an exception to this trend and, while his requests were ultimately unfulfillable, he was able to express anger during his testimony in
a way that highlighted his concerns and contributed to the larger conversation about the experiences of witnesses at the TRC. Despite the great
achievements of the Truth and Reconciliation Commission in South Africa, the dynamic between the commissioners and witnesses surrounding moments of anger hampered opportunities to cultivate trust and a
greater responsiveness to the needs of citizens.

CHAPTER THREE

The First Skeptic

Hannah Arendt and the Danger of Victim Testimony

In the first chapter, I showed how Hannah Arendt displayed great ambivalence toward the decision to allow victims to take the witness stand during the trial of Adolf Eichmann. In her coverage of the trial, she wrote that the emotional manipulation catalyzed by victim testimony and orchestrated by chief prosecutor Gideon Hausner gave the trial the air of a "mass meeting." She was frustrated with victims who focused on their suffering rather than on the guilt of Eichmann and who could not relate their experiences to the judges and spectators in a rational and organized way. She also expressed discomfort at having to hear in public content that would have been difficult to appreciate even in private. In her biography of Arendt, Elizabeth Young-Bruehl writes, "Many people who read her five-article series in the *New Yorker* . . . concluded that Hannah Arendt was soulless, or that she lacked what Gershom Sholem called *Herzenstakt*, sympathy. They thought that Arendt felt no emotional involvement with the fate of her people. She, on the other hand, thought that she had finally been cured of the kind of emotional involvement which precludes good judgment." It is precisely this relationship between "emotional involvement" and "good judgment" that motivates the current chapter.[1]

Writing in a more journalistic form, Arendt did not connect her observations recorded during the Eichmann trial to her broader theoretical frameworks, but her orientation toward political judgment, in a recapitulation of the role of the impartial spectator in the writings of Adam

Smith, offers a persuasive framework with which to analyze her appre-
hensiveness about the value of victim testimony. Arendt's theoretical
writings, particularly in *The Human Condition* and *On Revolution*, provide a rich foundation for thinking about the political significance of victim testimony. Most interestingly, her writing appears to both support
and deny its political potential. In the first part of this chapter, I elaborate upon two strands of Arendt's thinking that seem to be working
in opposite directions when applied to the case of victim testimony at
truth commissions. On the one hand, Arendt depicts action in the public sphere as the highest form of politics, which suggests that testimony
in public has the potential to usher in something truly new for politics.
On the other, she argues that certain emotions, such as love, compassion,
and pain, are inappropriate for public life and have a destructive impact
on the important work of action. In the final section I advocate for a resolution of this tension based on Arendt's fear of the *social*, as well as on
her understanding of judgment.[2]

Victim Testimony as Action

According to Arendt, *action* represents the most important form of behavior in human life; it is oriented to the highest questions of freedom
and human flourishing and can take place only in the public sphere in
the presence of others. She has been called the theorist of new beginnings, and it is through action, the activity of creating for the sake of the
collective, that new beginnings take shape.[3] Arendt's theories about the
centrality of action for defining the political, and the inclusion of words
and narratives in the concept of action, provide support for my argument
about the importance of victim testimony in the period after mass violence. In her writing on action, Arendt draws on the ancient Greek perspective found in Aristotle that suggests that the public world of political
action is the only space for truly important endeavors.[4] The endeavors
that take place in the public sphere must have the support of fellow citizens who are also committed to governance and the flourishing of the
polis. Action relies on a movement away from the individualized concerns of household and family, spheres that are defined largely by pragmatic and mundane questions, and toward generalizable concerns about
what is necessary for freedom.[5] Narrow self-interest, especially based on
class or social group, represents for Arendt the antithesis of the politi-

cal outlook that is necessary for action. Action, which refers to initiatives undertaken in public for collective progress, cannot take place in the home or in the market of economic transactions; it must be visible to others. To be in public is equivalent to being political—when an event is seen by others, it enters into a collective reality that then becomes the inspiration and precedent for future action.

Arendt's particular definition of action in the public sphere relies in large part on what it is *not*, just as Aristotle's understanding of the polis was largely based on how it contrasted with the institution of the family. Arendt takes from Aristotle the categorization of the private realm as primarily concerned with the economic and reproductive needs of the household.[6] The tasks that occur in the private realm are driven by necessity—especially that of biological and economic survival—leaving little time or space for the task of freedom, the highest political goal. Arendt uses a three-part classification of labor/work/action to highlight action in the public sphere as the highest goal. *Labor* is the primary task of the household, and it serves as Arendt's term for the activities needed to sustain life. In contrast to *work*, the activities that shape the material world, labor is repetitive and has no lasting product. Work is able to materially change the world and can even lead to products that outlive individuals and contemporary society, but it is still constrained by instrumentality and a commitment to predetermined ends. Only action in the public sphere is able to transcend the constraints of labor and work and provide the space for non-survival-oriented, noninstrumental ways of thinking and being with others. Additionally, the private realm is governed by hierarchies, both in the family and in working life, as opposed to the equality granted in the public sphere. As a citizen, one is afforded the respect of being an equal among equals, one who has the responsibility to rule and be ruled in turn. Although Arendt does not carry into her framework the restrictions Aristotle placed on the political participation of women and slaves, scholars have argued that she continues to see the responsibilities of reproduction and child rearing as obstacles to the most valuable type of action.[7]

Action, as Arendt understands it, is connected to the pluralism of humanity: since we cannot assume homogeneity in experience, perspective, or preferences, politics must be oriented toward recognition of this variation. As such, there must be a space where people can both assert themselves as individuals and form alliances with others. The public sphere is the arena for both of these activities because it allows for *logos*, reasoned speech, the feature Aristotle understood as most distinctly human. The act of speaking not only proceeds naturally from human nature but also leads to a moment of recognition and inclusion in the larger species group. The ability to share thoughts and to conceive of a new action, and then to enact the action with an awareness of its unpredictability, is what separates human beings from all other species.[8] However, while the practice of speech reflects the commonality of all people, it also shows the human drive for uniqueness: just as we seek recognition as part of the species, we struggle to define ourselves as unique individuals.

The Role of Speech

Arendt is adamant that speech makes action in the public sphere possible. It is through speech that individuals assert their uniqueness and their power to initiate new action. Speech allows for common concerns to emerge, unites individuals in a shared goal, and acts as the conduit for political change.[9] The following excerpt makes clear the relationship between speech and action as the defining feature of public life.

> In man, otherness, which he shares with everything that is, and distinctness, which he shares with everything alive, become uniqueness, and human plurality is the paradoxical plurality of unique beings. Speech and action reveal this unique distinctness. Through them, men distinguish themselves instead of being merely distinct; they are the modes in which human beings appear to each other, not indeed as physical objects, but *qua* men. . . . This is true of no other activity in the *vita activa*.[10]

Speech is thus both a necessary precursor to action, because it allows individuals to see themselves as distinct as well as part of a larger group, and an action itself. Arendt repeatedly speaks about the power of storytelling to communicate individual experiences and to promote interpersonal alliances that are based on these experiences. Speech allows for the process of distinguishing oneself from another through the "disclosure of 'who' in contradistinction to 'what' somebody is—his qualities, gifts, talents, and shortcomings, which he may display or hide—is implicit in everything somebody says and does."[11]

Arendt argues that revealing aspects of one's personal identity through narrative is a part of political life, one that is important in the drive toward human interaction.[12] The stories we tell about our lives are the core of our experiences as political animals, and this is especially true in the aftermath of mass violence. Self-disclosure connects an individual to others, including those who, by listening to that person's life story, can interpret and apply it to their own experiences or become a part of it themselves.[13] Still, Arendt insists that we can never be the authors of our own life stories because there are too many unpredictable elements that will interfere with any straightforward unfolding of events. The meaning of a story can be revealed only in retrospect, and most likely this will be done not by the instigator of the action but by a storyteller or historian.

Nowhere is Arendt as poetic about the art of storytelling as in her references to Isak Dinesen.[14] No other figure so thoroughly embodied the craft of storytelling for Arendt and had a life (as author, traveler, lover) that made lucid its power. In describing Dinesen's writing, Arendt emphasizes that it is the ambiguity of interpretation suggested in Dinesen's writing that is most valuable and that storytelling, ironically, through imagination, ends up bringing one back to the possibilities and constraints of reality, in a way that would not otherwise be possible. Dinesen's gift, according to Arendt, was to allow the story to guide her eventually to the silence of acceptance: "The reward of storytelling is to be able to let go: 'When the storyteller is loyal to the story, there, in the end, silence will speak.'"[15]

Victim testimony can, at first glance, seem to be a compelling case of Arendtian action through speech. The importance that she attributes to being seen in public as a marker of the political can apply to the significance of public testimony of victims, rather than to their written submissions, for example. The public space of a state-sponsored truth commission allows for the expression of narratives that affirm the uniqueness of individual stories while also allowing larger patterns and similarities of experience to emerge. Private expressions of grief and mourning, along with artistic interpretations, serve an important role in thinking about the psychological legacy of war, but the public testimony of victims could, in an Arendtian framework, be seen as playing a singular role in political life. The South African TRC allowed previously disenfranchised and second-class citizens, such as blacks, Asians, and "coloreds" in South Africa, to testify in public and thus represented the first political institution to offer those groups the dignity and equality that Arendt understands to be foundational to political life. The hierarchies of fam-

ily, ethnicity, and economic power, while visible, were counteracted by
the dignity afforded to all participants, and the commission thereby set
a precedent for future political interactions among citizens that was not
based on narrow group identity. The publicness of the testimony of witnesses at the TRC acted as a more ideal "public" than had been seen
before in modern South Africa and allowed individuals who had never
considered themselves to be citizens to engage in the political process.[16]

Furthermore, victim testimony fits into the framework of Arendtian
action because it is concerned with questions that go beyond necessity
and material concerns. Freedom and justice are the emergent themes,
and they function as reflections on the violence of the past and its influence on political life in the present, rather than as "technocratic" or
instrumental resolutions of political problems. Similar to what Arendt
hopes for the practice of politics, victim testimonies reflect the plurality of experiences of mass violence, and the narrative form of the testimonies opens up possibilities for new ways of thinking about freedom.
Through the many voices that are allowed to speak in public, the commission and the audience are able to see relationships between private
identity and public experiences that have likely not been recognized
before.

The act of testimony is consistent with Arendt's descriptions of disclosure and the value of the individual story for revealing insights that
are useful for political life. For example, when witnesses are asked about
human-rights violations they have experienced, they are solicited to re-
peat the facts of the events (which they have already submitted in writing
to the commission), but they are also able to include more commentary
on the significance of the events and how it affects them in the present.
For Arendt, the nature of disclosure makes it impossible to control what
is revealed about the subject and how it will be interpreted, and this supports my thesis about the political importance that stems from the open-
ended nature of victim testimony. The political value of testimony comes
from the willingness on the part of the commissioners and the broader
audience to examine explicitly and implicitly disclosed information
about what the victim thinks is necessary for justice and a rebuilding of
trust after war. The fact that stories may be interpreted in ways that the
author did not intend is not something to be feared. As Arendt writes,
"You should not try to hold your hand now on whatever may happen to
what you have been thinking for yourself. You should rather try to learn
from what other people do with it."[17]

Bonnie Honig's agonistic reading of Arendt's understanding of action would also buttress an argument for testimony as action, provided that testimonies do not reify a singular conception of identity.[18] She extends Arendt's reading (to a place Honig acknowledges Arendt might not have chosen to go) to argue for a performative approach to action, one that is about a disruption of stable and expected categories in favor of the contingent, unexpected, and incomplete. The "doing" of action is more important that the "being" of an established identity as a woman, Jew, or victim. In Honig's reading, the division between public and private is not marked so much by the content of concern (the body, household, etc.) as by the extent to which the expression of the concern is open to innovation and resistibility. If the action, regardless of content, brings into existence something new and is not beholden to the state, it has the possibility of being considered worthy of Arendt's highest designation. Victim testimony could, therefore, arguably fit this description, as long as it is oriented toward the unprecedented opportunities for politics and not toward rigid categories of racial or ethnic identity or the stifling identity of perpetual victimhood. Honig's argument is a provocative but, on balance, distorted reading of Arendtian agonistic action. Instead of using her approach to suture the tensions between my argument for testimony and Arendt's understanding of action, I am more persuaded to live with, and learn from, the incompatibility between the two.

Thus far, I have shown that Arendt's theory of action in public, the core of her understanding of political life, can be applied to the experience of victim testimony in the context of truth commissions. Victim testimony fulfills many of the aspirations Arendt sets forth in her ideal description of action and is arguably a persuasive example of the power of a narrative to act as a conduit between individual experiences and collective understandings of politics in the aftermath of mass violence.[19] However, there is another strand of Arendt's thought that calls into question these assumptions about victim testimony as a manifestation of action. This orientation is centered on Arendt's understanding of the role of emotional expression in politics and its corrosive effects on relationships between citizens and what should be considered "political."[20] Compassion, love, and pain all serve as paradigmatic examples of aspects of emotional life that, for her, should be confined to the private sphere. When these emotions are allowed to permeate political discussions, both the public and private realms are negatively affected. If they must enter public life, they should go through a process of translation that makes them

less individualized and less private. She writes, "Compared with the reality which comes from being seen and heard, even the greatest forces of
intimate life—the passions of the heart, the thoughts of the mind, the de-
lights of the senses—lead an uncertain, shadowy kind of existence unless
and until they are transformed, deprivatized and deindividualized, as it
were, into a shape to fit them for public appearance."[21] This excerpt captures the paradox of Arendt's understanding of the significance of emotions: although they lead only a "shadowy kind of existence" in the private realm and so have a natural desire to be expressed in the elevated
space of public appearance, they have no place there, at least not without
being substantially transformed.

Compassion: The Dangerous Emotion

Although she is critical of almost all forms of emotional expression in
the realm of politics, Arendt is especially critical of the assumption that
compassion has a role in the public sphere. Moreover, she extends her
critique of compassion to those who consider individual suffering to be
an entry to politics.[22] Both the victim, who emphasizes her suffering, and
the responder, who is manipulated by it, are in the wrong. In one of her
most memorable historical examples, Arendt uses the French Revolution to illustrate the disastrous consequences of focusing on material deprivation ("misery") rather than generalizable political goals.[23]

Arendt does not doubt that the multitudes who participated in the
French Revolution were burdened by the conditions of poverty, but she
does not think that this is an issue that should motivate political upheaval. It is an administrative and practical question, and one that does
not require an "enlarged mentality" or the ability to think from the
standpoint of another. Unlike the American Revolution, which privileged the political questions of equality, representation, and institutional
design, the French Revolution was beholden to necessity, the material
conditions of poverty, to the extent that all other considerations lost their
urgency.[24] Poverty is an intractable reality, and as unfortunate as this is,
Arendt does not see the value of initiating a social movement around its
existence. She acknowledges that poverty has the power to inspire action ("the cry for bread will always be uttered with one voice"),[25] but it,
along with the pity that it engenders in response, carries devastating consequences. These consequences include forcing men to remain in "a con-

stant state of want and acute misery" without any generalizable political goals—a state that effaces political identity and leads to a warped view of human nature. The Jacobin focus on poverty caused compassion, the seemingly most appropriate response, to be held up as the highest political virtue during the French Revolution.

Compassion, in Arendt's formulation, is not an emotion suited for politics because of the relationship that it assumes between the one in pain and the respondent. The instinct of compassion, the desire to identify fully with the one in pain, closes the distance that is necessary for politics. She writes, "Because compassion abolishes the distance, the worldly space between men where political matters, the whole realm of human affairs, are located, it remains, politically speaking, irrelevant and without consequence."[26] This description considers compassion to be antipolitical because it destroys the politically necessary distance of the "in-between." The in-between is Arendt's way of envisioning the distance between citizens, who have relationships based on respect, as distinct from the distance between family members and friends who have much closer relationships and from the greater distance between strangers. Because politics is located in this in-between space that is neither too close nor too distant, it allows for an understanding of multiple perspectives that is necessary for judicious action. Compassion causes such a strong identification between the sufferer and respondent that it does not allow for the necessary deliberative space of politics; instead, the narrative of suffering may become reified and immune to criticism. Moreover, the expression of suffering is a highly subjective experience, as is the compassion that it provokes in response, and therefore is a difficult basis for collective political action. Arendt does not describe what, in place of compassion, a response to the pain of others *should* include, but she suggests that although psychological, moral, or political factors may play a role in internal motivation, they should not be considered part of the realm of political action: they are part of the private identity of the individual, an aspect of interior life that should not permeate the political sphere.

Arendt is critical of expanding the role of compassion in politics not only because it closes the in-between that she sees as necessary but also because it attempts to transform human nature into that of a more altruistic species, driven by the moral quest to end the suffering of others. Arendt addresses this concern in the following passage in which she makes a distinction between compassion, a specific response to the pain of an individual *qua* individual, and pity, a generalized sentiment: "Compassion, by its very nature, cannot be touched off by the suffering of a whole class or a people, or least of all, mankind as a whole. It cannot reach out farther than what is suffered by one person and still remain what it is supposed to be, co-suffering. It can comprehend only the particular. The sign of Jesus' divinity was his ability to have compassion with all men in their singularity."[27]

The reference to the compassion of Jesus is notable because it is suggestive of Arendt's fear that compassion is a sacred virtue and this quality makes it otherworldly and inappropriate for politics. When it comes to the mundane interactions between fallible human beings, acts of compassion should be the exception and not the rule, as would be the case in a Christian framework. Arendt finds any desire to instigate more virtue and more acts of goodwill in secular life antithetical to the work of politics. "Compassion with all men in their singularity" is an unattainable goal, and even if it were possible, it would not lead to the type of action that Arendt advocates for the political realm. When brought into politics, the goodness of compassion "will shun the drawn-out wearisome processes of persuasion, negotiation, and compromise, which are the processes of law and politics."[28] Compassion, which takes its justification from a sacred authority or a benevolent view of humankind, does not respond to "persuasion, negotiation, and compromise," the tools used by citizens in the service of collective political decision making. Thus, for Arendt, compassion sees only the particular and in its selective blindness reifies both the private identity of the individual and the material claims that are inaccurately considered to be political.

Pity is the more generalized sentiment that corresponds to the intense particularity of compassion. As such, it loses the authenticity and religiosity of compassion, but this makes it even more politically dangerous. Arendt writes, "Pity, taken as the spring of virtue, has proved to possess a greater capacity for cruelty than cruelty itself," and it is this willingness to inflict violence in the name of the material deprivation of others that Arendt finds most objectionable.[29] Pity as a generalized sentiment also reveals the deceit and hypocrisy that Arendt understands to be connected to compassion.[30] Although Arendt would concede that compassion is a virtue—a virtue that would allow one to feel more like Jesus Christ—it relies on a display of one's inner life that is incongruous with public life. The interior aspects of the self include the psychological experiences and motivations that shape decision and actions. These are parts of one's private identity: they are revealed in the private realm and in modern times have become a constitutive part of intimate relationships with others. In the public realm, however, Arendt posits that they should be submerged to allow one's political identity, the self that is a citizen and not a sufferer or an altruist, to be at the foreground. Assuming this type of public identity of a citizen is, for Arendt, a liberating moment. With such an identity, an individual is not confined to the particularities of experience or background and is given the opportunity to participate in a new, collective process.

Arendt suggests that, in contrast to compassion and pity, solidarity is the sentiment best suited for collective action around universal political concerns. Elizabeth Spelman writes, "Solidarity focuses on what nonsufferers and sufferers have in common—for example, their shared humanity, or dignity—not on the conditions of want, deprivation, misery, or humiliation which distinguishes."[31] Solidarity allows for the similarities of the human condition, including suffering and loss, to be present in the public sphere, without closing off political possibilities. While engaging with particular stories of pain can coerce a compassionate response and thus cause the relationship between sufferer and nonsufferer to be closer than is desirable for politics, solidaristic ties are based on dignity and respect and allow for the presence of multiple perspectives. Still, expressing solidarity is an effective way to acknowledge the severity of a situation without being moved to compassion or anger. It is worth noting here that solidarity is compatible with an Arendtian approach to judgment, although it fulfills a very different function within her framework. While judgment is a way to assess particular stories, solidarity does not rely on the same process of impartiality and enlarged mentality that I will discuss below; rather, solidarity refers to the temperament that is most suitable for interactions between citizens. It represents a desirable orientation toward those who are experiencing suffering, but it is not about the translation of information and subsequent evaluation that is necessary for judgment.

There is a moment in Arendt's own life when she chose to persuade and foster solidarity in a different way. Her work *Origins of Totalitarianism* preceded both *The Human Condition* and *Eichmann in Jerusalem*, and her reactions to the reviews of the book reveal a different philosophy about the expression of the emotions. When she was criticized for the tone of moral outrage, she wrote: "To describe the concentration camps *sine ira* is not to be 'objective,' but to condone them; and such condoning cannot be changed by a condemnation which the author feels duty bound to add but which remains unrelated to the description itself. When I used the image of Hell, I did not mean this allegorically, but literally."[32] Given the argument of this chapter, the passage is surprising because Arendt seems to be sympathetic to the integral nature of anger in the communication of certain events. Both rhetorically and ethically, Arendt refuses to take a neutral tone in her writing about the concentration camps. While this is unusual for her, I do not see her statement as a fundamental challenge to her more fully developed ideas of public and private in later writings, because of its isolated nature and the fact that she exercised her indignation in writing in a controlled and strategic way focused on certain events. I suggest that she would see this as a very different invocation of anger than what is heard at truth commissions and would not run the risk of the dis-empowerment of a witness through pity, as described above.

The Case of Pain

While love and compassion are emotions that blind individuals to the need for distance and persuasion in politics, pain is disbarred in Arendt's account for an entirely different reason—its inherent incommunicability: we can never express the pain we are experiencing in an accurate way that elicits the response we desire. In addition, the logic she uses to describe pain gives a clue as to why the emotions *writ large* pose such a difficulty for the political sphere within an Arendtian analysis. Pain is the most intense human experience, Arendt writes, and it is "at the same time the most private and least communicable of all."[33] Pain is situated in private and embodies a radical subjectivity that cannot be authentically communicated with others. Elaine Scarry has further developed this idea in a way that Arendt might have supported. Scarry has written that pain is a world-shattering event that makes language inadequate and communication impossible.[34] Medical attempts to understand and schematize the intensity of pain in order to improve patient care have continually been at a loss for the "right" words, lending support to Scarry's argument that pain can be described only through metaphor.[35] While Scarry elaborates on connections between material and existential reconstruction in light of pain, Arendt's writing focuses on the political implications of its incommunicability. Arendt finds that pain, like other passions, is preoccupied with the self and its immediate reality; it cannot take on a larger political significance. But unlike the other passions, including love, it is "uncommunicable"—the attempt to communicate it in public is destined to fail, which should act as a deterrent for those who want to challenge its role in public. The suffering that finds its way into the public sphere is an incomplete interpretation of the radical subjectivity that cannot be fully translated into language. The radical subjectivity engendered by the experience of pain is so self-referential that it does not seek to achieve solidarity with other individuals, a necessary task for action in politics. Expressions of respect or solidarity cannot take root with discussions based on pain, and, as mentioned above, compassion is an inadequate response to pain in the public sphere. Because of pain's radical subjectivity and incommunicability, and the fact that there is no appropriately political response to it, Arendt excises pain from the public world. The appropriate distance of the in-between is, as with compassion and love, impossible if the experience of pain is allowed in the public sphere. Arendt's discomfort with the presence of emotions in the public sphere acts as a counterpoint to the claim that anger should be confronted through victim testimony in the transitional period after war. I argue that reason and emotion cannot be separated in understandings of justice after mass violence, that anger reveals insights about what is necessary to rebuild political life, and that its communication becomes a prototype for a trusting relationship between citizens. Arendt's writings on compassion, love, and pain suggest that, at best, she would have been skeptical of this claim, and, at worst, she would have thought it was dangerous for the actual work of politics.

In light of these Arendtian concerns, the testimonies from the South African TRC would be considered as unhelpful for politics for a variety of reasons. First, the TRC was set up to hear experiences of the past and did not explicitly encourage deliberation about the future, an aspect that could be changed in future truth commissions. Arendt was concerned about individuals and societies being so consumed by past experiences that they lose the opportunities for new action that are possible in the present. One could argue that victim testimony at truth commissions is guilty of just this failing. Such testimony arguably serves to reinforce the role of the victim in society rather than celebrating the change in political structure and the possibilities that have emerged. However, in the framework I describe in chapter 5, victim testimony can be listened to with an orientation to the practice of citizenship. Arendt's criticism is valid, but it is not exhaustive of the possibilities of victim testimony.

Second, if the process of victim testimony encourages individuals to speak openly about anger, despair, and experiences of physical and psychological pain, then it sets up the impossible goal of trying to communicate pain. Attempting this task in a public setting, Arendt would suggest, is an even more frustrating experience because it occurs outside of one's private relationships—those that are based on love, friendship, empathy, and affection in a way that public relationships are not. The web of relationships could expand to include a commission and all those who hear an individual's story, but these relationships will not have the same commitment to listening and responding to the emotional experiences of individuals. Trying to communicate pain in the context of victim testimony, an Arendtian critic may say, would only lead to disappointment for the witness, who cannot fully express what she has experienced, and for the listener, who has no adequate way to respond in this context. If the listener chooses to respond with compassion, this, as mentioned above, would have the effect of closing off the distance of the in-between that is necessary for political action. Although I am convinced by Arendt's perception of compassion, this is not a reason to exclude the expression of anger altogether. Instead, what is necessary is an alternative way to listen and respond to it—one that can be cultivated in a truth commission, properly understood.

Although victim testimony includes questions from the commissioners and has a dialogic structure, one could argue that it is still not an active conversation about the past or the future. Witnesses are not asked to reconsider their own position in light of the positions of others, and they are not asked to compromise or negotiate about their demands. On the contrary, one might argue that victim testimony encourages the perpetuation of a single position, just as Arendt says occurs in a family, rather than asking that the position be understood as one among many. The deference that is shown to the "authenticity" of the emotions in the context of victim testimony, Arendt would argue, sets a negative precedence for political life after the transitional period. It does so by encouraging the unmediated display of emotions, not the type of "deprivatized" stories that are the most important for building political alliances and relationships based on respect.

While I disagree with Arendt's assertion that the boundary between

private and public is a firm one not to be crossed with emotional testimony in the private sphere, her critique of compassion in the public
sphere is significant for understanding victim testimony. In media coverage of the TRC, journalists often spoke about the moving testimonies
of witnesses and the feeling of empathy that they engendered in the audience members. There was a sense that a test of the effectiveness of the
commission would be whether it adequately encouraged compassionate
sentiment in fellow citizens. Compassion, or in Arendt's terms a "closing
of the distance" between individuals and formerly antagonistic groups,
was seen as a natural and desirable outcome of listening to the testimonies. But could the distance actually be closed, and was this the goal of
the commission? Neither the audience members nor the rest of the national and international audience could engage in face-to-face contact
with the witness and respond in a particularized way. When the compassion of the audience and the media had no clear outlet, a generalized
sense of pity was the more likely sentiment—a sentiment that Arendt
would say was frustrating for both witness and listener and could lead to
displaced outcomes, such as the violence of the French Revolution.

Forgiveness is a sentiment that Arendt, perhaps unexpectedly, insists
is necessary for politics. Along with the ability to make promises, forgiveness acts as a mitigating factor in a world characterized by uncertainty.
Each new action always gives rise to unexpected outcomes, and the unpredictable quality of action necessitates a response that has the power
to end it and allow another act to begin anew. This possibility is found in
the act of forgiveness. Arendt writes, "Without being forgiven, released
from the consequences of what we have done, our capacity to act would,
as it were, be confined to one single deed from which we could never
recover; we would remain the victims of its consequences forever."[36]
Arendt's understanding of the significance of forgiveness is profoundly
political, not theological: she does not connect forgiveness to confession
or repentance, nor does she rely on a sacred authority. Although we forgive for the sake of the person, her focus is on the pragmatic and political significance of it as an action that can end a cycle of vengeance
and hatred. Forgiveness is also not undertaken for the sake of love because this would necessitate a pulling away from the world of politics.

Arendt's understanding of the political function of forgiveness could
arguably fit well with the role of victim testimony in truth commissions.
After an experience of war or mass violence, there may be a great need
to interrupt cycles of violence or revenge through a language of politics.

An institution such as a truth commission that is not oriented to retribution but is premised on new alternatives after war could be seen to embody Arendt's understanding of the political role of forgiveness. As discussed in the previous chapter, Desmond Tutu allowed a Christian interpretation of forgiveness to frame much of the discourse of the TRC, especially in its initial stages. He applauded individuals who articulated a willingness to forgive and suggested that they were making a great sacrifice for the nation. While Arendt's formulation of forgiveness seems applicable in this context, the TRC's emphasis on forgiveness precluded victims from expressing anger, a concern that Arendt would not have harbored.

A Fear of the Social

Arendt's exclusion of compassion and pain from the public sphere reflects her great unease with the expression of emotions within political life. While her theory of action and the significance of narration could be used to support a justification of victim testimony, her understanding of emotion denies it political import. Her reservations about emotions in public life are representative of her broader concern about the forces that have the power to thwart political life—a cluster of phenomena that make up the *social*. In this section, I suggest that Hannah Arendt's negative responses to the victim testimony heard during the Eichmann trial are best understood as part of her fear of the *social*, an idiosyncratic term meant to encompass many of the threats to the vibrant political sphere that she envisioned.[37] Emotional expression is the part of the social that is most pertinent for victim testimony, and I posit that, for Arendt, the expression of emotions is dangerous for public life in two major ways. First, a singular focus on emotional expression and psychological exploration may distract individuals from the work of politics; second, taken to an extreme, a preoccupation with the emotions may replace politics altogether. I draw on Hanna Pitkin's understanding of the social as politics *manqué*—the missed opportunities of politics—to suggest that for Arendt victim testimony would be consistent with her fear that emotional preoccupation can become a replacement for politics.[38]

Arendt identifies the social realm by using many terms including "society," "mass society," and "the social," but the consistent trope is that activities that were previously tied to the private realm in Greek thought—namely, the tasks of the household—take on a life outside the household. The social becomes the location for these tasks and related attitudes, and it occupies a space that is neither public nor private. Although grounded in the idea that household and economic tasks erroneously become the focus on public discussion, Arendt's conception of the social is much broader and includes all the ways in which individuals squander the opportunity for collective action and public participation. When individuals see themselves as "laborers and jobholders" above all other identities, this represents the transformation of the public realm into the realm of the social. At the same time, private concerns involving intimate relationships and family life also make their way into the public discourse.[39]

The social is thus a third realm of human activity, one that has the potential to thwart the flourishing of both the public and private spheres. Because Arendt depicts the social as an undefined but dangerous entity threatening public and private, Hanna Pitkin describes Arendt's theory of the social as "the attack of the blob."[40] Arendt imbues the social with an impending sense of doom and describes its colonizing force in the following excerpt from *The Human Condition*: "The social realm, where the life process has established its own public domain, has let loose an unnatural growth, so to speak, of the natural; and it is against this growth, not merely against society but against a constantly growing social realm, that the private and intimate, on the one hand, and the political (in the narrower sense of the word), on the other, have proved incapable of defending themselves."[41] Just as the concept of the social pushes against the public and the private, victim testimony can also be seen as a third realm and one that challenges public understandings of action and private understandings of the emotions.[42] Emotional expression is the part of the social that is most pertinent for victim testimony, and I posit that, for Arendt, victim testimony would be seen as a blatant misappropriation of the public sphere for private concerns. Instead of encouraging people to think about what concerns they share with other citizens and the need for political solutions, victim testimony institutionalizes the rise of the social by sanctioning a public space for reflections on pain and suffering. Moreover, victim testimony encourages the practice of psychological reflection as political discourse rather than foregrounding the idea that individuals should break with the pain and disappointment of their private lives in order to embrace the role of citizen.

Although the emotional content of victim testimony might be reason enough for Arendt to banish it from the public sphere, I suggest that she would be even more concerned about the attitude of helplessness that would be encouraged in such a political institution. Such a sense of dependency and vulnerability may be the result of individual suffering, or a need for public assistance, but in both cases it is the unsatisfactory outcome of individuals seeking emotional understanding and expression in the public realm. Pitkin has argued that Arendt understood helplessness to be an empirical concern in totalitarian political systems where political participation was not a possibility, as well as a psychological orientation that would exist in many other political systems. For Arendt, to be passive in the face of political need was a sign of defeat and, in the case of democratic systems, a betrayal of the possibilities for collective action, both within and outside of formal institutions. Furthermore, the psychological orientation of helplessness is a result of the increasing tendency for contemporary individuals to become preoccupied with the radical subjectivity of private life. Throughout her writing, she intimates that dwelling on one's own story, with its experiences of disappointment and suffering, has a natural appeal but that this is an impulse to be resisted if one is to participate in politics. If emotions are to be brought into politics, they should be, as mentioned above, "deprivatized," and it is not clear how much of the original emotion Arendt would allow to remain after the process of "deprivatization."[43] She asserts the need for a transformation with regards to the emotions if they are to move from the private realm of concerns (the household, the body, visceral needs) to the public realm of universal, political questions. Arendt suggests that individuals who do not adjust their emotions accordingly will find it difficult to participate in political life, but this is not a cause for concern for her. The depersonalization of the emotions is necessary to encourage the type of exchanges between citizens that will lead to action. In short, for Arendt, emotional expression lies on the fault line she created to maintain a strict separation between the public and private spheres, but the line must be reconsidered to engage with anger in a direct and generative way after mass violence.[44]

While Arendt posits that emotional expression and psychological exploration are not appropriate for public life, she encourages them in the private realm and even sees them as necessary for the development of subjectivity. However, there are also times when she seems to disdain any exploration of psychological life, even when it is confined to the private sphere. The following anecdote recounted by Richard Sennett depicts this point of view:

> A friend of ours was once in the toils of a profound depression, unable to eat, a thirty-year-old moving with the gait of an aged man, tempted each day by suicide. The friend was also being smothered in advice, all of which ended in the injunction, "You must see a psychiatrist!" Arendt counseled against the chorus; she thought it would "trap him forever within the prison of himself." And it was this attitude, I think, that caused her to feel the reverberations of exile in the everyday lives of people who had never been menaced by dictators. They, too, needed to experience something like the rites of passage of exile from the past in order to release themselves from the prison of subjectivity.[45]

Although Sennett suggests that her comment was motivated by her experiences of exile, the exchange has important implications for understanding Arendt's fear that a preoccupation with psychological exploration is an unhealthy part of the rise of the social. In this anecdote, Sennett connects Arendt's dismissal of psychiatry to her belief that one must be willing to break with a significant element of one's past before being able to participate fully in politics. For Arendt and others who experienced totalitarianism, this rite of passage entailed a willingness to be a refugee and to start a new life in a different country. It also required a willingness to forego the resentment and apathy that may have defined one's emotional life in a dictatorship. For those who are not living in exile or with the memory of dictatorship, the rite of passage may require a break with the self. Without such a break, the self that is encumbered by past suffering will be stuck in the "prison of subjectivity"; indulging in psychological exploration will only forestall the process of escaping. Being confined to such a mental state would prevent an individual from engaging in political action because the increasing preoccupation with the self would lead to a decline in his ability to think from the perspective of an "enlarged mentality," a concept critical to the process of judgment described below.

I suggest that the above anecdote reveals Arendt's deep-seated fear that emotional life could easily displace political life, although this is a different interpretation than Sennett presents in his retelling.[46] Sennett ignores how Arendt's injunction may appear dismissive not only of the

benefits of psychiatric care but also of the problems—potentially significant ones—that have pushed the man described above to such a dire psychological state. Even if one were to agree with Arendt that a preoccupation with the suffering of the past is an impediment to political life, the
application of this claim to the current case is unconvincing. A man on
the verge of suicide is an unlikely candidate for the "rite of passage": the
prison of subjectivity is too immediate and urgent to allow for an "exile's" break with the past. Arendt's response to the suggestion of psychiatric help reveals much about her own preoccupations with the boundary between public and private, a concern that permeates her theoretical
framework. It appears that Arendt was so concerned about emotional
preoccupation as a distraction from politics that she took opportunities
to warn others of this phenomenon, even if it meant that she appeared
callous and unable to appreciate the burdens of psychological distress.
Such a high level of concern about maintaining the boundary between
public and private would make it difficult for her to fully explore the
benefits of victim testimony.

For Arendt, the entry of the emotions into political life represents a
moment of uncertainty and danger, and the power of emotions to displace political life has at least two manifestations in Arendt's theory of
the social: *distraction* and *replacement*. Both embody the psychological
orientation of a preoccupation with interior life that Arendt understands
as destructive for the necessary boundary between public and private.
When emotions distract from the work of politics, people are content
to dwell on interior life to the point that they no longer see larger concerns: emotional distraction supplants a desire for innovative action. In
this manifestation, political life is allowed to remain intact, but its relevance declines as individuals become increasingly preoccupied with
their own experiences and their need for expression.[47] Individuals turn
away from politics in order to delve further into their private and interior
selves, albeit while looking for public spaces to reveal what they discover.
Solipsistic individuals do not prioritize thinking about collective concerns but still want others to be attuned to their particular experiences
and opinions. The incident remembered by Richard Sennett exempli-
fies Arendt's fear of distraction. From Arendt's perspective, if the young
man were to see a psychiatrist, he would experience a type of "public" recognition of his psychological distress, which would lead to more
inward-looking behavior rather than to political action. For the young

man and others caught in the "prison of subjectivity," individual experiences, particularly those of pain and disappointment, become important in and of themselves. Individuals who are experiencing emotional life as a distraction from politics do not try to transform their experiences into politically useful ideas or generalizable narratives. By using their own emotional lives, rather than universal political ideas, as the basis for reflection, individuals are restricted to the private sphere or the realm of the social, which appears to be public but does not live up to the requirements of that realm.

The second way for emotions to affect politics is as a replacement for more universal questions in the public sphere. In this scenario, individuals do not allow emotions to hinder their entry into politics (the distraction model); instead, individuals' emotional experiences make their way into politics and change the nature of the discourse and its aims. By way of example, I offer that Arendt would understand *identity politics*—social movements that use past experiences of oppression to mobilize participants—as a replacement of universal political claims with claims based on resentment.[48] Once emotional expression is allowed to enter into the public sphere, it obscures the distinction between public and private identity that is necessary for collective action oriented toward freedom. I suggest that Arendt would have placed victim testimony in this category. By creating a political institution that is specifically oriented to testimonies of pain and suffering, the very nature of political discourse is being replaced by an inferior means of communication.

In short, Arendt would see victim testimony as an inappropriate replacement for politics. Hanna Pitkin describes Arendt's conception of the social as politics *manqué*: a poor alternative to politics, a missed opportunity that can never be regained.[49] This is an understanding of the social that is particularly relevant to an understanding of victim testimony because it implies both opportunity and loss. Pitkin writes: "If the social is the large-scale counterpart to behavior, as politics is to action, then the social must be politics *manqué*, the absence of politics in a context where politics is possible and desirable. Of course, in many situations nothing useful can be done, and in many others nothing needs to be done. Those would not illustrate the social. It would mean actual opportunities for politics, missed, denied, or avoided."[50] Seeing victim testimony as politics manqué is one way to resolve the apparently contradictory strands of Arendt's theory as applied to the case of victim testimony. The ways in which her theory of action supports victim testimony bolster its great potential, but the fatal flaw, that which necessitates the term "manqué," is the emotional content and tenor of the testimonies. Arendt's frustration with the expression of emotions in the public sphere is so acute precisely because often something "can be done" and "needs to be done" regarding the issue at hand. This is even more pressing in the case of transitional justice after war.

Judgment as the Final Constraint

It is only fitting that Arendt's work *Judging* was left unfinished at the time of her death because it is the topic that serves as the keystone to her understanding of the relationship between past events and political action.[51] While the social provides a structural explanation why victim testimony would be criticized by Arendt, her theory of judgment provides a clue to her thinking on the level of the individual. Although Arendt emphasizes the relationship between particular experiences and judgment—a relationship that could be attuned to emotional insights—she ultimately recapitulates a description of an "impartial" spectator that is evocative of the writings of Adam Smith.

Arendt enthusiastically adopts the term "enlarged mentality" from Kant as a way to describe the process of taking into account "the possible rather than the actual judgments of others," and an exploration of this concept again reveals her rationalistic understanding of judgment as an overture that claims to consider the particular viewpoints of the other but consistently undermines the possibility of the same.[52] Arendt celebrates how enlarged mentality allows us to imagine how others may respond to a situation or idea and then incorporates these judgments, in an impartial way, into our own account. Yet, this incorporation requires a filtering of "subjective private conditions." In her essay "Crisis of Culture," she writes,

> The power of judgment rests on a potential agreement with others. . . . This means, on the one hand, that such judgment must liberate itself from the "subjective private conditions," that is, from the idiosyncrasies which naturally determine the outlook of each individual in his privacy and are *legitimate as long as they are only privately held opinions*, but are not fit to enter the market place, and lack all validity in the public realm.[53]

For Arendt, the enlarged mentality necessary for judgment requires the ability to think from the point of view of another and becomes the prerequisite for participating in a debate among citizens. If one is unable to speak from the perspective of an "enlarged mentality," she forfeits her ability to be a fully engaged participant in the public sphere. Arendt makes the point that enlarged mentality is distinct from empathy because it is not articulated for the purpose of understanding the subjective experience or, to use the language of this project, the emotional orientation of another.[54] To mistake enlarged mentality for empathy would give too much weight to understanding the emotional and subjective conditions of others and would prevent a move to the general standpoint: it would mean exchanging "their prejudices for the prejudices of my own station."[55] Contrasting enlarged mentality with empathy, Benhabib writes, "[Enlarged mentality] is not empathy, in that it does not mean 'feeling with others,' but signifies instead a cognitive ability to 'think with others.' Judgment requires the moral-cognitive capacities for worldliness . . . and a firm grasp of where one's own boundaries lie."[56] An enlarged mentality is thereby necessary for the purposes of abstracting from particular circumstances to a general understanding of the issue at hand and cannot involve the affective connection between individuals that would emerge from empathy.[57] The distinction Arendt makes between enlarged mentality and empathy parallels her discussion of solidarity versus compassion, discussed above, as the proper basis for political action, evident in her response to the French Revolution. Solidarity between individuals based on mutual respect is far superior to action based on compassion, an attachment that denies the necessary inbetween of citizen relations.[58]

In Kant's writings, the concept of enlarged mentality is one step toward the idea of the *sensus communis* as a judgment of what would be beneficial for the collective. Translating sensus communis as "common sense" does not effectively capture the central idea of Kant's philosophical anthropology: to achieve the sensus communis man must reflect on his place among men; this is the primary way he is distinguished from "the animals and from gods."[59] Quoting from Kant's description of sensus communis, Arendt writes, "In itself there is nothing more natural than to abstract from charm or emotion if we are seeking a judgment that is to serve as a universal rule."[60] In Arendt's interpretation, perhaps even more than in Kant's own formulation, the *sensus communis* is best understood in contrast to communication based on the expression of emotions.[61] Both thinkers simultaneously democratize the practice of judgment (with a greater number of perspectives considered) while sanitizing the role of emotions.

It is the logos of speech rather than the intonation, gestures, and body language that is the basis of the *sensus communis*. The expression of emotion is a base instinct to be superseded by language and rational communication in order to be part of the process of judgment. Arendt goes so far as to cite Kant's observation that insanity is marked by an inability to move beyond the gestures of emotions to the sensus communis.[62] The mark of sanity is the ability to separate one's private experiences, including emotions, from what *should* be communicated in the public sphere. Put another way, the sensus communis along with enlarged mentality and the ideal of impartiality are all filters that work together in order to separate the emotions that are present in particular circumstances from the more valuable information (rationally justifiable content) that is necessary for the general standpoint. In such a framework, there can be no general standpoint that takes into account the information that emotional responses may contain, even when they go beyond particular instances and reveal patterns that are meaningful on a larger scale.[63]

Revealing how emotional knowledge becomes detached from content through the adaptation of an enlarged mentality, Arendt explains:

> Suppose I look at a specific slum dwelling and I perceive in this particular building the general notion which it does not exhibit directly, the notion of poverty and misery. . . . The judgment I shall come up with will by no means necessarily be the same as that of the inhabitants, whom time and hopelessness may have dulled to the outrage of their condition, but it will become for my further judging of these matters an outstanding example to which I refer.[64]

This example sharply illustrates the contrast between Arendt's understanding of enlarged mentality and the perspective I consider to be necessary when responding to victim testimony. At first, there is a parallel between Arendt's relationship to the inhabitants of the slum and the relationship between the commissioners at a truth commission and witnesses. Both are listening to testimony and finding patterns. However, Arendt perceives the hopelessness of the slum inhabitants as part of the particular attributes of slum experiences but is more concerned with their classification within the general categories of poverty and misery. She does not think that the hopelessness expressed should be carried into the next stage of seeing patterns. For her, the move from the particular to the general with increasing impartiality is a prerequisite for the process of judgment. My approach suggests that a consideration of the particular causes and consequences of hopelessness does not need to be left behind in order to do the work of judgment or for the formulation of a political response to the issues of poverty. The emotions expressed by the slum inhabitants are not epiphenomenal; they are influential in shaping the political horizon and thus are important for the spectator to consider in the process of judgment.

For Arendt, the most compelling approach to judgment is Kant's idea of exemplary validity—an approach, beholden to the Platonic form, which considers the particular to be entirely self-contained and able to generate the tools for its evaluation. She writes, "One may encounter or think of some table that one judges to be the best possible table and take this table as the example of how tables actually should be: the *exemplary table* ('example' comes from *eximere*, 'to single out some particular'). This exemplar is and remains a particular that in its very particularity reveals the generality that otherwise could not be defined. Courage is *like* Achilles."[65]

With the method of exemplary validity, there is an acceptance that there can be no further way of distilling the particular in order to obtain a more universal version of the event or concept. The particular refuses to be transformed to the general in such a way that the essence of its significance (its "tableness" in the above example) would be lost, and Arendt acknowledges the value that it gains from remaining as a particular. Moreover, I argue that the example she gives of courage suggests that exemplary validity is necessary when the components of the particular are related in such a nuanced or complex way that they cannot be abstracted further (i.e., courage demands a complex interaction of prudence, bravery, wisdom, action, etc., best understood through the metaphor of Achilles).[66] Arendt's recognition of the importance of exemplary validity acts as a reaffirmation of why she turned to reflective judgment, from Kant's aesthetic theory, in the first place: it provides a philosophical way to incorporate the particular into political judgment. More than rational precepts that have general validity, judgment requires an appreciation of the interdependence of experience, practical wisdom, and context, and it cannot be reduced to only one dimension. Furthermore, the significance of the particular is often best understood through a narrative for which the particular serves as a shorthand reference (the narrative of Achilles' life is necessary to understand the meaning and significance of courage). If one instance of victim testimony—an individual narrative—were considered to have the status of exemplary validity, this would highlight the complexity of the different components of the testimony, including the multiple dimensions of the significance of anger, the violence of the past, and hopes for the future political community. The interdependent relationship between these components cannot be disaggregated without diminishing their political significance and the information they carry about the needs of transitional justice. April Flakne's argument about what happens when a new narrative is compared to an exemplary one of the past is relevant to how audiences should hear victim testimony in relation to past stories of justice. Flakne writes, "The story to which I have compared my new story does not remain stable or unaltered. If the exemplifying act has been successful, I have offered a rival account of the evaluative concept under question; we will never be able to see the story of Achilles in exactly the same way again, even while we have not deprived him of his valor."[67] Similarly, applying the status of exemplary validity to testimony suggests that it could then later become part of a set of culturally specific narratives that in turn are shaped, and shape in turn, future exceptional moments that cannot be judged using universal and deductive reasoning.[68]

Based on Arendt's interpretation of Kant's concept, exemplary validity is thus a way to acknowledge the richness that particular examples have to offer, even when they cannot be transformed by the processes of impartiality and enlarged mentality in order to be fully generalizable.[69] In the context of my argument about the need for an engagement with anger as necessary to the practice of justice, Arendt's interpretation of the concept of exemplary validity is promising but falls short. It opens up a space for considering the expression of emotions such as anger within a framework that emphasizes their particular context and publicity but is undermined by her more dominant need to excise the emotions from understandings of political judgment. The concept of exemplary validity also disappoints as a way to conceive of an "intermediate range of perspectives" because it remains at the level of particularity without embodying a new way of conceiving of the *semi-particular*. It celebrates the singularity of a particular example (e.g., Achilles) but it does not create an intermediate level where certain particulars are understood as significant although they would not be able to take the form of the general standpoint. The significance of anger in the context of victim testimony depends on this imagined intermediate range of perspectives. At this level emotions would not have to give way to the impartiality and rationality required for the general standpoint but would contribute to a new understanding of the relationship between emotions and justice.

Were she to have written on the subject, I suggest that Arendt would have considered institutions of transitional justice such as truth commissions to be full of political possibility. The very act of gathering so many people together in a public space should encourage action, not just reflection on the pain and suffering of the past. For these reasons, Arendt would have found victim testimony in the context of truth commissions to be a near miss: a gesture that came close to initiating a new process in politics after mass violence but was thwarted by the content and behavior of the testimonies. Arendt would have been disappointed in the psychological orientation of focusing on the past and not the future, the display of emotions such as crying on the stand, the language of compassion, and the singularity of perspective.[70] Each of these things represented a turning away from politics and, taken as a whole, suggests that Arendt would have seen victim testimony as collective action without political direction. In her skepticism of victim testimony she identifies the ways it can, without the proper safeguards, collapse into a celebration of victimhood and shallow compassion.

CHAPTER FOUR

The Second Skeptic

Adam Smith and the Visualization of Sympathy

The following two quotations from Adam Smith's *The Theory of Moral Sentiments* capture that book's central tension regarding the communication of anger:

> He longs for that relief which nothing can afford him but the entire concord of the affections of the spectators with his own. To see the emotions of their hearts, in every respect, beat time to his own, in the violent and disagreeable passions, constitutes his sole consolation. (Book I.i.4.7)

> Too violent a propensity to those detestable passions, renders a person the object of universal dread and abhorrence, who, like a wild beast, ought we think, to be hunted out of all civil society. (Book I.ii.4.3)

In the first quotation, Smith takes seriously the need to share individual pain with others and receive the sympathy of spectators. While sympathy does not negate the pain, it is the most comforting response we can receive from others, and even when we express anger and resentment ("the violent and disagreeable passions") we hope for sympathy, and rightly so. At the same time, in the second excerpt, Smith is surprisingly caustic in relation to those who express the "detestable passions," taking the expression of these passions as a threat to civil society and the object of universal condemnation. Why does a theorist who pays so much attention to the complexity of the communication of pain take such a harsh position in relation to anger?

The answer lies with Smith's understanding of sympathy within the idiom of a visual model, one that balances a concern for sympathy with an emphasis on distance, clarity, and proportionality. The visual metaphor reaches its apex with the normative ideal of the *impartial spectator* and his skill in judging the value of emotional expression from a distance that is great enough to allow for objectivity but close enough to understand the context of the emotion.[1] However, I will show that this model is too exclusive and dismissive of the emotions that exceed its narrow limits—a frequent occurrence with anger and resentment.[2] Smith is aware of the limitations of his model of sympathy, especially in exceptional cases, and is aware of the way the expression of anger and resentment is difficult to productively incorporate into his visual paradigm. With this awareness, Smith unwittingly provides the impetus for a new paradigm that is based on listening rather than seeing and is not entirely beholden to social norms for assessing proportionality.

The Visual Model and the Impartial Spectator

In contrast to *The Wealth of Nations*, *The Theory of Moral Sentiments* is concerned with the noneconomic transactions that determine social and political life. Constructing an ethical framework to guide these transactions was, for Smith, a fundamentally political, as opposed to a metaphysical, project.[3] While still making normative assessments about political life, he is more concerned with the realities of human interaction as he observes them than he is with essences or theories of human nature.[4] The reality of pain, its inevitable presence in our lives, and the impetus to share the experience with others is of particular interest to Smith, and he writes: "That we derive sorrow from the sorrow of others is a matter of fact too obvious to require any instances to prove it."[5] The communication of pain is described within *The Theory of Moral Sentiments* using the terminology of the theatre: the one who has experienced pain and is expressing it is the "actor"; all those who see it and are given the chance to respond are "spectators."[6] With this language, the visual metaphor finds solid footing, and pain becomes a performance to be watched from an appropriate distance; Smith consistently uses the act of watching to describe the communication of pain. When Smith writes, "Men of the most robust make, observe that in looking upon sore eyes they often feel a very sensible soreness in their own," he is emphasizing not only the consequences of the act of looking but also the eyes as the critical organ.[7]

The visual model is not just applicable to bodily pain that is easily observed by a spectator. Smith considers both physical and psychological pain and argues that physical pain, such as a toothache, is easily forgotten, while psychological or psychic pain, such as is prompted by betrayal or loss, is much more persistent.[8] It is the legacy of the latter that is the most challenging for the development of sympathy and often prompts anger, hatred, and resentment—what Smith calls the unsocial passions—that initially seem to repel sympathy.[9] In contrast to the social passions of generosity and kindness, the unsocial passions are those "of which the expressions excite no sort of sympathy," and they are marked by their uneasy place in public life.[10] They challenge the bonds of citizenship, suggest social unrest, and are prone to exaggeration and inaccuracy, and thus they must be treated separately from the more straightforward illustrations of the social passions.[11] The volatility of the unsocial passions demands greater scrutiny of the actor. Because the unsocial passions can be very difficult for the spectator to hear and interpret, the burden is on the actor to adjust the intensity of her emotions so that they may "be brought down to a pitch much lower than that to which undisciplined nature would raise them."[12] This type of adjustment in pitch, tone, and intensity signals a willingness to communicate in a manner that is consistent with social norms and presents the actor as worthy of sympathy. Yet Smith notes that although an initial reaction to the unsocial passions may be that of aversion, the spectator has a responsibility, as with any other expression of pain by the actor, to determine their impetus.[13]

The Example of Mother and Child

The empathy experienced by a mother in reaction to the pain of her child is one of the strongest and most immediate human reactions and a stark contrast to the problems that emerge in Smith's discussion of the unsocial emotions. The following description of a mother and her child illustrates this intensity: "What are the pangs of a mother, when she heeds the moanings of her infant that during the agony of disease cannot express what it feels? In her idea of what it suffers, she joins, to its real helplessness, her own consciousness of that helplessness, and her own terrors for the unknown consequences of its disorder; and out of all these, forms, for her own sorrow, the most complete image of misery and distress."[14]

Here, Smith describes how the pain of a child is transmitted to the mother in a complete and visceral way, without the help of language or context. There appears to be very little distance between the child's "helplessness" and her own "consciousness" such that it is not an evaluative or intellectual process that precedes the expression of sympathy, but rather an affective attachment.[15] In addition to the intensity of empathy in this scene, the relationship is also marked by an acute sense of the innocence of the child as the victim of harm. An infant is the most extreme case of a human being who can bear no responsibility for the misfortune that befalls him, and the mother-spectator, too, is an extreme version in this case, entirely responsible for the child's survival and displaying a sympathy marked by maternal love and the potential for self-sacrifice. I suggest that the mother-child model stands outside the normal process of sympathy in Smith's framework and speaks more to a Rousseauian understanding of *pitié* in the state of nature. While sympathy, as Smith understands it, may be inspired by the communication and empathetic response that a mother has for her child, it cannot be replicated on a larger scale and is not particularly relevant for citizen relations. Moreover, the lack of distance is not desirable for the type of assessment of appropriateness and proportionality necessary for sympathy in public life as Smith envisions it.

Nonetheless, Smith retains a very important aspect of the mother-child example in his larger theory of sympathy: that of the desirability of the innocent victim.[16] This is the actor who can be seen as helpless, blameless, and perpetually vulnerable. This archetype will become more pronounced as the qualities of the impartial spectator are more defined. The innocent victim is important to the visual model because he or she represents a simple node for communication, and, in such a scenario, it is only the harm that must be assessed, not the motivations, character, or failings of the actor. The visual model of sympathy deployed by Smith suggests the high value he places on clarity and objectivity, qualities in the spectator whose cultivation is aided by an actor who is blameless and not burdened by the unsocial passions.

The Development of Sympathy

In most cases, however, the immediate empathetic connection evident between mother and child is impossible, and instead there is greater emotional and intellectual distance between the actor and the spectator. It is this distance that allows for the cultivation of sympathy and the skills of reception, assessment, and response. For Smith, sympathy is not the instinct of compassion but rather a mechanism by which we develop an understanding of social norms and proportional responses to injury and pain.[17] It is the spectator's ability to understand the issues at stake through cognitive and affective clues that allows for judgments about whether there is a basis for sympathy and how much. By judging the experiences of others and offering sympathy, the spectator is exposed to the passions without having to experience them firsthand, and this is part of an education directed toward self-command, the quintessential Smithian virtue that combines reason and emotion in a studied and reflective way.[18]

This belief that the emotions reveal a strong cognitive content can be traced to Smith's affinity for Stoic thought, a tradition that highlights the singular importance of the emotions in helping determine what we consider to be important while also warning of the dangers of attachment to emotion.[19] The presence of an emotion reflects a particular history and set of values and is grounded in interpersonal relationships. Through identifying an object, making this identification intentional, and understanding the value and significance of the object that is revealed through the emotion, the Stoics understood emotions to be a source of evaluative judgment.

Yet while the Stoic tradition sees the rich potential of the emotions to reveal information, it also regards them as dangerous because they represent forces beyond the control of the individual. At a fundamental level, emotions have the power to overtake and overwhelm and are, as Martha Nussbaum observes, "in effect, acknowledgements of neediness and lack of self-sufficiency."[20] Attending to the emotions requires that an individual surrender the illusion of self-sufficiency along with the ability to predict one's disposition in reaction to an event or information. Thus, for the Stoics, emotions have great power—but this is a power that often cannot be harnessed for desirable ends and requires the strong antidote of judgment.

While an emotion represents an upheaval that disrupts existing ways of thinking, it must be followed, in the Stoic conception, by an assessment of how the emotion fits with previously held beliefs.[21] Through this process, it emerges that the object that has caused the upheaval likely does not warrant further emotional expression. The emotions, in fact, become "extirpated" through philosophical reflection on how emotions should fit with beliefs.[22] I agree with Fonna Forman-Barzilai, however, that the language of extirpation is too strong for Smith's framework and does not account for his desire for certain emotions to be heightened at appropriate times.[23] For Smith, the challenge is moderation, not extirpation.

Moreover, in Smith's thought as in the Stoics, if the unsocial passion is warranted because of an injury done to the actor, then the spectator has a responsibility to act. Resentment, more so than any other form of communication or social mechanism, puts into motion a series of actions oriented to the pursuit of justice. The emotion alerts the spectator to the presence of an injury, imagination allows him to experience it vicariously, and rational inquiry determines its cause. None of these steps is optional, and Smith writes: "When we bring home to ourselves the situation of the person whom those scourges of mankind insulted, murdered, or betrayed, what indignation do we not feel against such insolent and inhuman oppressors of the earth?"[24] In such an instance, the injury is obvious and the spectator is motivated to move beyond the act of sympathetic resentment to acting with the goal of punishment and retribution for the "insolent" oppressors.

In addition to the practice of showing sympathy in response to the pain of others, the ethical education of the individual includes assessing oneself in terms of the expectations of sympathy.[25] The inward trajectory of sympathy begins with the ability to see oneself through the eyes of another and thus to want to be worthy of their praise.[26] Moreover, the true internalization of the mechanism of sympathy is to act in a way that is praiseworthy without actually needing constant praise to do so.[27] When turned inward, sympathy is the central way to control passions and prevent attachment in the Stoic sense because it provides the incentive to act in a way that others would understand as reasonable given the precipitating events. The development of sympathy is thus a path of self-improvement that will eventually eclipse the concern for the pain of the other that precipitated it.

Smith is explicit about detachment from emotional expression as a normative goal, as evident in the virtue of self-command; he writes "that command of the passion which subjects all the movements of our nature to what our own dignity and honour, and the propriety of our conduct, require" is the pinnacle of ethical education and the virtue from which all others flow.[28] Only the spectator who has developed this ability through experience, reflection, and discipline is able to maintain a proper distance from his own emotional reactions. But I argue that the tension between detachment and sympathy distorts Smith's framework in major ways such that the value of the sympathetic response to pain is superseded by the cultivation of restraint in the spectator. This dynamic is most clearly evident when he writes about the value of resentment for justice alongside disdain for those who express it. Yet, sympathy is sometimes the appropriate response to anger; Smith writes that when "we plainly see what is the situation of those with whom he is angry, and to what violence they may be exposed from so enraged an adversary, we readily, therefore, sympathize with their fear or resentment, and are immediately disposed to take part against the man from whom they appear to be in so much danger."[29] The exchange of sympathy in this situation does not necessarily shorten the distance between actor and spectator because this is not desirable, but it affirms the direct connection between the entities and a component part of a civic public.

While resentment is one of the most important of the unsocial emotions because of its direct connection to justice, there is also danger in the spectator identifying too quickly with the actor, and the visual metaphor serves to emphasize this warning.[30] A certain amount of distance is required while the process of communication takes place, and this distance is significant because it serves as a counterweight to the tendency to be repelled by the unsocial emotion or to be encompassed by its energy prematurely.[31] Once positioned at an impartial distance, the spectator is now poised to judge the legitimacy of the claim to sympathy. The determination of sympathy involves two metrics within Smith's framework: propriety and merit, that is, the legitimacy of the emotion (according to set standards) and the need for punishment or reward, respectively. Propriety depends on how the spectator assesses the appropriateness of the expression of suffering in accordance with social norms that can be used to judge the severity of the injury and expectations for others who may be in the same situation.[32] If there is a convergence between the expression of suffering by the actor and the reflective calculations about the nature of harm by the spectator, the standard of propriety has been met. In the language of the visual model, there is parity between what is perceived on the part of the spectator and the desired expression of the actor. If there is not convergence, the expression should be seen as unjustified or too extreme to be helpful for the process of justice.

As for the second task of judgment, Smith writes that the assessment of merit or demerit, a calculation similar to retributive punishment, is "made up of two distinct emotions; a direct antipathy to the sentiments of the agent, and an indirect sympathy with the resentment of the sufferer."[33] Such sympathy with the resentment of the sufferer, the basis for propriety, is not crucial for the assessment of demerit. A determination of merit is concerned with what should be done to the one whose actions precipitated the sentiment of the actor, regardless of the sentiment expressed by the actor.[34] The object of reflection is, then, not the type of sympathy offered but the punitive or beneficiary action that emerges from the communication. The goals of determining propriety and merit fit nicely with the visual model: both are dependent on clarity and rationally justifiable assessments. The visual model, along with these determinations, gives structure to an inherently amorphous process that is prone to the concerns voiced by the Stoics. Namely, the communication of pain and the desire for sympathy can be an overwhelming task that encompasses, in Smith's eyes, both valid and invalid motives as well as unacceptable intensities of expression. The ability to determine propriety and merit in an objective way represents a triumph of the mechanism of sympathy.

Resentment can play both a positive and a negative role in justice, and its role is so crucial for justice that Smith, in a manner reminiscent of Aristotle, is critical when an actor *fails* to show it in the appropriate situation. The spectator can rightly feel frustration with, and even contempt for, the actor "who tamely sits still, and submits to insults, without attempting either to rebel or to revenge them."[35] This observation reveals that it is possible to show too much stoicism in the face of the unsocial passions. Again, both acknowledgment and judgment are necessary for the impartial spectator who is committed to the process of negative justice.[36]

As mentioned above, both propriety and merit depend on maintaining an adequate distance between actor and spectator. While imagination closes the space between the two, an accurate understanding of what would be the appropriate display of sympathy depends on being able to "see" the situation clearly, something impossible to do at close range. Family or friends, or those otherwise emotionally tied to the actor, will not have the best vantage point. Instead, Smith gives the example of the relationship between neighbors as an ideal to be strived for, even in the situation of judging one's own actions.[37] The example of the neighbor captures for Smith a type of distance that is desirable because showing sympathy for a neighbor's suffering is a protection against self-pity and indulgent thoughts about one's own suffering while still encouraging concern about the misfortune experienced by others. If we experience sympathy as good neighbors, we will not be entirely emotionally invested or removed but will rather keep selfishness at bay when we "feel much for others and little for ourselves."[38] Yet this formulation reveals another tension within Smith's framework: the impartial spectator is expected to develop the capacity for sympathy with others while always holding himself to a higher standard.[39]

The Metaphor of the Mirror

The practice of being a spectator to expressions of pain and determining their propriety and merit is only the first step in the education of the sentiments. Through experience and reflection, the spectator develops the skills and insights that then shape how he himself experiences and expresses suffering. As mentioned above, the goal is to develop what Smith admiringly calls "self-command," and the skills developed in responding in a proportional and proprietary (according to social norms) way to the suffering of others should be used to direct one's own response such that excess sentiment is removed. One's experiences cultivating sympathy for others serve as a type of mirror, reflecting for oneself the best ways to contain emotional excess. Like the concept of the impartial spectator and the norm of neighborly distance, the idea of using sympathy as a mirror for self-assessment is another potent example of the power of visual metaphors for Smith. Sight, with its promise of clarity and objectivity, is the bodily sense that has the power to assess others as they really are.[40] Expanding on the theme of the mirror, Smith writes about the reciprocity and adjustment between actor and spectator: "As their sympathy makes them look at it, in some measure, with his eyes, so his sympathy makes him look at it, in some measure, with theirs . . . and as the reflected passion, which he thus conceives, is much weaker than the original one, it necessarily abates the violence of what he felt before."[41] The conceptual addition of the mirror to the existing visual metaphor makes the dynamic present in any type of sympathetic communication more complex. As the actor seeks a sympathetic response from the spectator, she is also called upon to put herself in the shoes of the spectator returning her gaze and adjust her passion according to what the spectator would consider proportional. Similarly, the spectator is also expected to see himself through the eyes of another and act in a way that he would find commendable.[42]

One of the consequences of the emphasis on self-command is a decreasing concern for responding to the actual pain of the other. By suggesting that the internalization of the mechanism of sympathy is more admirable than offering it in an interpersonal context, Smith shifts the focus from communication to self-cultivation, particularly of the elite male. The following quote demonstrates how the example of resentment is used as a case for drawing a contrast between the emotional actor and the stoic spectator:

> The insolence and brutality of anger, in the same manner, when we indulge its fury without check or restraint, is, of all objects, the most destestable. But we admire that noble and generous resentment which governs its pursuit of the greatest injuries, not by the rage which they are apt to excite in the breast of the sufferer, but by the indignation which they naturally call forth in that of the impartial spectator, which allows no word, no gesture, to escape it beyond what this more equitable sentiment would dictate.[43]

Here, the stoic response of the impartial spectator is most admirable when it is in reaction to anger, a sentiment prone to excess and worthy of being called "detestable." To be on guard against such emotion is a substantial challenge for the spectator, and it is this challenge, rather than the testimony of the actor, that Smith would like to investigate further.[44] All concern is now for the "cool and impartial spectator" rather than for the one expressing resentment: "We should resent more from a sense of propriety of resentment. . . . There is no passion, of which the human mind is capable concerning whose justness we ought to be so doubtful, concerning whose indulgence we ought so carefully to consult our natural sense of propriety, or so diligently to consider what will be the sentiments of the cool and impartial spectator."[45] For Smith, the predisposition of the spectator in response to anger should be one of serious doubt that mandates special attention to propriety. The stoic response is a sign of success in relation to the communication of anger, one that highlights the impropriety of emotional expression. The possibility that anger has a singular value within public life does not make sense within this approach because its cost seems inordinately high.

When Sympathy Is Not Warranted

If the expression of anger is out of proportion with the event that caused it, the spectator is not expected to further engage with the actor. While this is frustrating for the actor, it represents a necessary outcome of proportionality and convention for Smith and a central component within his logic of the value of sympathy. In the visual model, if the objectivity and impartiality exercised by the spectator have revealed that the actor cannot be the worthy recipient of the sympathy she wants, to offer it would be a betrayal of the ideals of the impartial spectator and a validation of undesirable types of communication. Moreover, what Smith's logic in these situations reveals is a bias, consistent with Stoic thought, toward those who seem to be asking for comparatively less sympathy than they deserve according to the spectator's assessment, while those who express overmuch are seen as less ethically mature. The latter group is also potentially forfeiting its entitlement to any sympathy at all because the sympathy that was held out as a possibility at the outset of communication quickly turns to disgust: "We are disgusted with that clamorous grief, which, without any delicacy calls upon our compassion with sighs and tears and importunate lamentations. But we reverence that reserved, that silent and majestic sorrow, which discovers itself only in the swelling of the eyes, in the quivering of the lips and cheeks, and in the distinct, but affecting, coldness of the whole behavior."[46] The visual metaphor of recognition from the appropriate distance is dramatically curtailed in this situation. It is as if the line of sight connecting the actor and spectator is blocked and the spectator must look away because of the undesirable form of expression that the actor has chosen. The quickness with which sympathy may turn to disgust is notable in Smith's writings on anger and again implies his new focus on developing the qualities of the impartial spectator rather than attending to the needs of communication in a difficult situation. The unsocial emotions have always been challenging for sympathy, but as the argument progress, Smith doubts whether there are any benefits to engaging with anything but the most straightforward cases.

The Exceptional Cases

Nonetheless, at some moments Smith recognizes the limitations of his understanding of sympathy and, by extension, of the visual model. He draws the reader's attention to cases that are unusual and do not fit the common standards of propriety and merit.[47] These are the moments where Smith is willing to temporarily overlook the ideal of self-command for the possibility of greater knowledge and stronger bonds between citizens and thus shift the attention back to the relational and particular role of sympathy. In fact, it was Smith's attention to the particular, Ryan Hanley suggests, that prompted his greatest criticism of the Stoic sages and their unyielding adherence to universalism.[48] With an awareness of the dangers of a universalist model, Smith was careful to avoid creating a sentimental order that was unable to deal with the moment that defied precedent:

> There are some situations which bear so hard upon human nature, that the greatest degree of self-government, which can belong to so imperfect a creature as man, is not able to stifle, altogether, the *voice* of human weakness or reduce the violence of the passions to that pitch of moderation, in which the impartial spectator can entirely enter into them. Though in those cases, therefore, the behavior of the sufferer fall short of the most perfect propriety, it may still deserve some applause and even in a certain sense, may be denominated virtuous. It may still manifest an effort of generosity and magnanimity of which the greater part of men are incapable.[49]

This passage is remarkable in several ways, most notably for Smith's change of tone in reference to anger. Rather than using a visual metaphor to show the volatility of anger, Smith employs the *voice* to initiate a challenge to predetermined norms and expectations. While this voice may be more symbolic (e.g., the voice of reason) than actually pertaining to sound, the point remains that human weakness persists. The perspective here is one that accepts human fallibility and imperfection and the burden is taken off the actor to fully adjust expression to the requirements of the impartial spectator. Instead, communication between actor and spectator may exceed conventional expectations because of the nature of the injury or its unusual emotional manifestation. The sentiment cannot be moderated or mitigated, but this does not nullify its value or the standing of the actor. Furthermore, previous standards of virtue achieved by using the visual metaphor are inadequate. Previously, for an actor to be considered virtuous, he had to refrain from expressing an injury that would make him vulnerable to charges of excess and weakness. Here, in contrast, Smith values authenticity and the courage to voice anger in a way that is surprising and provides an opening for an alternative way of understanding the expression of the unsocial passions. In their own way, they can "manifest an effort of generosity and magnanimity of which the greater part of men are incapable."

In another exceptional moment, Smith acknowledges that actors worthy of sympathy may in fact be partially to blame for their misfortune and their shortcomings in propriety. This is again a case that defies the ideal he has set up and insists on new modes of interpretation: "If you labour, therefore, under any signal calamity, if by some extraordinary misfortune you are fallen into poverty, into diseases, into disgrace and disappointment; *even though your own fault* may have been, in part, the occasion, yet you may generally depend on the sincerest sympathy of all your friends."[50] Just as with the exceptional case above, the emphasis here is shifted away from the impartiality of the spectator and toward the actor's complex reality. Smith acknowledges the actor may be worthy of blame and disappointment regarding how she has behaved or reacted but is still asking for—and is worthy of—sympathy. The spectator is aware that demands of propriety have not been met, and the exchange should not serve as a model for how the impartial spectator should behave; yet the actor is still worthy of sympathy. However, Smith is careful to point out that it is your friends, not neighbors (as in the description of appropriate distance), who can provide sympathy in such a moment. He goes on to use this example as a contrast to talking about situations that are not as "dreadful" and therefore must have stricter expectations of propriety.[51] The exceptional case of the culpable actor who still deserves engagement and sympathy is an unusual situation and cannot become the norm. Still, his assent to the idea of the exceptional moment is helpful to my argument; the period after mass violence may give rise to an engagement with anger that is not expected at other times.

The passages referencing the exceptional moment and the flawed victim are Smith's attempt to adjust what he realizes is a rigid system of sympathy with an overwhelming focus on the cultivation of impartiality. Smith recognizes that the ideal of the impartial spectator is in danger of enforcing inherited bias if there can be no standpoint from which to critique propriety. He may also have realized that the rigidity of his theory of sympathy is working against his understanding of the natural tendency toward concentric circles of sympathetic attachment, a model often attributed to him. In this model of human relationships, at the center are the experiences that are easiest to experience in an empathetic way, first of the self (the conflation of actor and spectator) and then those of one's nearest relations, such as mother and child. More distant rings include fellow citizens, strangers, and foreigners, and a salient question for scholars reading Smith is whether there is an obligation to resist the strength of familiar ties in order to sympathize with the more distant ones.[52] In Forman-Barzilai's interpretation of Smith, the answer is no; she suggests that while Smith accepted the Stoic account of the concentric circles of sympathy, he had no interest in creating a more cosmopolitan version of sympathy.[53] She calls him a troubled particularist, whose concerns are grounded in what is local, but who is not beholden to accepting its social conventions as truth.[54] For her, Smith is able to negotiate the interplay between the importance of social norms created by sympathy and propriety and the mandate to judge these norms as an outsider at the appropriate time. However, I do not see this type of fluidity when it comes to expressions of anger, except in the two instances mentioned above. The anxiety surrounding the expression of anger and the predisposition to interpret an actor's expression as extreme often fails to generate particularism—even a "troubled particularism"—but I agree that this would be a fruitful way to build an alternative approach to his theory of sympathy. While Smith was attuned to the dangers of universalism, he did not go far enough in attending to particulars when it came to expressions of anger.

The Problem of Sound

Smith asserts that an appropriate response to the unsocial passions cannot occur when the actor, in an undisciplined fashion, allows himself to cry or express lamentations, anguish, or rage that is disconcerting to an impartial spectator. His distaste for the physical expressions of suffering and his reactionary emphasis on emotional distance is partially due to Smith's persistent fear that our own fears and shortcomings will color our ability to respond appropriately. It is also the result of the belief that displays of emotions such as tears or anger are signs of weakness and will be used to manipulate the spectator. In infancy, tears substitute for language and reflect a physical need, but in childhood, language is meant to replace tears, and Smith advocates that teachers and siblings should help enforce the idea that tears are a reflection of immaturity. Smith does not acknowledge the possibility that tears may reflect a type of psychological pain that cannot be suppressed or translated into language. In describing how men of differing virtues respond to pain, Smith says that the weak man "abandons himself as before, to sighs and tears and lamentations; and endeavors, like a child that has not yet gone to school, to produce some sort of harmony between his own grief and the compassion of the spectator."[55] Crying is thus a sign of weakness and a desperate attempt to garner the compassion of the spectator who may be questioning the proportionality of the "weakest" man's expression of pain. In an exchange between an actor who is crying and a spectator who is meant to rationally assess the appropriate response, the tears become the clearest indication that it is the impartial spectator who should be admired.

Similarly, Smith suggests that, even when the expectations of propriety do not allow for communication, the reaction to the aural presence of anger is similar in one respect to the response to the emotions of "pure" suffering, such as in the example of the infant. Smith writes, "The hoarse, boisterous and discordant voice of anger, when heard at a distance, inspires us either with fear or aversion. We do not fly toward it, as to the one who cries out with pain and agony."[56] The sound of anger therefore is always cacophonous and, more so than the other passions, instigates strong reactions in the spectator that prevent him from acting with the cool impartiality of the ideal. The tools that protected the impartial spectator from becoming too close to the one in pain do not work with these types of threatening sounds.

Seeing versus Hearing

The experience of responding to suffering should, for Smith, be incorporated into a visual model through his emphasis on distance and impartiality, a process of translation that will protect both the actor and the spectator from inappropriate emotion. When the sounds of anger remain and continue to affect the spectator, the translation has not been successful. "Seeing," then, is not just a metaphor; it is an intellectual mechanism for responding to suffering in a way that holds the ideals of neutrality, objectivity, and self-command constant. Smith fears that the visceral response to sound will bypass the cognitive and reflective mechanisms that distance the *visual* spectator. This could explain Smith's inability to consider other ways to respond to resentment. In the narrow case, resentment is a catalyst for the investigation of a crime, and thus fits the move from aural to visual. The rational basis for the claim of injustice and its consistency with social norms means that the content of the emotional expression can be judged from a distance, without having to pay too much attention to the significance of the affective component. The impartial spectator in this situation has not responded with fear or anxiety and is able to assess whether an injustice has occurred and, possibly, who should be held responsible. However, when the relationship between emotion and justice is not clear, such as when anger seems disproportionate to the violation or is a result of a variety of causes, I suggest that a response is still possible, but it cannot come with the distance of the impartial spectator.

A broader engagement with the testimonies of victims requires listening to anger not only for the information it may reveal about justice but also for what it displays about the actor's hope for status and recognition. A model based on listening and responding would be able to explore the gradations of interpretation of anger in a way that the metaphor of sight would miss, especially because the visual model is meant to clear away the unsocial passions in order to uncover the cognitive value underneath. A focus on listening would also incorporate the harsh expression of anger as a necessary part of communication and the basis of a shared political reality. Instead of proportionality, the ethics of listening in relation to sympathy has the following goals: to communicate what the actor needs and fears about participating in civic life, to recognize the civic bonds that connect actor and spectator, and to provide the bridge between emotional expression and the work of justice. While the expression of resentment may also suggest the desire for punishment of those who caused injury, determining the legality and severity of the injury is not the focus in this new framework; neither is encouraging stoic responses from the spectators as a way to demonstrate superior discipline.

Smith is not deaf to the influence of sound on sentiment. On the contrary, the following observation about music uncovers the relationship of hearing to sympathy even in his intrinsically visual framework: "When music imitates the modulations of grief or joy, it either actually inspires us with those passions, or at least puts us in the mood which disposes us to conceive them. But when it imitates the notes of anger, it inspires us with fear."[57] In the visual framework, music serves as a way to prime the spectator to respond sympathetically to what follows, especially in the case of grief or joy, a point similar to George Marcus's argument about the role of emotions in political behavior.[58] Emotions help us recognize and develop patterns in response to stimuli; they also help us learn from prior experience. In Marcus's language, "reason depends on emotion" in ways beyond the reach of consciousness. Furthermore, research has shown that anger can be a priming device that can instigate willingness to compromise with political opponents, but this is only possible without the hatred that often accompanies it.[59] For Smith, though, a predisposition to anger works against the possibility of sympathy; it encourages fear and anxiety in the spectator. This happens not only with music but when the actor communicates anger or resentment in a way that is not "toned down to a pitch" where it can more easily be heard. The visual model thus sees the "noise" of anger as a source of distortion obscuring relevant details that are necessary for determining propriety and merit. An ethics of listening does not separate the affective component from the content in such a stark way. The sounds of anger are part of what is being communicated through speech and sound; it indicates departures from established norms and implications for the actor and his role in social life. Taking the sounds of anger seriously in the process of sympathy is a way to acknowledge that communication is not only a cognitive investigation of the other person; it is a way to engage in a more basic form of connection between actor and spectator, witness and audience, citizen and citizen.

My perspective on an ethics of listening is shaped by Charles Hirschkind's inquiry into the culture of cassette sermons in Egypt. He argues that the practice of listening to these tapes in the car or one's home results in an inculcation of affective responses such as piety and generosity.[60] These responses then allow the sacred teachings of the Quran, as well as their interpretation, to be more fully understood. Hirschkind further posits that cassette sermons encourage listeners to engage in the deliberative practice of comparing their own actions with those discussed in the sermons, a preliminary action which precedes political deliberation.[61] The key difference between Hirschkind's argument about listening and my own is that the desired interpretation of the sermon is already largely predetermined by the cleric recording it. There may be individual variations in how much of the sermon is understood or applies to a certain context, but the goal is a particular affective orientation to the Quran, the cleric, and faith itself. In contrast, the ethics of listening to testimony is much more open in terms of desired outcome. On one level, it is the actor's communication of a desired form of expression that is important: how she would like her testimony to be heard and interpreted acts as an ideal to be strived for through the practice of listening. On another level, however, the task of listening in the period after mass violence is a political one and entails connecting each individual testimony to other testimonies and ultimately to the work of justice in a way that is broader than negative justice. The outcome should be oriented to the construction of trust among citizens and a sense of shared political life, but the exact mechanisms for this can be determined only through the process.

Susan Bickford has argued that adversarial listening is an understudied part of the literature on democratic citizenship.[62] A focus on listening, she says, should not evoke images of caring and consensus; rather it is always marked by engagement with conflict. The practice of listening to testimonies of anger intrinsically puts conflict at the center and forces the type of listening to which Bickford attends. In response, she calls for a type of "genuine" listening that cannot be measured simply by the presence of silences, question asking, or argumentation, an option she claims proponents of communicative action rely upon for legitimacy.

Instead, Bickford uses Merleau-Ponty's writing on visual perception as an effective model for listening. Recounting Merleau-Ponty's characterization of the relationship between an object and the world, she writes, "Objects appear when we concentrate or focus on them, and the surrounding world becomes the background or horizon that allows that object to stand out. The crucial point here is that the figure-ground structure is not one in which the ground is invisible or absent; it remains present and is perceived as present, part of a 'unique totality.'"[63] In a similar way, Bickford says that in listening, the listener acts as the horizon and the speaker is the focus (the object). For there to be any semblance of meaning, interpretation, or communication, the listener must be aware of the particularity she brings as the horizon, but she must not let it overshadow the centrality of the speaker. The relationship between speaker and listener is not fixed, but it has certain contours and boundaries that shape and are shaped by the process of communication.

I take Bickford's use of the perception metaphor to be relevant for listening to anger on several points: first is the recognition of the imbalance in focus between speaker and listener. Active listening requires humility on the part of the listener to accept that, for the time being, her perspective does not carry equal weight to that of the speaker. To hear the unexpected, one must be sufficiently detached from what one wants to say or is planning on saying at the next opportunity. Bickford writes, "We cannot hear our inner voice and the other's voice at the same volume."[64]

At the same time, it is erroneous to think that one can listen without the weight of one's experiences and hopes for the future. The horizon of the listening self is finite and engages with an object in an incomplete way. However, both listener and speaker, along with what is spoken and heard, are part of a "unique totality." The experience of a truth commission can be this unique totality.

I also agree with her refusal to provide a shorthand mechanism for genuine listening; it can be achieved only when there is a full engagement with the testimony being communicated, including the most difficult parts of the unsocial passions. The benefits of this engagement may not be immediately apparent. Bickford argues for three possible outcomes: "a perceptual merging of perspectives on the world, a recognition of coexisting and discrepant perspectives, and an inability to make sense together at all," or for a mixture of these.[65] For Smith, the first option is what he hopes will emerge from the moderation of emotion necessary with the unsocial passions and the corresponding judgment of the impartial spectator. The latter two options represent for him a failure of the sympathetic process and are unhelpful for the practice of citizenship. Bickford sees these as realistic possibilities for conflict, and, like her, I argue that through listening we are prepared to engage with the conflicts rather than ignoring them in the wishful hope for harmony. An ethics of listening, rather than seeing, would provide a framework for these types of exchanges. In the next chapter I will discuss the specific value of anger for public life even when it results in the recognition of "discrepant perspectives" or an "inability to come together," all frustrations held by commissioners at the TRC, as well as by skeptics of the value of anger.

While I suggest that the concept of the impartial spectator and the metaphors of visuality he employs are not helpful for thinking about anger in victim testimony, Adam Smith's model offers several insights that can be carried over to a new paradigm for sympathetic responses to anger based on listening. First, Smith provides a justification for the value of sharing resentment, even more than other types of pain, with fellow citizens. An actor communicating resentment enters into an alliance with the spectator against those who are responsible for the injury; Smith writes, "They can easily avoid being friends to our friends, but can hardly avoid being enemies to those with whom we are at variance. . . . The bitter and painful emotions of grief and resentment more strongly require the healing consolation of sympathy."[66] While expressing resentment is not consistent with the highest virtue of self-command, Smith is insightful about how the sharing of resentment is an important step in forging loyalty between citizens. Thus the ability to sympathize with a situation that has caused resentment is one of the most significant types of citizenship exchange. Truth commissions cannot be solely concerned with forgiveness or the objective recording of facts; they are institutions that can and must allow for the communication of resentment.

Second, Smith's theory is one based on practice, cultivation, and experience, an approach that can be compelling when applied to the ethics of listening within the context of truth commissions.[67] Intrinsic responses to pain, such as a mother's feeling for her child, represent only a small fraction of the types of pain that are part of public life, and it would be erroneous to assume that innate reactions can guide the spectator throughout the process. Smith emphasizes cultivating the skills of judging, especially in relation to propriety and merit, which are, in fact, the basis for listening in the new framework. Attention to sound and language can assist in understanding the particular context for the vocal expression of pain as well as the conventions for how a certain type of pain has been communicated in the past. Yet determining propriety or merit is not the goal of the process, which is oriented toward increased trust between actor and spectator and the work of justice. An ethics of listening takes from Smith an emphasis on the learned process of sympathy but makes room for the reverberation of anger.[68]

Smith, a skeptic in the tradition of Seneca, also brings up the concern that even when justified, anger and the other unsocial emotions may be unpleasant for the actor, and he notes that the expression of resentment, while cathartic, may cause further feelings of disruption. Even where there is cause to express it, it may still be disruptive and upsetting for the actor and difficult to reconcile with a desirable self-image. Within a model based on engaged listening, a spectator can acknowledge this ambivalence without suggesting that such expression is inappropriate for public life or the mark of weakness in relation to an ideal of impartiality.

The visual model, for Smith, is a powerful way of communicating several qualities of the practice of sympathy in a concise way: impartiality, distance, objectivity, and stoicism in the face of volatile emotion. While this model includes the communication of resentment as signaling the presence of an injustice, it is a narrow one unable to account for the types of anger I see as useful in victim testimony. In fact, the sounds of anger are a way for Smith to show how the sentiment does not easily fit the visual model. A model based on listening rather than seeing can better capture the challenge of communicating anger and the possibilities of response. Such a model does not rely on an innocent victim or a superior spectator but rather sees anger after mass violence as within the possibilities of Smith's exceptional case. An ethics of listening will not follow a formula of valuing acceptable anger based on previous norms and dismissing all other types; rather, anger must be understood to have several communicative outcomes that are necessary for the beginnings of trust and the awareness of a shared political life.

CHAPTER FIVE

Three Values of Anger

My fear of anger taught me nothing. Your fear of anger will teach you nothing, also.
—Audre Lorde, *Sister Outsider*

Anger, like other emotions, is closely related to a cluster of affective predispositions, including resentment, sadness, and frustration. Insisting on a narrow definition of anger misses the way these emotions often overlap; conversely a broad interpretation of the emotions, writ large, lacks analytical specificity. Cutting through these parameters, this chapter provides a schematic for interpreting anger in the context of testimony after mass violence. Each of the three dimensions of anger described here—cognitive-evaluative, confrontational, and kinetic—highlights a different way in which anger is important to the process of transitional justice but is often missed because of a focus on material evidence or a defensive reaction of censure. The term *dimensions* of anger indicates ways of interpretation and guidelines for themes and structure and is tied to the practice of listening rather than to the speaker's explicit intent—the three dimensions of anger may exist concurrently in one testimony. Moreover, I am not suggesting that listening to anger can be broken down to a tripartite structure in all contexts or even that all dimensions are equally valuable. Identifying the different types of insight anger may hold through a variety of clues, patterns, and inferences is the focus, and it is a task to be practiced in future truth commissions. As such, this type of listening necessitates that the audience at a truth commission be aware of how anger can simultaneously reveal and obscure truths about the speaker and her perspectives on political life.

The Cognitive-Evaluative Account

The cognitive-evaluative approach to thinking about the emotions has been influential for several decades, with writings by Robert Solomon, Martha Nussbaum, and Anthony Damasio pervading much of the literature in political theory.[1] The central tenets of the cognitive-evaluative account include the following: emotions are intentional, they are directed toward an object (something or someone), and they are a form of judgment about what one values. The cognitive-evaluative account stands in contrast to theories of sensation that suggest that emotions are purely visceral sensations that are not intrinsically connected to a political or ethical worldview or, more moderately, that emotions cannot be interpreted as legitimate and accurate judgments. This dichotomy between cognitive and noncognitive, however, is no longer particularly helpful, and I agree with Remy Debes that it is better to think of emotions as holding a set of properties, both cognitive and otherwise, that are present to varying degrees.[2] Thinking about anger in terms of its many properties is a way to keep from thinking about anger in an overly narrow (cognitive) framework that denies its complexity and volatility in order to make it politically palatable.

An analysis of the significance of the emotions will almost always have a "cognitive" element—that is, an interpretation that assesses an emotion's meaning or function—but, ultimately, the question must be: To what end do we direct the cognitive-evaluative analysis? I suggest that from a cognitive-evaluative perspective, anger can reveal what citizens *need and fear* in political life in an unparalleled way.[3] Citizens need to be seen as agents who will be treated as equals in the political process, and their fears include the idea that their needs will be ignored and that the risks of politics will not be equally shared. Listening to the cognitive-evaluative dimension of anger in testimony is also a way to grasp the challenges of expanding the demos, while at the same time nurturing this expansion through an extension of trust. An appreciation of this dimension of anger, along with the confrontational and kinetic dimensions, is a necessary step for the type of communication that builds a sense of shared risk, a topic discussed in the next chapter.[4]

The cognitive-evaluative approach to the emotions is not new, and in addition to Aristotle, it has been strongly articulated by Stoic thinkers and later by Adam Smith. Proponents of the righteous anger model in the twentieth century built upon the significance the Stoics attributed to emotions as forms of judgment, but these proponents saw the value of anger as a catalyst for social justice movements in a way that went beyond the negative justice of Adam Smith.[5] The righteous anger model is open to anger as a response to structural injustices such as racism and does not assume that an "impartial spectator" will be the best judge of whether an injustice has occurred because one must take into account one's own prejudice or inability to imagine an alternative social order. It was righteous anger that propelled the civil rights movement, feminism, and the anti-apartheid struggle into public consciousness through media coverage and eventually led to street demonstrations and civil unrest. In retrospect, the cognitive-evaluative interpretations of anger in those cases might have initially seemed disruptive to the political order, but they were necessary to bring injustices to light. The righteous anger account also highlights that even when connected to a legitimate cause, anger must be expressed in the right way in order to have the desired effect. Leaders such as Martin Luther King Jr. and Nelson Mandela are exemplars because they were able to express anger in precisely the right way at the right time, actualizing the ideals of both a righteous anger account and—accounting for differences in perceptions of citizenship and slavery—an Aristotelian one.[6]

However, the type of listening that can happen at truth commissions should be seen as separate from the work of social movements or its catalysts (although they may be related in other contexts). Testimonies should be understood to reveal fears about status in political life and the promises of equality and dignity in the new regime. They also point to the motivations and injuries that continue to pulsate within political life, even when these are not formally recognized. The righteous anger approach often uses what I consider the "easy cases" when arguing for the significance of anger to justice—examples of anger that capture widely held perceptions of injustice. My task, with an analysis of the other dimensions of anger, is to look at the ambiguous cases that do not easily fall into the category of righteous anger and could therefore be summarily dismissed but which can still reveal much about victims' needs and fears in the aftermath of mass violence.

The possibility of uptake, or remedy, has long been a critical component in cognitive-evaluative interpretations of anger. The best evidence for the claim that anger is informative, one could argue, is the fact that we can imagine responses that ameliorate its causes. Uptake in response to anger at discrimination on the basis of sexual orientation, for example, is a willingness to take its impact seriously and implement antidiscrimination policies. For the Stoics and Adam Smith, the concept of uptake means an investigation of the injustice and an assessment of whether punishment is merited. For proponents of righteous anger, it might include a sustained investigation of how an injustice has been perpetuated and also how victims have been silenced. Feminist proponents of the role of anger in the process of consciousness raising have hoped for, among other things, the uptake of better legal policy with respect to sexism as well as the acceptance of the anger as legitimate.[7] All of these responses should play a role in the response of the audience to anger at a truth commission, as the cognitive-evaluative account reveals.[8] But another type of uptake should happen through the formal inclusion of the testimony in the recorded proceedings and in the final report of the commission and is important for connecting anger to future political life. The report at the conclusion of a truth commission is a critical part of the process and necessary to make a bridge between transitional justice and increased trust in ordinary political life. The patterns in the testimony that are described and analyzed in the report should inform what one sees as the next step in the process of restorative justice. In particular, it can answer the question: How can the disordered relationships that have been identified in the testimonies—between police, neighbors, and former enemies, for example—be specifically addressed in policy after the truth commission has ended?

In the service of uptake, an ethics of listening to anger requires an ability to deduce from anger a connection to political life even when it is not immediately apparent. This is a process of uncovering causes and desires, but it cannot be made so rational that the complex and sometimes contradictory values contained within anger are lost. Robert Solomon, a proponent of a cognitivist view of the emotions, offers a particularly rigid understanding of the cognitive component, one that has fallen out of favor even with those who were previously advocates. It is useful, however, to examine this perspective as a foil to the multivalent approach to anger described below. Solomon argues that emotions are commensurate with rational judgments: "Emotions can be rational in the same sense in which judgments can be rational. Judgments are actions. . . . But if emotions are judgments, and judgments are actions, though covert, emotions too are actions, aimed at changing the world (whether or not their expression actually does succeed in changing the world). In other

words, emotions are purposive, serve the ends of the subject, and consequently can be explained by reasons or 'in-order-to' explanations."[9] For
Solomon, the cognitive component of emotions means that there is always the possibility of persuasion, argument, and revision. If emotions
"serve the ends of the subject" through purposive and intentional orientation, then both the ends and the emotions are fallible.

The validity of the emotion in relation to these ends should be the
subject of discussion. Solomon takes the example of anger and asserts,
"Anger can be explained, not in terms of what it is 'about' or what causes
it, but in terms of its purpose."[10] The intensity of the emotion may be
disproportionate to its purpose, but Solomon still wants to focus on the
causes and intentions of emotions as the great benefit of the cognitive
approach. Emotions may indeed reveal information that one cannot get
through other means, but for Solomon, one must determine precisely
what is being evaluated. He acknowledges that it may be difficult for the
person experiencing the emotion to be able to articulate its purpose, but
this is not a reason to stop attempting to understand it. Solomon wants to
decipher the underlying code that would connect emotions to beliefs and
concludes that this is the responsibility of the agent and of those who are
in a position to respond.[11] Emotions, for him, are thus subject to contestation and revision, all in the service of revealing the most accurate normative judgments and insuring that the judgments and the emotions are
proportionate. Solomon's argument about the ability to revise emotions
through discussion can be seen as the upper limit of what may be argued
from a cognitive-evaluative standpoint, but it is a limit that I find implau-
sible, especially within the context of victim testimony after violence. By
focusing on narrowly determining the purpose and cause of an emotion,
Solomon is foreclosing the possibility of understanding the cognitive potential of emotions that are rooted in *many* causes and are simultaneously pursuing variable ends.

I suggest that this is a common scenario when trying to understand
anger that arises after violence. For example, the anger that a victim of
torture expresses on the witness stand is not solely directed at the perpetrators; it is also directed at the state, the community, and even peers
for their complicity or disinterestedness. It would be impossible to re-
duce the causes to any one overriding factor, nor should this be the task
of the commission. One can ask a witness to reflect upon the causes of
an emotion, although this may be difficult depending on the intensity of
the emotion, but trying to "solve" the puzzle of the causes and purposes

of an emotion is not the best way to uncover the insights that anger provides for societies in the aftermath of violence. During the process of
victim testimony, it is unlikely that there will be a single cause or purpose for any given emotion, and even if this is the case the witness may
not be willing to concede this or to reconsider the intensity of the emotion. The role of a truth commission is not to question the legitimacy of
anger expressed during victim testimony but rather to see that within
the complexity of causes and intentions exists information about what is
necessary to trust that fellow citizens are concerned with collective well-
being. Solomon's analysis reveals the danger of an extreme commitment
to cognitivism with respect to the emotions; such a position ends up attributing so much rationality to the emotions that they become indistin-
guishable from reason as traditionally understood.

Jon Elster provides an important distinction within the concept of intentionality when he separates emotions that are "triggered by a belief
about an action by oneself or another" from those that are "triggered by
a belief about one's own or another's *character*."[12] While both types of
emotions have intentional objects, the latter's focus on character, either
one's own or another's, is a very different type of object and is closer to
my interest in the character of citizens and citizens' relations with each
other. Anger directed at a specific injustice is one part of the cognitive
evaluation; it may also be directed toward the character of the perpetrators and bystanders, as well as the speaker's own complicity, guilt, or lack
of resilience. Elster's assessment, along with Tarnopolsky's response to
him in her analysis of shame, serves to highlight an inherent bidirectionality (outward and inward) in the expression of an emotion such that the
information conveyed is always about the self-perception of the speaker
as much as it is about an event or perceptions of other people.[13] In the
case of anger the inward- and outward-directed targets may reinforce
each other with ever-greater intensity in the cognitive-evaluative interpretation or else become intertwined in a way that is difficult to decipher
(making them a candidate for interpretation via the second dimension
of confrontational anger described below). The case of anger is a particularly complex one for thinking about bidirectionality because of the
fears of the escalation of violence and the chance that the inward grappling with one's perceived failings of character will be seen as tethered
to increasing hostility toward another.

It is Aristotle who builds on the intentionality of the emotions and
provides the most compelling link between anger and status within the

cognitive-evaluative account, a link particularly relevant to victim testimony. In the *Nicomachean Ethics* Aristotle refers to the development of proper emotion in the individual, while in the *Rhetoric* he is concerned with offering guidance to the orator, legal or otherwise, who is trying to persuade an audience.[14] Anger in testimony does not fit comfortably into either of these categories; it is not strategically significant as oratory or directly relevant to the cultivation of virtue as in the *Nicomachean Ethics*. Nevertheless Aristotle's understanding of the significance of anger for political life is relevant to thinking about how commissioners and the audience can conceive of and respond to testimony in the context of a truth commission: here, as in Aristotle's formulation, anger is fundamentally political, and it is part of the emotional education that is necessary for citizenship.

In the *Nicomachean Ethics* the virtuous man understands anger, just as he understands a range of other cognitive emotions, at the nexus between theory and practice. With emotional life as with virtue, it is not enough to have an abstract appreciation of what is good; one must know how to live it with others. Through practice, habituation, and reflection, the virtuous man will be able to decipher how to exercise anger at the right time, in the right way, and for the right reason.[15] In contrast to the Stoic preoccupation with controlling anger once its judgment has been assessed, for Aristotle, to fail to get angry when the conditions call for it is an act of cowardice, not restraint. It is cowardice because it shows a lack of respect for oneself as an equal member of the polis. Additionally it shows a failure to appreciate the communicative importance of the emotions as constitutive of virtue. The emphasis on defending one's self-respect and sense of worth is apparent in his frequently quoted definition of anger, "Let anger be [defined as] desire, accompanied by [mental and physical] distress, for apparent retaliation because of an apparent slight that was directed, without justification, against oneself or those near to one."[16] Thus, anger (*orge*) is defined as the legitimate response to a slight, an offensive action that is an affront to the respect one deserves as a member of the polis. From the beginning, legitimate anger is connected to specificities of status and its influence on all communication in the political space. Konstan emphasizes how specific the definition of slight is when used in relation to anger: it is explicitly focused on the act of making the other feel worthless.[17] Thus the catalyst for anger is to feel belittled, even more than it is to have suffered a violation of the body or one's property.[18] In this way, Aristotle's definition acts as a political counterpoint to the Smithian reading of resentment; while Smith aims for objective assessments of anger caused by material violations, Aristotle asserts that the disturbance of respect and dignity, including in its most subtle forms, can be the catalyst for anger (but only for those who already have standing in the community, a caveat discussed below).

If we apply Aristotle's understanding of the slight to the case of testimonies at the TRC, we are drawn to the many ways in which individuals express a desire to be recognized as equals in light of previous slights. Victims talk about this desire with reference not only to government policies during apartheid but also to the way they were treated by teachers, police officers, and neighbors. They also refer to how the ANC-led government seemed to ignore those who were good soldiers for the cause, causing a different type of slight for those who sacrificed much for the anti-apartheid movement.[19]

Anger also appears in Aristotle's writings as *thumos*, a term that connotes passion and spiritedness in addition to anger itself.[20] In Barbara Koziak's interpretation, where thumos is understood as an emotional orientation that is broader than anger, it refers to a spectrum of necessary affective relationships between citizens, including friendship. To know when anger is appropriate in the Aristotelian framework is to know the variations of its expression and the response it may provoke in others. The cultivation of this affective spectrum is part of what is required for one to be a fully participatory citizen because it is not enough to rationally assess one's role in the collective; one must have the proper disposition to others, and it must be developed through interactions over time. One of the challenges of developing an affective disposition to others is knowing how to respond to the pain of others in a way that connotes recognition of their worth. The cultivation of thumos is not only relevant when there has been a slight; it implies a level of attention to the emotional disposition of others and oneself even when there is no slight as such. In the case of thumos, the cognitive-evaluative interpretation takes the form of discerning how emotions can be harnessed to create functioning social relationships. Thinking about anger in terms of the Platonic discussion of thumos is a helpful way to move beyond the dichotomy of good emotions versus bad emotions. Instead the spiritedness of thumos is inevitable within political life and contains some elements that seem directly beneficial to political life and others that seem to hurt it, prompting Plato's defense of censorship of certain types of speech and art.[21] Yet, an attempt to control the expression of thumos only highlights its buoyant nature. Without a thumos-driven motivation for participation and the work of politics, all political endeavors will eventually stall.

The attention to the emotions of others captured by the concept of thumos is necessary for the kind of relationships and cooperation that Aristotle envisions in his understanding of political friendship. While not as all-encompassing as true friendships, political friendships (as a type of "utility" friendship) still require a willingness to respond to the pain of others in a way that is oriented to *eudaimonia* (flourishing), and this requires skillfully navigating one's own emotions and those of others, even in the most challenging circumstances. By including anger under the category of thumos, Aristotle gives it a normalized role in political life and suggests that developing the skills to respond to its expression in other citizens is part of the task of political friendship.

Responding to thumos (anger) with thumos (spiritedness) is thus a way to understand the demands of citizenship, especially during periods of transitional justice. The transitional justice period is distinctive in that the social contract is in the process of being redrawn (and political obligation reconsidered); as part of this process the community must respond to the most serious crimes on a large scale, a task more overwhelming than the work of everyday politics. Yet the role of thumos as an orientation toward other citizens and the emotional attention required for functioning relationships is the same. It must be, as Koziak said, "worked out over time piece by piece," and a truth commission can be a significant part of the process.[22] Koziak's account of thumos demonstrates on the individual level the larger significance of anger in the context of truth commissions. It demands an attention to the emotional lives of fellow citizens, and this is a task that cannot be accomplished by proxy. Listening to victim testimony is the manifestation of a new type of citizenship and the trenches of its practice.

The Anger of the Powerless

Despite the importance of anger and the cultivation of thumos in his account, Aristotle cannot extend this thinking to subordinates—women and slaves in ancient Athens—because of his understanding of the relationship between public and private. Those who are politically disenfranchised in the Athenian context do not have the right to express anger, even though from a contemporary vantage point they have some of the best reasons to do so. In ancient Greece, when those who were weak expressed anger, they were seen to be giving in to the baser and animalistic aspects of emotion rather than achieving the legitimacy afforded to the anger of the high-status male. The prohibition against women expressing anger in the political sphere was both a question of standing (their role was in the household) and of differentiated virtues; anger for the Greeks is about competition and sexual power, neither of which is desirable in women. In William Harris's estimation, the mythological figures of Clytemnestra and Medea capture the anxiety that characterizes Hellenic thinkers on the subject of women and anger.[23] The rage of these women as they took revenge on powerful men was seen as an example of the excessive emotionality of women and its disruptive power. While a few poets and tragedians saw this as an overgeneralization and investigated the degrees of justification for women's anger (as in *Electra*), Harris concludes that, "Anger . . . is—together with sexual desire—the emotion which most clearly requires, in the view of the Greeks, different rules for women and men."[24] These rules included its confinement to the private sphere and to issues of comparative unimportance.

Similarly, slaves were seen to lack the capacity for deliberation required for participation in the political sphere and were not eligible for citizenship. Their anger, while perhaps of concern in the private sphere, was not judged to be politically significant. The fact that their anger could be a precursor to a breakdown in the established division of labor was also a concern. The anger of slaves (and the opportunity of response) was not an opportunity to cultivate thumos or cooperative relationships in the Aristotelian polis because they were not equal members of society whose participation was valued. As with *ressentiment* described by Nietzsche, anger expressed by those who lacked political and social power was tainted by desperation and envy. This double standard of the legitimate anger of elites and the illegitimate anger of others parallels the tension of the emotion itself—at times it is perceived to be inferior to reason and a dystopic ideal for political discourse, yet it always enters political life and is integral to the spectrum of affective communication that exists between citizens.

These perspectives on the anger of women and subordinate groups are still with us. While men in politics may use anger to great effect, women who voice it may be seen as disruptive, unaware of their social roles, and potentially worthy of scorn.[25] Feminist scholars writing in the 1970s and 1980s focused on the ways in which anger played a critical role in consciousness raising about sexism because it was a departure from gender expectations. Allowing oneself to get angry at everyday forms of patriarchal dominance was an early step in identifying as a feminist and mobilizing for social change. Anger was also a shorthand way of expressing solidarity with the movement. The concept of "outlaw emotions" emerged from this context, and anger was redefined as a critical feminist act. That is, the emotions that had been seen as excessive or inappropriate for women could become the best tools for critiques of structural injustice.[26]

Elizabeth Spelman argues that the cognitive-evaluative approach to the emotions is even more telling when applied to the expression of anger by subordinates. She writes that the expression of anger "would mean both that the subordinates would have standards of conduct applicable to the dominants, and express and apply those standards; and that dominants would thereby be subject to the judgments of those they've deemed to be beneath them."[27] Here she emphasizes that the judgment that emerges from the cognitive-evaluative reading in this situation goes beyond particular injustices to standards of accountability that may have been overlooked because of the social hierarchy. The anger of subordinates is threatening on many levels because it represents not just a demand—potentially with an implied threat of violence—for greater equality but also an excoriation of the actions or perceptions of the listener.

The confrontation between those who were previously considered subordinates and are still identified as "victims" and other citizens is one of the most remarkable aspects of a truth commission.[28] During periods of transition, truth commissions are at the forefront of the expanding demos, and the state can acknowledge those who previously had not had the privilege or dignity of citizenship. New constitutions and voting rights have formal import, but the image of individuals testifying in public in the context of a state-sponsored commission is even more powerful. The respect they are accorded could be an early instance of democracy's promise. Truth commissions have the opportunity, more than other political institutions, to present a picture of what it means to have expanded the demos and fostered citizen relationships that make participation in this new demos a reality.

One might argue that all types of political inquiries, including surveys and polls, attempt to assess what citizens need and fear, and they do it without anger. Why, then, should testimony be different? My claim is that testimony that includes anger contains insights otherwise hard to access. For example, the anger surrounding sexual violence against men was an unexpected development during the TRC. Before the hearings, there was a sense that such violence was too personal to be expressed publicly and a potential cause of shame for witnesses. It also appeared to be more of a medical issue than one with a bearing on political participation. While it was not common, the fact that some men talked about their inability to father children due to the torture they experienced is important for restorative justice. Even though they did not explicitly connect this anger to how they felt about citizenship, identifying this connection between a diminished sense of self and participation in political life is part of the task of listening to anger in the context of victim testimony.

Examples of the Cognitive-Evaluative Dimension of Anger

Lendiso Richard Ndumo Galela was an anti-apartheid activist with the Pan-African Congress. He was tortured while in detention at Robben Island and also while in exile in Zimbabwe.[29] In this excerpt, the commissioners have just told Galela that he should keep his comments brief because the session is coming to a close. He speaks of the impact of past violence on his life:

> There is no amount of money that can pay for a person's dignity. That is a fact. I am the equivalent of a corpse, I do not have any dignity left, *I have been stripped of my dignity* and that is what I wanted to say and I would just like to say that even though my physical appearance seems like that of a man *I have been stripped of my manhood* and a specialist told me that it would give, it would take three months for me to be treated and if nothing happens, I should know that I would be condemned sexually. . . . What I am saying is that I do not see what the Commission can do for me, because so many of them were unsuccessful.

Galela's anger seems to come from many sources: his indignation at feeling rushed in his testimony, his belief that he has been "stripped of his dignity," his impotence and sexual dysfunction, and his skepticism that the TRC hearings will be able to restore what was lost through violence. He is not persuaded that the commission values his individuality, nor does he trust its ability to shape collective concerns. When he says that "no amount of money . . . can pay for a person's dignity," he questions whether through participating in the TRC and receiving financial reparations the victims were becoming complicit with the state, the perpetrator of violence in this situation.[30] His willingness to question the relationship between the TRC and the witnesses who took the stand, along with the candid nature of his remarks, reflects the type of testimony that should have been the catalyst for a discussion about what was necessary for justice in South Africa. Moreover, the statement "I am the equivalent of a corpse" is an articulation of an unsettling reality in his self-perception: he could no longer see the humanity in himself and thought the commissioners were rejecting him in a similar way. Most importantly, Galela's testimony reveals a connection between the individual psychological foundation of hopelessness and its implications for politics. His pain and frustration have led to such feelings of despair that there seems to be no reason for him to be involved in political life. Galela's self-perception as a man who has been hollowed out to the point of becoming a "corpse" precludes his existence as a citizen. His despair is so thorough that it is unclear what could be done to incorporate him into the emerging society of the new South Africa.

One could argue that there will always be members of society who turn away from politics after a traumatic event, but it is important to note the specific identity of the individual in this case. Galela, a member of the Pan-African Congress, spent much of his young adult life fighting for a revolutionary cause. Such a commitment suggests that he was inspired by the possibilities of political change and was willing to put himself at risk for the sake of political ideals. The transition to an ANC-led government and the end of apartheid could have been a triumphant moment when his work and that of others like him were vindicated. Instead, he felt diminished and unable to function as a complete human being. He had sacrificed too much—in his words, his "manhood"—and could no longer imagine what it would mean to participate fully in the community.

Two further examples show how a cognitive-evaluative approach elucidates the expression of anger in victim testimony and should be seen as relevant to the challenge of expanding the demos during the transitional period after the end of apartheid. First is the testimony of Ellen Kuzwayo, an anti-apartheid activist, teacher, and author in Soweto during the student uprising in 1976.[31] Kuzwayo expresses the belief that the Afrikaner regime made black children feel like animals and that they were not allowed to develop the skills necessary for maturity. The commissioners were unwilling or unable to engage with this insight and instead asked her if the teachers in her community communicated what was happening at the time of the uprising to the government. Kuzwayo's testimony reveals that she is highly educated, well traveled, and able to put the South African experience in a global context. At the end of her testimony, she focuses on how the South African state trained black children to play certain limited roles—roles that remain the same even when government structures change.

> MS KUZWAYO: I still believe to this day, I am still angry because I feel the Nationalist Party government did never see our children as children. Because the colour of their skin was not the colour of the skin of their children, they were not children, they were not human beings, they were children who were not given an opportunity to grow, to mature, to become adults like everybody. . . . *They turned our children into animals.*
>
> MS MKHIZE: Thank you very much Mamma Kuzwayo. Actually even if you see us interrupting you, it's not because it's irrelevant, but it's because we want to pick on some of the other things. . . . Because you have made emphasis on the drama of the day, how devastating it is, surely the question is what did the community do? Did they only talk among themselves? Did they make efforts to make sure that the government hears the impact of what they had orchestrated?
>
> MS KUZWAYO: . . . And today it's very difficult, we talk about violence in this country and violence that is carried out by young people in this country. They get you out of your car, or they see your car standing somewhere they come and take it away. *And these kids have been changed into murderers. And I want to believe that if Native Education had not been changed the situation would be different in South Africa today.* Now it gives an impression that Black children are thieves, murderers, they are everything else that is not good.[32]

Kuzwayo connects the pattern of crimes committed by young black males to the legacy of apartheid, but the commission is unable to respond.[33] An approach based on listening to the cognitive-evaluative significance of anger would instead have focused on how she identified the challenge of expanding the demos to include those whom the education and legal system had deemed to be destined for criminality. This challenge fell within the scope of the TRC investigation and was precisely what a transitional institution like the truth commission was poised to take on. It could have identified which relationships needed greater attention and resources within a framework of restorative justice. When Kuzwayo says, "They turned our children into animals," she invokes the hierarchies of political life that previously excluded blacks altogether and still excluded those who are uneducated and poor. Their anger is transmitted through her testimony. Testimonies such as this one could have changed the parameters of what was previously considered to be the scope of the investigation by pointing to obstacles to expanding the demos.

Another example shows the value of the cognitive-evaluative approach even for cases that many would rather dismiss as reactionary and makes for a complex case of righteous anger. Johannes Frederik Van Eck is an Afrikaner who was on vacation at a game reserve when he lost four members of his family to a land mine planted by the ANC. The year was 1985.

> MR VAN ECK: I'm expecting from the ANC, through this Commission, to answer the following questions . . . Is this your way of doing things to citizens and families and friends, to give them this pain by killing their loved ones? Is this your way of doing things that you justify all your murderous acts by linking it to a struggle against a regime? Is this actually habit or your policy to differentiate between just and unjust, murder? *Is this your way of doing things or policy to call a killer of innocent women and children a freedom fighter?* . . . Chairman, I think it was very clear in my submission, all I'm asking, my only request is that it should be consequent, I said, leave those people as they are, leave them where they are, but then we should look at who we are hunting for in vain. In other words, the Commission stands for equality and justice. That's all I'm asking for, for justice and nothing more.[34]

Van Eck suffered a tragedy and wanted those who planted the land mine to be punished, but he extended blame to the larger strategy of violence employed by factions of the ANC. In addition to punishment of the perpetrators, he wanted a public investigation of the actions of the ANC and he was bitter that these actions were not scrutinized at the TRC in the same way as those of the apartheid state. This is an unusual case that fits with a righteous anger response to a violent crime but could also be seen as a reactionary move to shore up the crumbling racist order. Yet the framework for engaging with anger that I am proposing should be applied to examples such as this. The cultivation of thumos requires that citizens try to understand the anger expressed here and what it connoted about Van Eck's fears about his value in future political life. Van Eck's fear can be interpreted as a concern that his family and those like him will not be part of the emerging South African political life in the post-apartheid era. They will be seen as aggressors and losers of the struggle, and the fierce protection of their material assets may be the only way to retain power. For Van Eck, and whites like him, the TRC inspired a fear of victors' justice. But attention to the demands of Aristotelian political friendship and trust (discussed in chap. 6) would also require that the commissioners and the audience accept that the anger expressed here might not quickly dissipate in the new South Africa and that cooperative relationships would take time to build. Van Eck's anger reveals his complex position in relation to the creation of trust in the new political landscape: the ANC and those in the anti-apartheid movement have acquired political power and amnesty for past crimes, while he feels that his suffering has gone unacknowledged.

In these examples the commissioners did not directly engage with the anger expressed by those who testified, and their avoidance represents a conventional way of thinking about anger in politics. In the case of Ellen Kuzwayo, they did not explore the connections between the violence and ideology of the past and the challenge of reconstructing the political realm. Focusing on the material evidence and facts about the past was the more obvious way to respond, but an ethics of listening means that the audience (including the commissioners themselves) should be more attuned to the cognitive-evaluative significance of anger as expressed in the testimonies through their assumption and understanding of its value. What is revealed through anger in the testimonies is part of the risk that is then shared by the victim and the audience. The needs and fears expressed in testimony should be considered as the content for the future work of restorative justice. This content takes into account the questions from the commissioners, the official report, and the actions that are begun after the truth commission has concluded its work. The cognitive-evaluative approach relies on active listening in order to determine the complex causes of anger, along with the desires for status and power that are embedded within it. The potential for uptake also provides an opportunity for a tangible response to anger, which may be the best indicator of shared risk necessary for the development of trust. With uptake to the cognitive dimensions of anger, its causes and implications become part of the reality of the audience and not solely that of the victim.

The Confrontational Dimension of Anger

Listening to testimonies of anger includes considering the type of anger that does not fit the righteous anger model because it is disproportionate, extreme, or erroneous. One reason why proponents of righteous anger suggest these demarcations is because they allow for the distinction between unhelpful rage and helpful anger where only the latter is considered as legitimate. In the aftermath of mass violence, this is not an easy distinction to make, and it necessitates other frameworks for understanding anger, namely, a second important dimension of anger I have termed the *confrontational* dimension. The confrontation contained in the term refers to anger that goes beyond the contained adversarial quality of righteous anger by eschewing obvious solutions or reparations. The confrontational dimension of anger is difficult to respond to and even to coherently follow because of the various antecedents and objects found within its expression.[35] Still, the confrontational dimension of anger often exists alongside the cognitive-evaluative dimension such that a single testimony necessitates both interpretations in order to make sense of its significance.

The confrontational dimension is likely to encompass other negative emotions such as despair as an excessive form of sadness, or hopelessness, and they can be interpreted along the confrontational dimension even though they may not initially be read as anger. The listener should identify the confrontational dimension when she hears parts of the testimony that do not seem to be connected to specific events or to relate to the events in a way that challenges expectations of response or proportionality. They may also appear to be extradiegetic; that is, beyond the purview of the expected narrative of egregious rights violations. The anger that necessitates a confrontational interpretation is often not stated explicitly with a self-identification of anger by the speaker (e.g., "I am angry"). Rather, anger fulfilling the confrontational dimension is distinguished by the cadence of speech, repetition, and turns of phrase that together indicate that the witness is grappling with intense sentiments that are connected to her own faults, her need for acceptance by an audience that may not understand, and the paradoxes of participating as a citizen when one cannot stop thinking about the past.

Jean Améry's writing in what Brudholm refers to as the "Zustand" passage captures the confrontational dimension of anger in a powerful way. Améry describes the feelings found in resentment, what he calls "ressentiment," as so conflicted that they give rise to a warped conception of time. He writes, "It did not escape me that *ressentiment* is not only an unnatural but also logically inconsistent condition [*Zustand*]. It nails every one of us onto the cross of his ruined past. . . . *Ressentiment* blocks the exit to the genuine human dimension, the future. I know that the time-sense of the person trapped in *ressentiment* is twisted around, dis-ordered, if you wish, for it desires two impossible things: regression into the past and nullification of what happened."[36] Améry's perspective is powerful for showing exactly how interdependent the backward- and forward-looking aspects of resentment can be. He can identify the promise of the future while demanding a nullification of the past. It is not just that the past and the future happen to co-exist in the worldview of a survivor; they are two powerful forces in battle. While indebted to him, Améry cannot follow Nietzsche in his understanding of *amor fati* as the solution to *ressentiment*; embracing the past through a love of fate is an impossible proposition even for someone who understands how *ressentiment* must be "logically inconsistent." Instead, Améry hopes that the listener will also eventually have an unreconciled vision of the past and a sense of the perpetual uneasiness based on what he hears in the anger of victims.

Even without the self-awareness evinced by Améry, the confrontational dimension of anger is valuable (beyond the cognitive-evaluative dimension) for what it reveals about the complexity of the process of citizenship of the period after mass violence, including (1) the speaker's perceived costs of the triumph of restorative justice over retributive justice, (2) the speaker's understanding of the pervasive yet intangible effects of past violence, and (3) the synchronous struggle of the speaker to configure her own life narrative while also communicating a desire for a change in the sphere of the political. On the first point, the confrontational aspect of anger may be an expression of frustration with the process of restorative justice, rather than directed to an instance of violation. If retribution through punishment is one of the goals of anger, then the fact that punishment is, at best, a deferred possibility at the South African TRC gives rise to the need for alternate paths. One is the path of righteous anger discussed above; another is a more diffuse anger that serves as a type of protest against the assumption that the witness will communicate in a conciliatory manner. The "confrontation" embedded in the category is also reflective of the possibility of confrontation with fellow citizens with this type of expression. The excess and variable nature of this dimension of anger seems to be an escalation of emotion, yet it should also be seen as a way to get a more dynamic picture of the lived experiences of the victim and citizen.

The second value of the confrontational approach is to draw attention to the way anger can reveal the invisible and intangible consequences of years of violence. They may be the secondary effects of violence, including the loss of optimism in the future, rather than the primary effects (torture, death, etc.) of human-rights violations. Lastly, attention to the confrontational dimension may include a witness's frustration with herself in her response to the violence, at the time or on the stand. The speaker may be frustrated that her intensity is undermining other things she hopes the listener will get from her testimony, including details about the violence or desired punishment or a greater incentive to trust her in the future. The witness's anger may also include the conflict of wanting to let the anger of the past go but resisting because the event had such a profound impact on one's life. In this way, the confrontational dimension of anger may occupy a space between demanding recognition as a victim and wanting to be seen as a citizen, even when one is unsure of what that means. Attentiveness to the confrontational dimension of anger means that the audience may pick all these things up and will be attuned to the ways that expressing anger is a challenge for the speaker, including a challenge to the speaker's self-perception of character.

Maria Lugones coins the term "second-order anger" to refer to a type of anger that is decidedly not seeking uptake. More emphatically, uptake may be impossible given the context and content of "second-order" anger. I see strong affinities between her conception and the confrontational dimension of anger in victim testimony as she is critical of how a view of anger as "righteous" is dependent on the largesse of a dominant class for the recognition of its worth. Those who express second-order anger in Lugones's account refuse to accept the righteous anger approach as the only legitimate grounds for anger, which is anger that is legible to the dominant class. Anger, in her mind, must be understood much more broadly than the case of subordinate groups petitioning those who are more powerful. Second-order anger is about the irreconcilability and ultimate incommunicability of the subjective experience of the angry self and other realities. She writes, "This anger echoes or reverberates across worlds. It is a second-level anger. . . . It recognizes this world's walls. It pushes against them rather than making claims with them."[37] Second-order anger, consistent with what I am calling the confrontational approach, is a type of existential angst that does not merely want the recognition of membership in the demos or the chance to be on equal footing with elites; it is communicating a more complex reality. Not relying on the assumption of a coherent self, Lugones characterizes this type of anger as evocative of the divided self that desires contradictory ends and is frustrated by the difficulty of communicating them to others. The very attempt at communication may feel like a betrayal of the intensity of experience.

Confrontational anger also finds affinities with Sianne Ngai's description of "ugly feelings," such as envy and paranoia, that she describes as noncathartic and therefore often overlooked as central to action. Ngai contrasts these feelings that are "associated with situations in which action is blocked or suspended" with conventional understandings of righteous anger in political life. The noncathartic feelings she describes are notable because of their long duration; over long periods of time they render visible the nature of obstacles to action and the relationship between different types of obstacles. Ngai's insight can be applied to anger that does not feel like anger, conventionally understood, including the type of anger that appears as irritation or paranoia on the stand. These expressions, following Ngai, should not be read as a weakened instantiation of righteous anger or as the confused communication of a witness who is unsure of the merit of her case. Instead, I take her to be supporting the need for an alternate approach to a cognitive-evaluative account of the emotions that demands that they be connected to action in a direct way in order to be seen as politically significant. An analysis of the confrontational dimension is one such alternative that would be applicable to emotions of lesser intensity, as well as to heightened ones like rage, because it focuses on what the emotion can communicate in terms of broader political life and about the relationship between the speaker and the audience.

The monograph *There Was This Goat*, by Antjie Krog, Nosisi Mpolweni, and Kopano Ratele, provides an example of the type of narrative that lends itself to the confrontational interpretation of anger.[38] The authors focus on the testimony of Notrose Nobomvu Konile, one of the mothers of an activist killed as part of the Guguletu Seven.[39] When Konile testified about her son's murder at the hands of the police, the commissioners found it difficult to make sense of her fragmentary ideas and uneven recall of the relevant events. In particular, it was hard to determine whether Konile was presenting the events in chronological order, given that she included a discussion of a dream and parts of conversations with her son from different time periods. As a radio reporter covering the trial, Krog attested to the seeming incoherence of the testimony; yet in retrospect, Krog and the other authors find themselves moved by Konile's language and intrigued by the ways her testimony refuses to submit to easy practices of interpretation. Unsatisfied with the way Konile's testimony was translated and understood at the TRC, the authors explore it further in two critical ways, first through retranslation and then through a visit to Konile's home.

Retranslation entails listening to the testimony in Xhosa, Konile's native language, and then comparing the new English translation with the less accurate one recorded simultaneously during the TRC. Krog and her coauthors are sympathetic to the challenges of simultaneous translation, but they are happy to find that in the retranslation the testimony becomes less fragmented through details about the village where Konile lived and the specific content of her dream. For example, it becomes clear that the dream of the goat represented a bad omen for Konile and the first sign that her life was about to change in a dramatic way. Krog and her coauthors write, "The sequence of forebodings every time Konile saw Pheza, plus the story of the goat dream, indicated that culturally these incidents were connected for her. Konile was communicating a message to the Truth Commission audience that effectively said, 'Long before I heard of my child's death, I was already in pain through the premonitions and the bad dream.'"[40] Greater attention to the language and imagery of the testimony revealed an internal logic to her testimony that made it more politically relevant.

Ten years after her appearance at the TRC the authors visited Konile in her hometown, a rural village in the Eastern Cape known for its agriculture and coal production. The unusual landscape of the village further clarified the symbolism present in Konile's testimony, including the salient imagery of the goat and coal. The authors observed improvements in Konile's situation since the TRC, particularly in her increasing ability to use the resources available to her (including money from the TRC Reparations Committee) in order to secure a home and take a leadership role in a textile collective.[41]

The attention Krog, Mpolweni, and Ratele direct toward Konile's testimony and her life afterward is exceptional in its detail. They pay close attention to her choice of linguistic and cultural references, her psychological state, and the perspectives of those around her in order to better understand her experiences of violence and life in the present. Their efforts have lasted far beyond the scope of the truth commission and would have been impossible to replicate for every witness, but their findings are still helpful in considering normative possibilities for interpreting testimonies. First, as mentioned above, their engagement affirms the value of examining the language and emotions of testimonies that seem incoherent or excessive. Konile's recollection of the dream with the goat and its ominous presence in her life reflected the way that the violence of apartheid became integrated with her conscious and subconscious reality. Other references, too, initially point more to Konile's psychological life than to shared concerns but can later be seen as part of a longer story of claiming a civic identity after being identified primarily as a victim.

The confrontational dimension of anger is also relevant in testimonies that contain an elliptical structure and compounded emotions. A cognitive-evaluative approach would miss the impact of the serial concerns expressed, such as in the following testimony. Nomakula Evelyn Zweni was a black anti-apartheid activist who was detained multiple times in the 1960s and 1970s. Testifying about her detention in response to her anti-apartheid activism in those decades, Nomakula Evelyn Zweni said,

> We burned these places up, there was a bar where I used to live, we burnt it—I am telling you we burnt it. Because they use to call us kaffirs how can you call a person kaffir, what is that—what is kaffir, what is that, what is that? I don't want apartheid at all. You will be beaten up—you would be beaten up in your land by the boers [sic].[42]

This short excerpt touches on many concerns: concerns about the apartheid land use policies, arson, the slur "kaffir," and violence committed by white South Africans against Zweni and members of her community. All these concerns become elided, and Zweni's anger is decoupled from any particular incident. Her anger should be seen as tied not only to the violence she experienced but also to the structural implications of apartheid, including the lack of economic opportunities coupled with easy access to alcohol in establishments owned by white South Africans. Similarly, her anger at the term "kaffir," a derogatory term that is now considered hate speech under South African law, is powerful because it refuses uptake or rectificatory response. The multiple objects of her anger reveal part of the interplay between the structural, linguistic, and economic legacies of apartheid and how they cannot be separated in an accounting of the political climate. A cognitive-evaluative approach to her anger could point to the specific experiences that caused Zweni pain, but a more expansive way to engage with her anger is through its confrontational dimension. Note how it provides commentary on the transitional moments that would be difficult to get otherwise.

The confrontational dimension of anger, as seen in the examples of the dream with the goat and the psycho-linguistic response to the term "kaffir," is important because of the way it references the intangible structures of apartheid. The fact that language itself has been shaped by the terms used to implement and enforce the violence of apartheid and the relationship between violence and liberatory goals cannot be easily recast in the utopic space of the truth commission. It is interesting to note that although Zweni's anger and frustration are notable, there is a change in the middle of her testimony. When asked to reflect on the process of testifying at the TRC, she says, "On this date, on the 22nd I do accept reconciliation with both hands."[43] She implies this is reconciliation with God, rather than with those who were the perpetrators of crimes in the previous regime. The juxtaposition of these two affective states, anger and reconciliation, within a single testimony further speaks to the importance of having multiple approaches to understanding the relationship between anger and political life. Expecting a contradiction in expressions of anger may be the most productive place for the listening audience to start. The response from the commission under ideal conditions is, as described by Améry, to allow the paradox and incommunicability of the testimony to be heard and allowed to exist without coercion or extensive mediation. The confrontational dimension of anger does not necessitate immediate uptake but demands a type of attention that shows acknowledgment of the risk taken in its expression.[44]

The Kinetic Dimension of Anger

The kinetic dimension of anger refers to anger's significance as a source of energy for political life. It is not connected to the conceptual issues of redress or contradiction as found in the cognitive-evaluative and the confrontational dimensions. Instead, the kinetic dimension operates on the level of visceral experience and the recognition of shared humanity.

Appreciating the kinetic dimension of anger means understanding it as the potential for social change. This is akin to appreciating the inspiring quality of a mass protest or an impassioned musical performance, even if one does not agree with or relate to the content. Those tasked with maintaining institutions may try to deny this type of energy by insisting on impartiality and evenhandedness, or they can appreciate it as the enlivening force of thumos. The most urgent and compelling political questions carry with them a high level of intensity, and this intensity should be better appreciated on the questions' own terms, distinct from the cognitive-evaluative and confrontational dimensions.

In considering the effects of anger's intensity, Robert Thurman makes a useful distinction between anger as energy and anger that is bound up with hate.[45] Thurman structures his essay *Anger* around forging a path between these two different ways of experiencing anger. He uses the term "resigning to" anger to refer to a wide range of perspectives that see the power and volatility of anger as integral to human life and as necessary for defending religious ideals or fighting against oppression (this is similar to the righteous anger account discussed above). In truth, much of my argument here could be seen to fit Thurman's category of "resigning to anger." He might point out that while giving anger a more central place in discussions of transitional justice may seem new, the feeling that anger should be justified and excused is long-standing and misguided. On the other side of the debate, he writes that there exists a tradition of "resigning from anger" that is equally misguided. This perspective is found in Seneca's discussion of the futile attempt to control, harness, and understand anger as well as is in the Buddhist tradition that situates anger in an understanding of nonattachment (to objects or concepts) and nondualism. In the Buddhist tradition, anger is another type of delusional attachment that gives the individual self-illusory importance and meaning.[46] An ontology of nondualism further reveals how anger relies on a dualism between victim and perpetrator, a vision which betrays the reality of the interconnectedness of all things. Anger directed at an oppressor does not make sense in Buddhist thought because it must be directed at oneself as well since the self is the conduit of experiencing anger. This makes the possibility of resolution difficult to fathom. Thurman suggests that while these concerns must be kept in mind, a middle path is also available, one of appreciating the particular energy of anger. As he describes it,

Anger's explosive energy becomes the bright blue-black sapphire radiant laser light of absolute purity wisdom, the completely inexorable, relatively absolute energy that absorbs all differences and oppositions, that destroys all obstructions, dissects all complexities and knots of resistance to freedom, that consumes death and life and all between in the infinitely free. It is so powerful in its destruction of all egotism and confusion it cannot be opposed. It is freedom itself, it is freedom that is free of freedom even, free of being free, and so is infinitely present in every level of sensitive and creative relationships.[47]

While not completely rejecting the ideal of resigning from anger that comes from nonattachment and nondualism, Thurman recognizes that anger remains a fundamentally creative force and the most powerful energy to which human beings have access. By calling it a "freedom that is free of freedom even, free of being free," Thurman suggests that anger is not trapped or defined by established concepts of freedom and restraint because it is the force that creates such a tension in the first place. Anger is not dependent on being released, expressed, or accepted; this is an erroneous way to think of its power. Rather, it is a force that destroys "differences and oppositions," but to allow it such power necessitates a paradoxical resignation from it. Thurman suggests holding on to the raw energy of anger while detaching from the specificity of its cause, a perspective that could be fruitfully carried over into the political sphere.

Engaging with the raw energy of anger in witness testimony is perhaps best accomplished in person, or in the video or audio recordings of a truth commission. Written transcripts, which may be useful for understanding the cognitive-evaluative and confrontational dimensions, cannot capture this aspect. Catherine Cole's writing on the TRC argues that this is precisely the aspect many people have overlooked in their commentary about the TRC. She references the testimony of Nomonde Calata, who broke into a mournful scream, and says, "The importance of this sound—a wail that transcended language and, in doing so, captured something elemental about the experience of gross violations of human rights—indicates the degree to which the physical expression was central to the TRC."[48] Here Cole is talking about the energy of that cry as paradigmatic of the TRC, but at the same time, she intuits an interpretation of it that is similar to righteous anger. Thurman's analysis pushes for a way to separate these two interpretations: Calata's scream can provide

energy for political life apart from being connected to the desire for revenge and the punishment of her husband's killer.

The kinetic dimension of anger should not just be seen as the irra-
tional backdrop for the rationality of the logos as embedded in anger.
I follow Cavarero in suggesting that the voice, the visceral and sono-
rous expression of the human body, is important for politics in ways that
go beyond reasoned speech because of what the voice reveals about the
uniqueness and relationality of a person (the ability to share experiences
with strangers).[49] The particular tone, modulation, and cadence of an
individual's voice are highly idiosyncratic and can betray the speaker's
fears and skepticism even when the words she uses suggest otherwise.
The voice is the instrument that connects the witness who begins as a
victim to her subsequent identity as citizen, and attention to voice via the
kinetic dimension of anger draws attention back to the process of listening. Cavarero desires a shift from the metaphor of sight, which she claims
has dominated Western metaphysical thinking, such that truth becomes
unconcealment against a perceived stable landscape, to that of hearing,
an activity marked by attending to the succession of sound amidst a dynamic field.[50]

Like the scream of Nomonde Calata, Antigone's mournful cries have
been interpreted as a type of primitive reaction to grief and a univer-
sally recognizable female gesture of putting commitment to one's family
against the needs of the state. Honig finds this reading to be a disservice
to understanding Antigone's political significance and to the concept of
natality, which I would also consider a kinetic force. Part of Honig's analysis on *Antigone* involves rethinking the meaning of sound. She writes,
"Parody, mimicry, and citation postulate not just worded repetition but
also intonation and inflection" and says further that sounds can be listened to not just as a complement to the "logos" of language but also as
forces that disrupt and inspire it in explicitly political ways.[51] The sounds
of anger, the very things that make it difficult to interpret using a cognitive-evaluative lens, can provide greater meaning and significance to the
other parts of the testimony because of the relationship between sound
and word, often through homonyms and wordplay. Just as Antigone's
cries and screams put forth resistance and hopes for an alternate political order, so do the sounds of testimony heard at a truth commission.

Sartre's understanding of the emotions provides another perspective
on the kinetic dimension. For him, expressions of emotion are magical
transformations of the world; starting in the body but finding a home in

the world, they are responses to events and obstacles that disrupt automatic causal linkages.[52] He considers emotions to be magical because of their unexpected force and location within the physiology of the body, as well as the connection that is forged between the body and the object that initiated the response. Moreover, they defy patterns of logic in their ability to foment intensity and attachment. The strong intentionality of the emotions present in Aristotle and Solomon is found again in a different capacity in Sartre's reading because of the connection he wants to draw between the object of emotion and the subject. Yet, it is his description of the quickening sensation of the emotions that warrants attention here; as audience members listen to testimony, the expression of anger, even when they do not agree with or understand its antecedents, is in Sartrean terms a powerful impulse to transform the world, and the kinetic energy of anger allows individuals to forge connections with others through its communication, even when retribution and repair are not possible. To witness anger is to experience how the energy of anger circulates, permeates, and electrifies all who encounter it. Anger is not death; it is the opposite of death and has an impact on those who listen to it that is not dependent on being able to respond but rather comes from its expression of the visceral human desire to survive and be heard.

The three dimensions of danger described here—the cognitive-evaluative, the confrontational, and the kinetic—speak to the understanding of anger as a complex life-giving force. Expecting anger's contradictions and the movement between different dimensions in the process of listening can open up a transformed type of communication between victim and audience. Each of the dimensions of anger reveals insights about the speaker's experiences and the challenges to establishing a new political culture with an expanded demos. Thus, the goal is not the disclosure of anger for its own sake or for the purpose of catharsis, but for civic interactions that are generative of trust, the focus of the next chapter.

CHAPTER SIX

Trust Enough to Tarry

Danielle Allen, in *Talking to Strangers*, takes distrust between citizens of different races as a powerful indicator of the stalled project of the civil rights movement in the United States. While legal protections have provided a formal equality of citizenship, the lived experiences of black and white Americans (along with those of other races) continue to be marked by a sense of division at best and fear and animosity at worst. She calls this dynamic "fossilized distrust" and describes the outlook of some citizens in the following way: "For decades, white Southern citizens had been accustomed to maintaining key public spaces as their exclusive possession; for the sake of preserving life and stability black Southern citizens had been accustomed to acquiescing to such norms and to the acts of violence that enforced them."[1] The public sphere continues to be the site of distrust, and Allen draws attention to the lack of friendly everyday interactions between people of different races in schools, churches, and on the street; a similar description could apply to perspectives about public spaces in South Africa during the transition from apartheid to democracy and the fossilized distrust that exists in its wake. The public sphere in South Africa was dramatically transformed during the 1990s by a new constitution and legal changes that promised greater equality (as in the United States during the civil rights era). Coeval with the legal changes was the evolution of social norms of citizenship, and the Truth and Reconciliation Commission served as a foundational space for their enactment.

I suggest that an engagement with anger provides an opportunity for truth commissions to serve as incubators for trust and to lay a path for future everyday interactions. The very aspects that make anger a challenge for communication could heighten the possibilities for trust, but this requires a number of changes from previous iterations of truth commissions. First, the commissioners and the audience must approach the witness in the spirit of trust, including trust in the value of communicating anger that seems to militate against the short-term goal of cooperation.[2] Next, the experience of the testimony, including the introduction, witness statement, questions, and responses, should be seen as moments that foster trust. Through the victim's expression of anger and the audience's response there is the chance for all parties to show a willingness to bear the risks and dependencies associated with political life. Last, the trust that is cultivated during the testimonies can set a model for new practices of citizenship after the truth commission has ended.

Trust is, in itself, practically a subfield of political science, relevant to every part of the discipline and integral to the analysis of collective life. At the outset of a truth commission, engaging with anger as it appears in testimony depends on an affective openness to the significance of victim testimony and to the idea that a shared goal exists between victims and the audience.[3] Yet to do so requires a motivation. Philip Pettit has argued that loyalty, virtue, and prudence are the conventional foundations for trust, and it is telling that none of these is relevant to victims (or family members of victims) of violence during the apartheid regime as the basis for trusting the state or fellow citizens. Rather than loyalty to the South African state, victims of state-sponsored violence were likely to feel betrayal and resentment.[4] The language of virtue also rings hollow for all those involved because of the gross violation of every imaginable ethical code. Prudence as the basis for trust would have been appropriate only for those who were bystanders and not direct perpetrators or victims of the violence. In addition to these reasons, Pettit introduces another motivation for trust that emerges from the granting of trust itself: the good opinion of others. The very act of placing trust in someone else generates a reason for that person to act in a way that maintains the trust. Even if the trusted person feels no connection to the ethical norms of loyalty or virtue, the desire to have the good opinion of another can be a motivation that stands alone. Thus the decision to trust can foster trust in *the absence of* other rational reasons to do so. Pettit's schema highlights how the period after mass violence raises questions about trust that are more vexed than in other periods because of the legacy of distrust that remains. I would argue that the distrust is so great that even the motivational power of trust is diminished because of the distance and hostility between citizens. When established reasons cannot hold, Pettit notes the great creativity involved in ushering in new reasons for trust, and this is part of what should happen in the discourse that frames a truth commission. Like Arendt's celebration of forgiveness as necessary for new beginnings, the initial sparks of trust between citizens are signs of the new and powerful as catalysts for political change.

Like other new beginnings, participation in civic relationships at a truth commission cannot be fully accounted for using rational assessments of the costs and benefits of trusting, yet such participation may be critical for future successful interactions. Pettit writes that for trust to emerge in institutional contexts, several conditions must be met, including other instances of trustworthiness known to all parties, a lack of ulterior motives, and freedom of expression.[5] In the context of a truth commission, I interpret his suggestions in the following way: a truth commission should demonstrate an awareness that even if the testimony has a confrontational tone, it may still be valuable in the process of building trust; testimony should be autonomous from the demands of state-sponsored nationalism (i.e., it cannot be an alternate form of propaganda for the state); and, last, the victim should have the freedom to tell his story in the way he chooses without coercion, as long as it does not become hate speech. Establishing clear institutional expectations of the victim at the outset is critical for creating an orientation toward trust because of the fine line between a predisposition to trust the victim and the predisposition to pity him. Pity does not allow for the transformation of identity from victim to citizen that is at the core of this inquiry (and of Arendt's critique) because it is tethered to a situation in which experiences of pain and suffering are interpreted only in a backward-looking way.[6] With an orientation toward trust, the victim is neither impotent nor infallible but rather an agent in an emergent political landscape who can affect the discourse in varied ways. As with Aristotle's description of entechnic speech, Pettit shows that *before* testimony can even be communicated, the institution must signal both trust in the speaker (that she is offering testimony in the spirit of civic participation) and the potential trustworthiness of the audience (to encourage such participation even when the content and tone of the testimony are challenging to hear).[7] Furthermore, being disposed to trust, for both the commissioners and the witnesses, includes the rational orientation that others will not betray or hurt you, that you are not being deceived, and that you share similar goals.

In addition to the self-actualizing potential of initial displays of trust described above, there is an additional reason why attention to trust is necessary even before testimony begins: this concerns the very nature of trust as an affective orientation to another rather than a narrowly cognitive one. In fact, the particular affective attitude we display toward those we trust is the best indicator that the trust exists.[8] The affects of generosity, interdependence, and reliability are not just the symptoms of underlying trust but make up the attitude of trust itself. Another way to think about the particular set of affective indicators of trust is found in Connolly's term "critical responsiveness."[9] Critical responsiveness, as mentioned in the Introduction, is a presumptive generosity to the presence of another, an approach that indicates a willingness to listen for what lies beyond the familiar and the comfortable. Stephen White provides an evocative description when he says that critical responsiveness is "receptiveness to human presencing, even when, on our first over-coded glance, it may appear abject, abnormal, unimportant, or threatening."[10] White finds critical responsiveness an appealing proposition, but he suggests that it needs greater direction in terms of its goals. In this project, the focus on anger provides a rejoinder to the critique; an engagement with anger with the goal of trust gives a focus to critical responsiveness that is underspecified in other contexts.

Trust and Restorative Justice

Restorative justice is a way of envisioning the process of justice as much broader than retribution for criminal acts.[11] Instead of narrowly focusing on punishing the injury committed by the perpetrator, the restorative justice approach focuses on rebuilding (or establishing for the first time) relationships that were damaged by the crime, and, along the way, the community is implicated in both the causes of criminal behavior and the possibilities for reparation afterward.[12] When a crime has occurred in a small community, this approach includes face-to-face encounters between victims and perpetrators, mediation, and restitution. As a subcategory of transitional justice, restorative justice initiatives on the national level such as victim testimony and material reparations are motivated by a concern for the broader relationships that were affected by mass violence including those between perpetrators, victims, families of victims, witnesses, and so on. A theory of restorative justice also takes as central the idea that the process of justice should foster cooperative relationships between individuals in a way that goes beyond punishment and instead encourages the cultivation of trust.[13] The relationship between anger and trust in the service of restorative justice also serves as a rebuttal to those who have criticized theories of restorative justice for being shallow and assuming too much good will on the part of the participants.[14] The model here starts with participants who may be angry and isolated and moves to relationships that demonstrate the beginnings of trust, thus nurturing (and not assuming) the connections upon which restorative justice depends.

While the terminology of restorative justice emerged in the late twentieth century, it is grounded in a long-standing tradition. The central concept of restorative justice, that of attending to the impact of the crime on the entire community, is vividly captured in Allen's essay on anger in ancient Athens and the yearly ritual of a mock stoning and the banishment of two people in the community as "scapegoats."[15] While the ritual of mock stoning is violent and could represent the worst parts of engaging with anger, Allen emphasizes that the ritual included a self-reckoning on the part of the community when its members considered the unjustness of the banishment and their own culpability in the decision. The ritual was meant to reveal that "we solve the problem of anger—of its ugliness and that of the violence of punishment—by defining those whom we have to punish as being outside society because of what they are— fools, beasts, cursed by nature—rather than because we have put them there. We do this rather than admitting that we punish because of what we need and that we are all implicated in this need."[16] The engagement with the anger of the community thus becomes a ritualized version of an agonistic political space, which is similar to the process I have described in relation to truth commissions. Instead of affirming the infallibility of the process of justice or its proponents, the ritual was a way to attend to the remainders of the process and the aspects of political life that are often overlooked in the interests of "peace," consensus, or the closure of decision. The remainders included the difficult questions of who was systematically excluded from political power or asked to sacrifice for the sake of the collective. Engagement with anger in the political space, then and now, evinces an awareness of the volatility of anger and the possibility that it will be misused or misdirected with tragic consequences. The role-playing involved in the ritual highlights the difference between blaming and presumptive generosity. Furthermore, annual attention to the problematic of anger reveals the need to cultivate cooperative relationships during times of peace as well as during those of conflict. Anger should not be thought of as important only when it has reached a pinnacle of intensity. Truth commissions can fulfill these multiple roles: they are not just forums for the expression of guilt or catharsis but permit investigations into anger past and present. The ritual described by Allen, just like the formal space of testimony, provides a space for the formal consideration of anger and a commitment that the interaction will be taken seriously and may possibly lead to trust.

Trust and Previous Experience

A skeptical retort to my argument for the presence of trust at the outset of testimony can be found in Russell Hardin's claim that trust relies on prior experience. Individuals are strongly shaped by the experiences they have with others where trust is either affirmed through mutual support and concern for well-being or denied because of betrayal and deception. A deliberate and concerted attempt to trust, however well-meaning, is difficult to achieve. Moreover, he argues, the majority of one's formative experiences with trust are outside of one's control, including family relationships, economic opportunity, and racism. While recent experiences lead to Bayesian updating of one's predisposition to trust, ensuring Hardin's model is not a static one, yet his point still holds: it is difficult to conjure trust (e.g., the idea of "choosing to trust") just because it would be valuable in a certain situation. Simply put, one trusts or does not, and the choice is only whether to act on this trust.

Applying Hardin's framework to the context of a truth commission is illuminating: first, the violence at issue in a testimony is a powerful example of an experience that one could not control but which shaped the predisposition to trust nonetheless. This is particularly true of one's relationship to the state. The negative experience of the recent past may be more influential than anything else when thinking about trust. Also, if one cannot choose to trust, then does it still make sense to say that the witness and audience must approach testimony in the spirit of trust? Yes, but I acknowledge that this trust is, at best, tentative *until* there are new actions and experiences that allow individuals to offset prior negative associations with trusting. This possibility of incubating trust is precisely part of the constructive benefit of truth commissions that I am suggesting. The engagement with anger is one opportunity to embark on a different type of relationship between the formal political institutions of the state and individual citizens. The process of engagement itself becomes the experience that will solidify the initial goodwill described above into a different type of trust in the aftermath of a truth commission.

Defining Trust in the Process of Testimony

While the generous predisposition to an engagement with anger is an initial instantiation of trust, it can develop into a different type of trust once it is grounded in the actual interplay between the witnesses and the audience. I follow Annette Baier in thinking about the meaning of trust in the context of a relationship. She offers a perspective that is consistent with the three-place model of trust (A trusts B to do C). In the three-place model, trust is not a generalized sentiment toward another person regarding all things, as in the case of a love relationship, but a more focused responsibility on a specific object of care known to both parties. The entire process of trust carries within it *the risk that the object of care will be harmed or ignored* and that the vulnerability of either party will be exploited. In the case of a truth commission, the object of care is the testimony itself, a personal accounting of a violent event and its aftermath. The personal nature of the testimony, as well as its power to make the witness a target of criticism, makes it an object of care during a truth commission. But beyond that, the object being entrusted to the audience is even more comprehensive. Political life requires that we trust fellow citizens to consider our best interests as part of collective well-being.

A related marker of trust, and one essential to a sustained level of trust in ordinary political life, is the awareness of shared risk among citizens. Risk can be understood in two ways: first, as the probability of a negative outcome, and, second, as increased dependency and potential for harm because of the access that trust allows. An engagement with anger suggests that audience members take on both types of risk because of the suggestions of violence that anger can imply (the first type), as well as the risk of becoming dependent on someone who has already experienced misfortune (the second type).[17] The victim is likely not particularly concerned about the first type of risk but has a heightened sense of risk as dependency because her testimony may be ignored, chastised, or mocked. Yet this testimony and the citizen identity that grows out of it can become the object of care discussed above. If there is a sense of

shared risk and the object of care is threatened, the event will reverberate negatively for both parties. Shared risk also entails the sense that one
party should not unequally bear the burdens of participating, whether in
the case of friendship or in political life. The uncertainty of disclosure
and of the outcomes of events in both contexts necessitates an understanding that engagement entails risk (as dependency) and that this risk
can be either fairly or unfairly distributed. With the goal of nurturing
trust, all parties will try to recognize and calibrate that risk to the best
of their ability such that there is a sense of mutual dependency. The challenge of trust is thus to treat others' needs and hopes as important, even
when the outcome of a political decision or negotiation is uncertain and
may carry negative consequences for one's perceived interests.

The concept of shared risk evoked here also incorporates Allen's insights about some of the causes of distrust in the wake of the civil rights
movement. She argues that there was a failure of recognition of the sacrifices made by fellow citizens, particularly African Americans, for the
sake of desegregation and legislative change. Although later amended,
Arendt's initial reading of the Little Rock incident is a pithy example
of the blindness to the sacrifices made by African American families.[18]
Without the recognition of sacrifice, shared risk is impossible because
there is a lack of transparency about what has been ventured and lost.
Risks are seen as zero-sum transactions with distrust as the predominant
affect, including distrust of motives, communication styles, and political
loyalties. When sacrifices are overlooked, they become fodder for future
distrust. Such a precedent also increases the likelihood that the same
groups will bear the brunt of future sacrifices. In thinking about the fo-
menting of trust through a truth commission, ensuring that sacrifices are
recognized is one factor for achieving the larger goal of shared risk.

The risks of engaging with anger differ for witness and audience. The
witness risks criticism, dismissal, and reproach for communicating an
emotion that runs counter to the spirit of future cooperation and civil
peace. Even for the witness who gets some pleasure, as Aristotle notes,
from its expression, anger can be exhausting. The listening audience
faces the risk of feeling uncomfortable, ill-prepared, accused of moral
failure (falsely or legitimately) or of having their efforts to engage rejected. Sharing risk in the expression of anger is dependent on the commitment of the listener to do the necessary work of guardianship. The
potentially disruptive nature of anger in the context of victim testimony
is precisely what makes engagement with it an important practice for the

development of trust. By developing a range of responses to anger, citizens expand their repertoire of affective connections with other citizens: a repertoire that can then be the basis for expanded participation in the new demos after the work of the truth commission has ended.

The *awareness* of what is at stake by all parties in the process of trust is part of what connects it to the larger hopes of civic life and restorative justice. When individuals are aware of the way trust is being enacted and nurtured, they should be able to see it as part of a larger political vision. Awareness of the process of trust that occurs through an engagement with anger provides a way to move beyond a narrow calculation of self-interest in matters of politics or criminal retribution. Baier goes so far as to consider the awareness of the expectations of trust as the best test for its presence. She writes, "Trust, I have claimed, is reliance on others' competence and willingness to look after, rather than harm, things one cares about which are entrusted to their care. The moral test of such trust relationships which I have proposed is that they be able to *survive awareness* by each party to the relationship of what the other relies on."[19] The space of testimony is an arena for such a moral test. When anger is expressed, the violation of trust is made audible along with the fragility of the possibility of trust in the future. Yet the benefit of a truth commission is that it focuses on the types of actions and micro-actions that can help encourage trust.

Margaret Walker connects trust to an engagement with resentment after mass violence. Under the broader rubric of "moral repair," she sees the need to move beyond the case of righteous anger to include the more ambivalent cases of resentment, yet she still sees the possibility for the strengthening of civic relationships. She focuses on three conditions necessary for such repair: "People are confident that they share some basic standards for the treatment of each other. People are able to trust each other to abide by those standards or at least to acknowledge fault if they (or others) do not abide by them. And so, finally, people are entitled to be hopeful that unacceptable treatment will not prevail. . . . Hopefulness, we have seen, is not the icing on the cake, but it is the pan in which the cake is baked."[20] While hopefulness plays the solidifying role in her theory, an awareness of shared risk occupies that space within mine. Hope is still an important affect necessary for participation in a truth commission, but the concept of shared risk is more inflected by the actual gains and losses of political life. As for the idea of shared standards, truth commissions are well poised to contribute to these outcomes. One can agree with others that a shared standard has been broken without confidence that others will understand how to make sense of the conflicting emotions that lie in its wake. The process of trust as shared risk emerges from the navigation of these conflicting emotions and formulating a response.

Expressing and listening to anger in victim testimony prefigures the type of political exchange that will follow the transitional period. Politics, like the economic market, is premised on repeated transactions, and the outcome should not be rigged to favor one winner. Instead, the possibility of "winning"—that is, being happy with the outcome and believing in the integrity of the process—should be open to the full range of participants.[21] Citizens should not expect only one group to perpetually bear the uncertainties and losses of the political process, such as the loss of economic opportunity or previous subsidies. During periods of transitional justice, a new pattern for politics emerges, and there is the possibility that both risks and opportunities will be shared in a more equitable way that marks a conscious break with the past. A truth commission should be seen as a conduit for this transformation. When witnesses come to speak about human-rights violations, they are usually not the beneficiaries of the old regime but its victims. However, through the process of testimony they are given the opportunity to be treated with greater dignity in the public sphere than they have before, and, as Arendt has argued, the dignity shown to victims must extend to their being seen as citizens—worthy participants in the political process who will not consistently bear all its losses. Victims must be able to assume the risk of expressing difficult emotion without fear of reprisal or rebuke, but they must also recognize that later they will be called upon to respond to the risks taken by others.

Power and Trust

A theory about the genesis of trust between parties is deeply intertwined with the relative power and status of these parties. Great power imbalance such as that of an infant and mother leads to a relationship of dependency but not to trust in the sense that I build on here. One could argue that the infant must "trust" the mother to look out for her survival, but it is not an accurate term because the infant does not have the ability to decide otherwise, either cognitively or practically. Great disparities in power make it impossible to fully participate in a relationship based on trust, especially when understood as shared risk. In those situations, it is coercion or necessity that prevails. The move from distrust to trust in the period of transitional justice should be concurrent with a move from great disparities in power to lesser ones, although these changes may not have been fully realized. The expression of anger within a truth commission is part of a confrontation with preexisting patterns of power and how they facilitated the violence at issue. However, there is a danger that an engagement with anger will depend on an individual or a group's being forced to perform a type of vulnerability or dependency. Such forced vulnerability cannot be the conduit for trust, either in the narrow context of testimony or in the broader context of political negotiation. Pettit captures the dilemma of providing an open space for the expression of anger without insisting on narrow victimization: "Only by guarding against forced vulnerability can a society facilitate the voluntary assumption of vulnerability—the voluntary assumption of limited vulnerability—that is associated with trust."[22] The way in which the commissioners and the audience engage with testimony is a test of forced vulnerability. An argument for active listening in the context of victim testimony is not dependent on the assumption that victims are morally superior or infallible but is premised on the assumption that communication by equal agents has the potential to encourage trust. At the same time, the freedom from forced vulnerability also carries with it a responsibility to take on the roles of citizen, spectator, and respondent for others. An affective attitude of critical responsiveness and generosity contributes to this type of climate. The challenge of allowing for vulnerability without demanding it is my response to Arendt's fears about the structure of testimony as potentially antithetical to action in public life. Properly conceived, victim testimony should be about voluntary vulnerability and the beginnings of trust.

Russell Hardin, in particular, is critical of those who conflate individual and institutional actors when thinking about trust.[23] The thick descriptions used to show the subtleties of the trust relationship between parents and children or close friends cannot be translated into the context of large-scale institutions. For him individual and institutional processes are fundamentally different, and institutions must rely on sanctions and enforcement for trust, not on assessments of personal character. Some may criticize my model for doing just this. By asking commissioners to engage with anger in a way that is open to its multiple possibilities and affirms the citizenship of the witness, some may argue that I am asking for an essentially small-scale personal response in the context of a mass experience. This is accurate in the sense that I am calling for a high level of attention to individual testimony and attention to responding to, valuing, and interpreting patterns across different testimonies. It is not enough for victims to know that they have been formally recorded or documented at a truth commission. On the other hand, the attention that the commissioners and the audience provide is not the same as that of a doctor or therapist. Bernard Williams has written that in the absence of thick relationships, modern collectivities must find alternative ways to foster trust. Both egoistic (derived from self interest) and nonegoistic (based on a shared ideal) motivations have a place, and Williams emphasizes that there can be no generalizable answer about what the proper balance between the two should be.[24] I agree that the problem of trust cannot be solved at the abstract level; rather, an engagement with anger is a specific way to include members of the political community who have little incentive to trust other citizens.

The Weight of Premature Trust

While a predisposition to trust and attention to the particulars of each testimony provide a context for trust, there is a danger that the trust will exceed the listener's ability to act on what she hears. An anecdote from Thomas Dumm's elegant book *Loneliness* is helpful for understanding this danger of premature trust.[25] Dumm recounts an episode from his childhood where, as the seventh youngest of nine children, he is called on to watch his brother while they are playing outside. He is five years old; his brother is two. Suddenly Thomas notices that his brother has wandered into the street and, joined by a neighborhood dog, has sat down in the path of oncoming traffic.[26] The young Thomas realizes the danger and wants to rescue his brother, but he is paralyzed by the words of his mother, who told him never to go into the street. He cannot determine a course of action that will fulfill his responsibilities to care for his brother but also obey his mother. All he can do is shout at his brother from the sidewalk to come inside. His older brother arrives home from school soon enough and immediately picks up the little boy from the street and brings him inside.

Dumm recounts this story as a way to explore his relationship to his mother, her loneliness, and its impact on him in childhood and after. I see it as a parable about trust: Thomas was entrusted with the care of his younger siblings, a practice that was modeled by his older brothers and sisters and made explicit to him by his mother. Although he understood the gravity of the trust placed in him, he was confronted with a situation in which his capacity to judge fell short of his responsibility. He did not refuse the trust placed in him (nor did he want to), but he could not fulfill it.

In the period after mass violence, a similar dynamic may be present in truth commissions. While some people will be skeptical about an engagement with anger, others may be willing but unaccustomed to it and unsure of how to proceed. The decision to participate in a truth commission, as a witness, commissioner, or listener indicates some willingness to learn how a different relationship between citizens is possible. Yet Dumm's parable raises the question: *Do citizens have the capacity to actualize trust in light of the difficult circumstances of testimonies of mass violence?* There is the danger that the citizen, like Dumm, does not know how to fulfill the responsibility with which she has been entrusted because it is so different from what she has done before and because of the experiential distance between her and the witness. Moreover, all of the proxies used to establish commonality between citizens, such as race and social class, have been delegitimized, making it harder to begin a relationship based on trust. The context of testimony at a truth commission, with its embedded complex emotions, presents a challenge to the audience in terms of responding to the testimonies and acknowledging the sacrifices. In the incident above, both Thomas and his mother display the affective aspects of trust and the object of concern (his brother) in evident ways. The parable reveals that the next challenge is to translate this trust into action that fosters the well-being of all parties. Trust makes such action possible but does not ensure it because of the role of judgment and capacity. Paralysis caused by ignorance or fear may overwhelm the possibility of action.[27]

The near-tragedy from Thomas's childhood might have been avoided if he had heard from his mother how to navigate the right course of action between two expectations (protecting his brother and following the rule about staying away from the street). Engaging with anger at a truth commission can be seen as charting a subtle course between "resigning to" and "resigning from" anger, as discussed in the previous chapter. The expression of anger may feel, to some listeners, like a hostile demand not worthy of a trusting response. The end of a testimony may very well have diminished the affect of generosity that existed in a listener before, but a response is still necessary to fulfill the promise of trust. This is the listener's moment of paralysis between trust and action—analogous to Thomas watching his brother in the street; greater guidance on the different possibilities of response would be an asset. The leadership of the commissioners can help in the process through the questions they ask and their attention to the multiple ways in which anger is significant. Furthermore, the listener should be able to trust that the anger will not preclude other ways of communicating in the future. Responding to anger in the context of a truth commission also serves as a model for future civic engagement when citizens will encounter dissensus or the intensity of the unsocial passions. The testimonies are critical moments in political life that can be interpreted as threatening to collective peace, but nonaction or denial is not the only path. There is another, albeit demanding, response of substantial engagement with anger even when it goes beyond the cognitive-evaluation dimension, but it must be learned and practiced. Attention to the three dimensions of anger and the different responses they engender is one of the most concrete ways that listeners at a truth commission can translate trust into action—with the overall goal of greater trust in the body politic.

Cultivating Trust in Response to the Three Dimensions of Anger

The practice of responding to anger in a way that encourages trust varies along the dimensions I have previously described. The cognitive-evaluative dimension of anger, with information that could be used for reparation or compensation, has a direct relationship to forging the relationship between trust and action. In this context, the commissioners indicate that they take the witness's testimony seriously, not just as voices to be added to a collective but as citizens who provide insights into the sites of fear and mistrust that must be addressed. Anger that is legible through a cognitive-evaluative lens should elicit a type of recognition and uptake from the audience. A commitment to right the injustice through whatever channels are available is part of the negotiation that suggests the sharing of risk in the future. The response to the cognitive-evaluative dimension is one place where the paralysis that was present in Dumm's anecdote could appear because the possibilities for action may be legally foreclosed. But this is precisely where a formal openness to an engagement with anger in a truth commission and a set of responses modeled by the commissioners could fill the gap between desire and ability.

Responding to the confrontational dimension of anger sets up a different type of relationship between witness and audience; specifically, it requires an audience that accepts the contradictory impulses of this type of anger, which is powerful in its representation of someone on the *cusp* of civic engagement. The anger itself may seem to reject civic life as a possibility, but the fact that the witness has chosen to take the stand also suggests a desperate hope for communication. Confrontational anger represents a desire to be heard even when the content may indicate the opposite. Karen Jones's gloss on the phrase "trust yourself" is helpful as a way of thinking about the dynamic of confrontational anger and its response.[28] The phrase is usually invoked as a way of encouraging the speaker to be confident in her ability to complete a task—that is, trust that you have the adequate preparation, skill, and ability to accomplish what you have set out to do. Yet Jones notes that it also has to do with assuaging the fear that one can undermine one's own ability through self-doubt or fear. Continuing this line of thinking, Jones writes, "'Trust yourself' has application precisely because parts of ourselves can sometimes stand in the kind of external relation to other parts that makes their interaction more like the interaction between two persons. We need to trust ourselves when we are worried about the possibility of self-sabotage, about the possibility that some not fully conscious part of ourselves might be operating from motives other than our professed ones."[29] The possibility of self-sabotage or, more moderately, the possibility of contradictory expressions is part of what makes the expression of confrontational anger difficult for the witness and difficult to interpret. Yet instead of trying to unite the disparate perspectives in a testimony or in the variations of response, the initial stages of trust in this context would suggest making room for all of them. Trust can develop with the expression of confrontational anger when both the speaker and the listener are open to the contradictory insights that emerge. The challenge of reflecting on past, present, and future in a constrained amount of time in front of a public audience is complex, and the coherence of the "message" of the testimony is not the most important aspect. If the phrase "trust yourself" were to be applied to witnesses at a truth commission, it would not be in the context of having the confidence to complete a task, but rather in that of trusting in the dynamism of the process of listening and responding to anger. There is always the possibility that the anger veers to the edge of inconsistency and excess, but the speaker and the audience have the power to treat this edge with care, and this is a step in the process of trust.

Examining the kinetic dimension of anger highlights the fact that the affective predisposition of the audience (and its relation to trust) exists prior to any content. Listening with presumptive generosity to the kinetic dimension of anger—that is, to the sheer power and intensity of its energy—is often where the process of testimony begins and one of the first places of risk for the audience. The kinetic dimension of anger forms the crucible where this model of trust takes shape. Anger is powerful in part because of its disruptive or destructive potential, and when the listening audience can be generously open to the force of this emotion and the sense of the testimony's importance to the future of political life, an affective attitude is initiated that provides a foundation for trust, akin to Connolly's critical responsiveness. Responding to the kinetic aspect of anger is the most challenging of the three dimensions, but it can also set a new tone for the inclusion of the passions (including anger) in political life, in a way that is neither disruptive nor diluted.

After the Truth Commission

In contrast to deliberative democratic models that emphasize reciprocity in communication, I am maintaining the prerogative of the witness to narrate her experiences in the way she chooses rather than in the manner of a cross-examination. Thus, despite the emphasis I place on the nature of the responses of the commissioners and the audience, the testimony of a witness at a truth commission is more monologic than dialogic. Still, the questions that the commissioners ask to further engage with the emotions that witnesses express and the affective orientation of the audience is important for the foundation and practice of civic trust. These responses put into motion the type of communication that will be necessary for the sharing of risk in political life and the sense that citizen identities are not fixed as victims, perpetrators, and bystanders. Testimony is an important space for the engagement with anger, but it will have to continue in other spheres in order for there to be greater trust

in the everyday interactions of democratic life. For example, a follow-up
to the testimonial portion of the truth commission could be a series of
public discussions for witnesses. These discussions would invite those
who had testified to make connections between their own testimonies
and others that they had heard. The goal is not to produce more detailed
accounts of specific events or even the experiences of specific individuals, but rather to explain the patterns and relationships between them.
Here witnesses are asked to move from the perspective of "I" to that of
"we," even if that docs not imply a unified voice. The focus in this context would not be on their role as victims but on the possibility that they
are uniquely placed to think about how to foster stronger civic relationships with other citizens given their experiences. In contributing to such
a discussion, they would be developing their skills in listening to the experiences of others while examining their aspirations for political life af-
tcr the truth commission has ended.

A discussion where witnesses make connections between their experiences and those of others while attending to the well-being of the collective is not a return to a type of consensus-based deliberative democracy. The expectation is not that each witness will speak in a universal
register providing public reasons for one's claims; the language may still
be informal and grounded in subjective claims. The goal is also not to
weigh the trade-offs of different policy options but to publicly acknowledge that there are similarities among some of the most difficult emotions expressed by witnesses and that their future political involvement
will be shaped by these emotions but not limited to them. In this new
type of forum, victims are called to act on the trust that others placed in
them when giving testimony while drawing on the trust they placed in
the audience during their own testimony. The sharing of risk that began
with the practice of listening to anger is extended when thinking about
the risk of the collective. An intermediary institution, such as this forum, could bridge the gap between victim and citizen and between testimony and political debate.

In Allen's description of the challenges that followed the civil rights
movement, she unknowingly provides the critical test for truth commissions: *Can they nurture practices and relationships of trust for the future?*
The period of mass violence, by its very essence, is about the abuse of
trust by perpetrators and bystanders. The purpose of the commission is
not just to acknowledge the acts of violence themselves but also the culture of abuse and the sense of betrayal of trust among citizens who ex-

pected the state and the police to care about their security. Against the background of this type of distrust, the challenge of nurturing new forms of trust is significant, but it can be initiated via a range of practices. An affective orientation to trust and the presumption of generosity in interpreting testimonies of anger are places to start, but more lasting trust requires new types of interaction between victim and audience. In such interactions, all parties will find themselves taking on the risks of disclosure, vulnerability, and the need for responsible action. Commissioners can set a precedent for responding to the three dimensions of anger in different ways, acknowledging that some forms of anger are harder to understand than others. The temporally bounded space of a truth commission is, thus, not only a compromised space for reckoning with past crimes and recording the experiences of victims but also an experiment in forging new types of civic interactions within a political institution.

Epilogue

Now that I have described what an engagement with anger would look like and how it might contribute to the fostering of trust, it is worth revisiting the concerns of the most important skeptics. The crux of Arendt's fear, based on her perceptions of witnesses at the Eichmann trial and her writing in *The Human Condition*, is that physical and psychological suffering, while relevant to individual narratives and political history, is not a desirable way to foster equal respect or trust. The argument I have presented here diverges from Arendt because I do not think it is possible to bracket the suffering of the past or the way it will continue to shape political participation in order to focus on more collective experiences of citizenship. The process of testimony in a truth commission, if administered in the right way, carries the possibility of transforming victims into citizens. For this to happen, the commissioners and the audience must engage with the various dimensions of anger and the indirect ways in which anger provides insight into what shared risk means during transitional justice and after. There is still a danger, as Arendt predicted, that engaging with anger in testimony will be frustrating for both the victim and the audience because an accurate communication of the intensity of pain may elude them both. This is not a reason to avoid the practice altogether. Even if the response that is offered in relation to anger is less than ideal, it still has political value because of the way it works through the challenges of distrust. The causes and symptoms of violence and anger are both private and public, and it is understandable that testimony about them will reverberate in both spheres. These spheres are renegotiated at a truth commission as part of the refounding of civil life after mass violence, and the improvisation of testimony and response is part of the process. Arendt's defensive reading of the public/private boundary and disdain for stereotypically feminine modes of emotional excess would prevent her from seeing the radicalism of social change that could emerge from an engagement with anger.

Adam Smith was concerned about anger that was beyond the resentment that could be legitimized by propriety and merit. Anger, in its proper form, is a catalyst for justice, but he worried (1) about the disruption of the social order and (2) about the norms of stoicism and neutrality tethered to the ideal of the impartial spectator. As Smith developed a normative theory that grew from his intuitions about emotions in everyday life, the possibility for a broader understanding of anger became less relevant. In its place was the development of an ethical exemplar who could distance himself from precisely this type of emotional discharge. The theory of engagement presented here follows Smith's method of drawing on lived experiences of anger but shifts the focus from the spectator, who views suffering with the appropriate analytical and physical distance, to the audience member, who listens as fellow citizens express needs and fears for the future of political life. Such listening invites a response that should indicate awareness that the witness has entrusted something to the public through the testimony and that the vulnerability on the part of the witness and the audience is part of what inspires a more trusting relationship going forward. In response to Smith's concerns, the theory here takes the unpredictability, excessiveness, and physicality of testimony as a given. The challenge of finding a response is part of the building of a new repertoire of civic relationships. The response to anger is not derived from another set of commitments for political life—it is a commitment in itself.

The shift to an aural model of judgment from a visual one is the linchpin that holds my theory together. With listening, the audience is brought into a more intimate relationship with the speaker, one that is close enough to suggest responsiveness but is not equivalent to a therapeutic relationship. Unlike in the visual model, greater distance in listening only makes it harder to understand the subtleties of language and does not improve clarity. The act of listening suggests being attentive to what is not expressed directly and what is communicated through tone, mood, and silence. Most importantly, the skills of listening developed through an engagement with anger during a truth commission can be marshaled for the sake of democratic participation in the future. Contra the impartial spectator, individual ethical development is not the focus of this framework, but rather the collective development of citizens in a previously divided society in a way that does not rely on pity or compassion as such.

Since my argument for three ways of interpreting anger is more expansive than previous conceptions, I have been asked whether there is an "illegitimate" anger that falls outside of my framework, such as anger that is strictly personal or outrageously misguided. Possibly—hate speech would not be encompassed by my framework, but highly personal or disproportionate anger would have a limited place. Filtering them out would be more of a danger for this model than allowing them to be expressed, but they are not valuable in isolation or detached from a broader context. These types of anger, potentially falling under the kinetic dimension, are unlikely to be the only sentiment expressed in a testimony and would thus be only one part of the significance of anger. Similarly, the confrontational dimension of anger provides another way to incorporate seemingly illegitimate or apolitical anger into the process because it can be interpreted as a reflection on the limits of politics and the lingering consequences of the violence in everyday life, including private life. Not all anger should be seen as equally valuable for the process of restorative justice, but a truth commission should be one of the most ecumenical political spaces for listening to the range of possibilities. The compilation of the truth commission report, however, should be focused on the patterns of anger and what they reveal about what citizens need and fear in the aftermath of mass violence. Highly particularized or idiosyncratic expressions of anger will be less influential here without being erased from the record altogether.

Although attention to the three dimensions of anger will have beneficial effects for the cultivation of trust and the goals of restorative justice, this does not imply that the expression of anger is without cost. These costs are significant, and to ignore them would be as shortsighted an approach as to deny the value of anger altogether. I agree with Lisa Tessman that anger should be seen as a "burdened virtue," that is, a class of virtues that are "disjoined from their bearer's own flourishing."[1] Even though burdened virtues may sometimes be necessary for social transformation and the realization of political ideals such as equality and dignity, they deserve a much higher level of scrutiny than other virtues. Tessman's contribution represents a key development in the debates on anger in the public sphere; she shows that the axis of analysis does not go from "no value" to "great value" but encompasses a consideration of the burdens, costs, and consequences of expressing anger, including the ability of the witness to experience other goods. While I disagree with her retreat from the political value of anger, her writing is a strong antidote to the tendency to glorify its expression and her writing cautions against using a strident tone.[2]

Another possible cost is the risk of perpetual anger without cessation. The bounded nature of a truth commission works against this possibility, as does the idea that upheaval must be followed by a period of judgment about which of the actions that emerge from an engagement with the testimonies deserves priority. A framework based on listening is not one of perpetual upheaval; it is meant to delimit an exemplary period in political life in which there is self-consciously a greater openness to risk than is found at other times.

Those who supported the Nuremberg and Eichmann trials for their roles in postwar retributive justice could never have imagined such a prominent role for an engagement with anger. Testimonies in truth commissions rely on a different set of procedural assumptions than that of criminal trials and rightly so. The forum of a truth commission should now be amended to make the most of its ability to bridge some of the most difficult divides in politics, including the division between those who have been excluded and the elite; those who seek accountability for the past and those who want to focus on the future; and those who hold onto consensus as the ideal and those who see the value in an agonistic exchange of ideas.[3] An engagement with anger in the context of a truth commission will not necessarily emerge on its own, and the case of the South African Truth and Reconciliation Commission shows that even well-meaning overtures to take anger seriously can become sidelined by other concerns. Articulating and appreciating the three dimensions of anger is a way for the commission and the audience to focus attention on anger even in light of other goals. Victims, commissioners, and audience members will develop a basic vocabulary for appreciating the dynamics of anger and the larger evolution of thinking about the difficult emotions tied to previous violence. The current scholarship on transitional justice has moved away from analyzing the outcomes of "truth" or "reconciliation," instead viewing institutions as capable of only partial processes.[4] An engagement with anger is one of these processes, tied neither to retributive justice nor to a lofty ideal of reconciliation, and it can be an important step in building relationships of trust between strangers and adversaries.

Anger is not an emotion I would wish on anyone, nor is it one that deserves to be romanticized. It is dangerous because it is powerful, but it should not be celebrated as powerful because it is dangerous. Rather, its power comes from the many ways in which it is at the crux of political life and the basis of trust. The expression of anger is a reminder of the need for democratic institutions, just as it shows the limits of consensus within them. In much of political debate, the tendency is to sideline anger for the sake of "constructive" arguments, but the period after mass violence demands a reconsideration of anger as a type of constructive exchange, one that challenges victims and listeners to relate in a way that contributes to the sharing of risk and reward.

Notes

Introduction

1. Testimony of Godfrey Xolile Yona, TRC Upington, October 2, 1996, Case Number CT/00695.

2. Addressing the role of victim testimony in truth commissions is especially important at the current time because of the need to better define how the International Criminal Court can work in a compatible way with truth commissions, especially on issues of jurisdiction and the sharing of evidence. Alison Bisset, *Truth Commissions and Criminal Courts* (Cambridge: Cambridge University Press, 2012).

3. Emotions as cognitive evaluations of the world and indications of worth find extensive elaboration in the work of Martha Nussbaum. See Martha Craven Nussbaum, *Upheavals of Thought: The Intelligence of Emotions* (Cambridge: Cambridge University Press, 2001), and *Hiding from Humanity: Disgust, Shame, and the Law* (Princeton, NJ: Princeton University Press, 2004).

4. See Antonio R. Damasio, *The Feeling of What Happens: Body and Emotion in the Making of Consciousness* (San Diego: Harcourt, 1999); Barbara Koziak, *Retrieving Political Emotion: Thumos, Aristotle, and Gender* (University Park: Pennsylvania State University Press, 2000); George E. Marcus, *The Sentimental Citizen: Emotion in Democratic Politics* (University Park: Pennsylvania State University Press, 2002); Christina Tarnopolsky, "Prudes, Perverts, and Tyrants: Plato and the Contemporary Politics of Shame," *Political Theory* 32, no. 4 (2004); Nussbaum, *Hiding from Humanity*; Sharon Krause, *Civil Passions: Moral Sentiment and Democratic Deliberation* (Princeton, NJ: Princeton University Press, 2008). Brian Massumi, *Parables for the Virtual: Movement, Affect, Sensation* (Durham, NC: Duke University Press, 2002).

5. Ruth Leys has argued that the new turn to affect in the humanities and social sciences has often underplayed the cognitive influence on the emotions and instead ended up reinforcing paradigms about basic emotions that rely heavily

on neurological data. Ruth Leys, "The Turn to Affect: A Critique," *Critical Inquiry* 37, no. 3 (2011).

6. See Fonna Forman-Barzilai, *Adam Smith and the Circles of Sympathy: Cosmpolitanism and Moral Theory* (Cambridge: Cambridge University Press, 2010); Michael L. Frazer, *The Enlightenment of Sympathy: Justice and Moral Sentiments in the Eighteenth Century and Today* (New York: Oxford University Press, 2010).

7. While much useful work has been done on the relationship between reason and emotion, I am aware of the argument that for some the category "emotion" is so vague as to be unhelpful and analytically empty. This critique has been waged from the perspective of attention to particular cultural constructions of what is even considered to be an "emotion" and from that of those interested in rhetoric. I agree that grouping all emotions together as a category of inquiry might be futile; however, attention to the particularities of specific emotions, such as anger, is more valuable. With my assessment of the multiple ways anger is significant, there will be parallels with other emotions, but the goal here is not to provide a universal theory about the significance of emotion *writ large*. See James R. Averill, *Anger and Aggression: An Essay on Emotion* (New York: Springer-Verlag, 1982); Anna Wierzbicka, *Emotions across Language and Cultures: Diversity and Universals* (Cambridge: Cambridge University Press, 1999); David Konstan, "Aristotle on Anger and the Emotions: The Strategies of Status," in *Ancient Anger: Perspectives from Homer to Galen*, ed. Susanna Braund and Glenn W. Most (Cambridge: Cambridge University Press, 2003); Michael S. Kochin, *Five Chapters on Rhetoric: Character, Action, Things, Nothing, and Art* (University Park: Pennsylvania State University Press, 2009).

8. See Marilyn Frye, "A Note on Anger," in *Politics of Reality* (Trumansburg, NY: Crossing Press, 1983); Macalester Bell, "Anger, Virtue, and Oppression," in *Feminist Ethics and Social and Political Philosophy:Theorizing the Non-Ideal*, ed. Lisa Tessman (New York: Springer, 2009); Cynthia Burack, *The Problem of the Passions: Feminism, Psychoanalysis, and Social Theory* (New York: New York University Press, 1994); Jiwei Ci, *The Two Faces of Justice* (Cambridge, MA: Harvard University Press, 2006); Philip Fisher, *Vehement Passions* (Princeton, NJ: Princeton University Press, 2002); Maria Lugones, "Hard-to-Handle Anger," in *Overcoming Racism and Sexism*, ed. Linda A. Bell and David Blumenfeld (Lanham, MD: Rowman & Littlefield, 1996); Max Scheler, *Ressentiment* (New York: Free Press of Glencoe, 1961); Robert A. F. Thurman, *Anger: The Seven Deadly Sins* (Oxford: Oxford University Press, 2005); Kenneth S. Zagacki and Patrick A. Boleyn-Fitzgerald, "Rhetoric and Anger," *Philosophy and Rhetoric* 39, no. 4 (2006).

9. Jeffrie G. Murphy and Jean H. Hampton, *Forgiveness and Mercy* (Cambridge: Cambridge University Press, 1988); Margaret Urban Walker, *Moral Repair* (Cambridge: Cambridge University Press, 2006).

10. In the psychological literature, the distinction between the anger of hope versus the anger of despair functions in a similar way. See John Bowlby, *Attachment and Loss, Vol. 2: Separation* (New York: Basic Books, 1973); Erin Halperin et al., "Anger, Hatred, and the Quest for Peace: Anger Can Be Constructive in the Absence of Hatred," *Journal of Conflict Resolution* 55, no. 2 (2011).

11. For Athenian understandings of concepts similar to restorative justice, see Danielle S. Allen, "Democratic Dis-ease: Of Anger and the Troubling Nature of Punishment," in *The Passions of the Law*, ed. Susan Bandes (New York: New York University Press, 1999).

12. Although my interest in victim testimony is connected to the scholarship on trauma by Cathy Caruth, Shoshana Felman, and others, there are important divergences. I agree with the work of Stevan Weine, whose writings herald what I see as a new turn in trauma studies. He maintains that earlier approaches to trauma, such as those seen in the work of Dori Laub, highlighted clinical approaches to the experience of trauma and were primarily focused on its unconscious and self-regarding meanings. Instead, Weine advocates an approach to testimony that is less oriented toward clinical interpretations of trauma and more concerned with the *historical* and *contextual* specificity of testimonies. I, also, am primarily concerned with the specific political meaning of testimonies and see the value in connecting experiences of trauma to present perspectives on everyday life—the conscious reflections on history and politics that can emerge from testimony which are interesting and necessary in ways we are just beginning to understand. Dori Laub, "Bearing Witness, or the Vicissitudes of Listening," in *Testimony*, ed. Shoshana Felman and Dori Laub (New York: Routledge, 1992); Cathy Caruth, ed. *Trauma: Explorations in Memory* (Baltimore: Johns Hopkins University Press, 1995); Shoshana Felman, *The Juridical Unconscious: Trials and Traumas in the Twentieth Century* (Cambridge, MA: Harvard University Press, 2002); Stevan M. Weine, *Testimony after Catastrophe: Narrating the Traumas of Political Violence* (Evanston, IL: Northwestern University Press, 2006).

13. Barbara Herman uses the case of the TRC to show how moral improvisation during exception periods can lead to new political obligations. Mandela demonstrated this type of moral improvisation with his discourse of forgiveness and turn away from retributive justice. Anger may be a consistent remnant of these kinds of improvisatory shifts. Barbara Herman, "Contingency in Obligation," in *Moral Universalism and Pluralism NOMOS XLIX*, ed. Henry Richardson and Melissa S. Williams (New York: New York University Press, 2009).

14. Aristotle, *On Rhetoric*, trans. George A. Kennedy (New York: Oxford University Press, 2007), 2.1.

15. For a humorous take on anger's role, see Elizabeth V. Spelman, "Anger: The Diary," in *Wicked Pleasures: Meditations on the Seven 'Deadly' Sins*, ed. Robert C. Solomon (Lanham, MD: Rowman & Littlefield, 1999).

16. The excellent history of anger in the United States by Carol and Peter Stearns evinces how history has shaped emotionology, the term they use to chronicle the way "we feel about feelings." They argue that the preoccupation with managing and repressing anger in the twentieth century, particularly at work in the context of child-rearing, is disproportionate to the frequency of its expression or disruptive consequences. The substantial attention to repression within a society at a given time thus changes one's experience of anger and corresponding consequences for one's social status and relationships. This finding, and its correlates in other historical and geographical examples, might suggest that a universal theory of anger can only be rudimentary, yet although the particulars of how institutional, cultural, and medical norms have shifted to envision anger in various ways, at base there exists an ongoing confusion around its appropriate role. The level of anxiety accompanying this confusion waxes and wanes, but its historical analysis confirms the orientation of this book: anger perpetually eludes a stable interpretation, especially in political life. Carol Zisowitz Stearns and Peter N. Stearns, *Anger* (Chicago: University of Chicago Press, 1986).

17. Konstan, "Aristotle on Anger and the Emotions."

18. In contrast to Aristotle, my definition of anger is not as closely tied to retaliation, nor is it as reliant on a cognitive justification.

19. For a treatment of Butler and Smith together, see Alice McLachlan, "Resentment and Moral Judgment in Smith and Butler," in *The Philosophy of Adam Smith: Essays Commemorating the 250th Anniversary of the Theory of Moral Sentiments*, ed. Vivienne Brown and Samuel Fleishacker (New York: Routledge, 2010).

20. I acknowledge that I move between the legal and political models for understanding anger; while they overlap, they are not identical. The impetus for this comes from my desire to see a shift in emphasis from a retributive model of justice handled by the courts (predominantly legal) to a restorative justice one (both legal and political) during periods of transitional justice.

21. This is the ideal for retributive justice, but courts of law systematically fall short of the ideal, especially along lines of race, class, and gender.

22. Thomas Hobbes, *Leviathan*, ed. Herbert W. Schneider (New York: Macmillan, 1958), 244.

23. John Rawls, *A Theory of Justice* (Cambridge: Belknap Press, 1999).

24. It is interesting to note that Robert Dahl wanted a way to account for the intensity of preferences in democratic decision making. Robert A. Dahl, *A Preface to Democratic Theory* (Chicago: University of Chicago Press, 1956).

25. This is not to say that Habermas denies that anger can be a form of moral response. It can, but it is not salient once the emphasis has shifted to valid and binding norms. Jürgen Habermas, *The Theory of Communicative Action* (Boston: Beacon Press, 1985).

26. See Thomas McCarthy, "Practical Discourse: On the Relation of Moral-

ity to Politics," in *Habermas and the Public Sphere*, ed. Craig Calhoun (Cambridge, MA: M.I.T. Press, 1992).

27. Fisher, *Vehement Passions*, 187.

28. Reflecting on the social contract tradition may be useful here. Anger expressed during the process of marking the contractual boundaries of the "people" has often been ignored. Truth commissions are unusual in that they provide a forum for reflection on the demos during this period of implementing a new contract.

29. Karl Marx and Friedrich Engels, "Capital," in *The Marx-Engels Reader*, ed. Robert C. Tucker (New York: W. W. Norton, 1978). Some might argue that while justice in the Marxist tradition cannot escape from its ideological formulation, freedom can function in a similar way in relation to anger.

30. Robert C. Solomon, *A Passion for Justice: Emotions and the Origins of the Social Contract* (Reading, MA: Addison-Wesley, 1990), 240.

31. Beltrán uses the term "festive anger" to refer to a desirable form of agonistic action in reference to immigrant communities. Cristina Beltrán, *The Trouble with Unity* (Oxford: Oxford University Press, 2010).

32. The gray zone was coined by Primo Levi to describe a space where victims are coerced to become perpetrators in order to save their own lives. The ethicality of these victims' actions presents a challenge to accounts of righteous anger and to thinking about future citizen relations. The engagement with anger I am suggesting would allow greater space for reflection on what Card calls the "the burdens of guilt and the obligations of perpetrators" alongside "the moral powers of a victim" within gray zones. Claudia Card, *The Atrocity Paradigm: A Theory of Evil* (Oxford: Oxford University Press, 2002), 219.

33. James Ptacek, "Resisting Co-optation: Three Feminist Challenges to Antiviolence Work," in *Restorative Justice and Violence against Women*, ed. James Ptacek (Oxford: Oxford University Press, 2010).

34. See James Dignan, *Understanding Victims and Restorative Justice* (Berkshire: Open University Press, 2005).

35. In his argument for greater inclusion of anger at truth commissions, Muldoon shows how the premise of restorative justice "frequently elides the dimension of struggle from the process of recognition, making it appear much less precarious and less paradoxical than it actually is." Paul Muldoon, "The Moral Legitimacy of Anger," *European Journal of Social Theory* 11, no. 3 (2008): 302.

36. For a broader view of testimony, see Nora Strejilevich, "Testimony: Beyond the Language of Truth," *Human Rights Quarterly* 28, no. 3 (2006).

37. See Richard A. Wilson, *The Politics of Truth and Reconciliation in South Africa: Legitimizing the Post-Apartheid State* (Cambridge: Cambridge University Press, 2001); Fiona C. Ross, *Bearing Witness: Women and the Truth and Reconciliation Commission in South Africa* (London: Pluto Press, 2003); Catherine M. Cole, *Performing South Africa's Truth Commission: Stages of Transition*

(Bloomington: Indiana University Press, 2010). See also Nir Esikovitz, *Sympathizing with the Enemy: Reconciliation, Transitional Justice, Negotiation* (Dordrecht: Republic of Letters, 2009).

38. Thomas Brudholm, *Resentment's Virtue: Jean Amery and the Refusal to Forgive* (Philadelphia: Temple University Press, 2008), 84.

39. See Lisa Tessman, *Burdened Virtues: Virtue Ethics for Liberatory Struggles* (New York: Oxford University Press, 2005).

40. Brudholm, *Resentment's Virtue*, 144.

41. See Danielle S. Allen, *The World of Prometheus: The Politics of Punishing in Democratic Athens* (Princeton, NJ: Princeton University Press, 2000); Seneca, "On Anger," in *Moral and Political Essays*, ed. John M. Cooper and J. F. Procope (Cambridge: Cambridge University Press, 1995).

42. See Allen, "Democratic Dis-ease," 194.

43. Anger, for her, is the knot in liberal theories of justice. Rawls does not want to emphasize the retributive value of punishment, because of its sanctioning of violence, and Allen suggests that it is a discomfort with the proximity of retributive punishment to vengeful anger that is to blame. In this way, it is not just the ability of anger to clarify necessary tensions within a community; a refusal to engage with the emotion of anger during the process of justice can perpetually create uneasiness within theories of justice.

44. Allen's recapitulation of punishment in Athens explores the idea that for anger to play the central role that it did, many types of constraints were formalized so as to prevent it from destroying social institutions. These included making anger the exclusive province of propertied men and emphasizing its inappropriateness for slaves and women. (In contrast to the polis, the household could not command the same attention to honor or breaches of honor.) One of the most frequent ways in which anger was mitigated was through the prohibition against sycophancy—a term that literally means "revealing of figs" and makes obvious the relation between anger (*orge*) and sexuality in Greek thought. Used in relation to the courtroom, sycophancy refers to an opportunistic display of anger for personal benefit without attention to the norms that govern the display of public anger. Allen suggests that these norms include precedents, statutes of limitations for anger, understandings of anger in tragedy and literature, as well as expectations for gradations and consistency. Allen, *The World of Prometheus*, 55, 160, 75.

45. Ibid., 168.

46. Seneca, "On Anger," 1.12.6.

47. Ibid., 1.13.5.

48. Hobbes defined anger as "sudden courage," and it seems that Seneca's response would understand it as the cheapest type of courage. Those who have courage will not need the "sudden" rush of anger.

49. He writes: "Anger is useless, even in battle or in war. With its wish to

bring others into danger, it lowers its own guard. The surest courage is to look around long and hard, to govern oneself, to move slowly and deliberately forward" (29, 1.11.8).

50. See Judith Butler, *Precarious Life: The Powers of Mourning and Violence* (London: Verso, 2004); Bonnie Honig, "Antigone's Laments, Creon's Grief: Mourning, Membership, and the Politics of Exception," *Political Theory* 37, no. 1 (2009); Nicole Loraux, *Mothers in Mourning* (Ithaca, NY: Cornell University Press, 1998).

51. Seneca, "On Anger," 1.12.4.

52. I see Martha Minow's formulation of the problem as representative of the perspective of many legal and political theorists. She writes, "Does the TRC chart an exemplary path between vengeance and forgiveness? Or does this truth commission illustrate an inevitable residue of feeling, moral outrage, and justice's demands—that exceeds the reach of legal institutions? . . . If the goal of healing individuals and society after the trauma of mass atrocity is elevated, truth commissions could well be a better option than prosecutions, although limitations in the therapeutic value of commissions for individuals and limitations in our knowledge of social healing makes this a line of future inquiry rather than a current conclusion." Martha Minow, *Between Vengeance and Forgiveness: Facing History after Genocide and Mass Violence* (Boston: Beacon Press, 1998), 57.

53. See Diane Orentlicher, "Settling Accounts: The Duty to Prosecute Human Rights Violations of a Prior Regime," *Yale Law Journal* 2537 (1991).

54. I find affinities with the work of Weinstein and Halpern, who draw attention to the ongoing fear and suspicion that exists between neighbors long after a conflict has ended. They suggest that a rehumanization process that develops over time and includes the communication of the "distasteful" emotions is one hope for reversing the trend. Jodi Halpern and Harvey M. Weinstein, "Rehumanizing the Other: Empathy and Reconciliation," *Human Rights Quarterly* 26, no. 3 (2004).

55. See, for example, the case Bruce Ackerman makes for emotional restraint in his discussion of the requirements for public deliberation. Bruce Ackerman, "Why Dialogue?" *Journal of Philosophy* 86, no. 1 (1989).

56. For a discussion of how psychoanalytic processes of abreaction and repetition could be applied to the TRC, see Mary Tjiattas, "Psychoanalysis, Public Reason, and Reconstruction in The 'New' South Africa," *American Imago* 55, no. 1 (1998).

57. See Charles Segal, "Spectator and Listener," in *The Greeks*, ed. Jean-Pierre Vernant (Chicago: University of Chicago Press, 1995). I acknowledge there is debate about this characterization; for example, the fact that actors wear masks when performing a tragedy suggests that it is the power of words and listening that is equally important to the communication of truth and knowledge.

58. Ibid., 214.

59. In nineteenth- and twentieth-century political philosophy, the metaphor of vision has been particularly important in considering how to respond to the pain of others. For a discussion on how technology in early American history worked to foster a distrust of listening, see Leigh Eric Schmidt, *Hearing Things: Religion, Illusion, and the American Enlightenment* (Cambridge, MA: Harvard University Press, 2000).

60. Jean-Luc Nancy, *Listening* (New York: Fordham University Press, 2007), 6. See also Susan Bickford, *The Dissonance of Democracy: Listening, Conflict, Citizenship* (Ithaca, NY: Cornell University Press, 1996).

61. Charles Hirschkind has written on how cassette sermons shape the practice of listening and cultivate particular affective responses necessary for Islamic devotional practice. He considers the function of emotion in this context to be not solely instrumental but part of the religious teaching itself. Learning to listen is a critical part of this education. See Charles Hirschkind, *The Ethical Soundscape: Cassette Sermons and Islamic Counterpublics* (New York: Columbia University Press, 2006).

62. See Chantal Mouffe, *The Democratic Paradox* (London: Verso, 2000); Bonnie Honig, *Political Theory and the Displacement of Politics* (Ithaca, NY: Cornell University Press, 1993); William E. Connolly, *Identity/Difference: Democratic Negotiations of Political Paradox* (Ithaca, NY: Cornell University Press, 1991).

63. William Connolly, *Pluralism* (Durham, NC: Duke University Press, 2005), 127.

64. James Tully, "The Agonic Freedom of Citizens," *Economy and Society* 28, no. 2 (1999): 169.

65. Friedrich Wilhelm Nietzsche, *On the Genealogy of Morals*, trans. Walter Kaufmann (New York: Vintage, 1967).

66. While I think truth commissions will always be vulnerable to this critique, institutional design can work against this trend by encouraging and connecting testimonies of the past to the work of restorative justice in the present. The designation of "victim" in my account, contra Nietzsche, is markedly temporary.

67. See Hannah Arendt, *The Human Condition* (Chicago: University of Chicago Press, 1958).

68. See Wendy Brown, "Wounded Attachments," *Political Theory* 21, no. 3 (1993); Alyson Cole, *Cult of True Victimhood: From the War on Welfare to the War on Terror* (Palo Alto, CA: Stanford University Press, 2006).

69. See Diana Tietjen Meyers, "Narrative Structures, Narratives of Abuse, and Human Rights," in *Feminist Ethics and Social and Political Philosophy: Theorizing the Non-Ideal*, ed. Lisa Tessman (New York: Springer, 2009).

70. Butler, *Precarious Life*; Honig, "Antigone's Laments, Creon's Grief."

71. See Hannah Arendt, *Eichmann in Jerusalem: A Report on the Banality of*

Evil (New York: Penguin, 1994); Judith N. Shklar, *Legalism: Law, Morals, and Political Trials* (Cambridge, MA: Harvard University Press, 1986).

72. See Priscilla B. Hayner, *Unspeakable Truths: Facing the Challenge of Truth Commissions* (New York: Routledge, 2001).

73. Arendt, *The Human Condition.*

74. Adam Smith, *The Theory of Moral Sentiments* (Oxford: Clarendon, 1976).

75. Emilios Christodoulidis identified early on the unhelpful mitigation of risk by the legal language and goals of TRC. Emilios Christodoulidis, "'Truth and Reconciliation' as Risks," *Social and Legal Studies* 9, no. 2 (2000).

76. My focus is on anger during a period of transitional justice, when the causes of anger include extreme examples of violence and exclusion, but the argument about the relationship between anger and the cultivation of trust can be extended to other periods. In fact, a truth commission can serve as a crucible for forging the skills of listening and the foundations of trust that will change the parameters of acceptable communication in the future.

77. This is related to what Lugones calls "second-order" anger. See Lugones, "Hard-to-Handle Anger."

78. See Thurman, *Anger: The Seven Deadly Sins.*

79. See Adriana Cavarero, *For More Than One Voice: Toward a Philosophy of Vocal Expression* (Stanford, CA: Stanford University Press, 2005).

Chapter One

1. Antjie Krog, *Country of My Skull: Guilt, Sorrow, and the Limits of Forgiveness in the New South Africa* (New York: Times Books, 1998), 32.

2. Ibid.

3. Priscilla B. Hayner, *Unspeakable Truths: Facing the Challenge of Truth Commissions* (New York: Routledge, 2001), 14.

4. "The idea for a truth commission was proposed as early as 1992, but it was not until after Nelson Mandela was elected president in April 1994 that serious discussions began about what form a national truth commission would take. . . . The act designed the commission to work in three interconnected committees: The Human Rights Violations Committee was responsible for collective statements from victims and witnesses and recording the extent of gross human rights violations; the Amnesty Committee processed and decided individual applications for amnesty; and the Reparation and Rehabilitation Committee was tasked with designing and putting forward recommendations for a reparations program." Ibid., 41–42. For a political analysis of the process that led to the truth commission, see Anne Leebaw Bronwyn, "Legitimation or Judgment? South Africa's Restorative Approach to Transitional Justice," *Polity* 34, no. 1 (2003).

5. Arendt uses the term "cheap sentimentality" to refer to what she sees as misplaced expressions of guilt among German youth. Hannah Arendt, *Eichmann in Jerusalem: A Report on the Banality of Evil* (New York: Penguin, 1994), 251.

6. Adam Smith, *The Theory of Moral Sentiments* (Oxford: Clarendon, 1976), 35.

7. Gary Bass argues against the dominant view of the Nuremberg trials as the first, or most unique, tribunal for war crimes. He writes, "War crimes trials are a fairly regular part of international politics, with Nuremberg as only the most successful example. International war crimes tribunals are a recurring modern phenomenon, with discernible patterns. Today's debates about war criminals in Rwanda, Bosnia, and Kosovo are partial echoes of political disputes from 1815, 1918, and 1944." Gary Jonathan Bass, *Stay the Hand of Vengeance: The Politics of War Crimes Tribunals* (Princeton, NJ: Princeton University Press, 2000), 5.

8. See Robert H. Jackson, *The Nürnberg Case* (New York: Knopf, 1947).

9. Leonard suggests that the "victors' justice" label is, in some respects, accurate because war crimes committed by the Allies could not be punished. He writes, "It should be noted that this court was a military court and therefore, the Allies established it to try those individuals accused of criminal activity only if they were part of the losing side. This was not a court to try all crimes committed during the Second World War; it was a court to try crimes committed by the Germans, as was the IMTFE [International Military Tribunal for the Far East] a court to try crimes committed by the Japanese." Eric K. Leonard, *The Onset of Global Governance: International Relations Theory and the International Criminal Court* (Hampshire: Ashgate, 2005), 24 n. 24.

10. Bass, *Stay the Hand of Vengeance*, 24.

11. On November 21, 1945, Jackson said, "That four great nations, flushed with victory and stung with injury, stay the hands of vengeance and voluntarily submit their captive enemies to the judgment of the law, is one of the most significant tributes that Power has ever paid to Reason. . . . The German people should know by now that the people of the United States hold them in no fear, and in no hate. It is true that the Germans have taught us the horrors of modern warfare, but the ruin that lies from the Rhine to the Danube shows that we, like our Allies, have not been dull pupils." International Military Tribunal, *The Trial of German Major War Criminals: Opening Speeches of the Chief Prosecutors* (London: Under the Authority of H.M. Attorney-General by His Majesty's Stationery Office, 1946), 3, 6.

12. Nuremberg Trial Proceedings Vol. 1, Indictment: Count One, Count Two, Count Three, Count Four. *The Avalon Project at Yale Law School*. http://avalon .law.yale.edu/imt/count.asp (Accessed July 26, 2011).

13. Eric Stover and Rachel Shigekane, "Exhumation of Mass Graves: Balancing Legal and Humanitarian Needs," in *My Neighbor, My Enemy: Justice and*

Community in the Aftermath of Mass Atrocity (Cambridge: Cambridge University Press, 2004), 93.

14. Jackson, *The Nürnberg Case*, 186.

15. Howard Ball, *Prosecuting War Crimes and Genocide* (Lawrence: University Press of Kansas, 1999), chap. 2.

16. Jackson, *The Nürnberg Case*, 186.

17. Lawrence Douglas, *The Memory of Judgment: Making Law and History in the Trials of the Holocaust* (New Haven, CT: Yale University Press, 2001), 17.

18. Ibid.

19. International Military Tribunal, *The Trial of German Major War Criminals*, 3.

20. Bass, *Stay the Hand of Vengeance*; Douglas, *The Memory of Judgment*; Martha Minow, *Between Vengeance and Forgiveness: Facing History after Genocide and Mass Violence* (Boston: Beacon, 1998).

21. Judith N. Shklar, *Legalism: Law, Morals, and Political Trials* (Cambridge, MA: Harvard University Press, 1986), 1.

22. Ibid., 10.

23. Ibid., 3.

24. Ibid., 134.

25. Bass draws on Shklar's understanding of legalism to develop his own interpretation of its significance in the context of punishing war crimes. He states that while Shklar's legalism is about generalized "rule following," he uses the term to refer to "rule following when it comes to war criminals" and the due process protections that should be accorded to this class of defendant. Bass's concern is with comparing how liberal and nonliberal states choose to deal with questions of war crimes, and he suggests that a commitment to legalism in the context of domestic political norms is the primary distinction between the two categories of regimes. He continues, "Liberal states are legalist: they put war criminals on trial in rough accordance with their domestic norms." Bass, *Stay the Hand of Vengeance*, 20.

26. Shklar, *Legalism*, 10.

27. Ibid., 169.

28. Ibid., 177.

29. See Bass's discussion of the Soviet orientation toward using war crimes trials to punish broader political offenses. Bass, *Stay the Hand of Vengeance*, 198.

30. I make the distinction between "show trials" where the outcome of the trial is predetermined and trials that may have pedagogic ends (such as educating the public) but are still providing appropriate protections for the defendant so that the outcome of the trial is uncertain. In contrast, Osiel suggests that all trials are, in fact, variations of show trials: "The orchestration of criminal trials for pedagogic purposes—such as the transformation of a society's collective

memory—is not inherently misguided or morally indefensible. The defensibility of the practice depends on the defensibility of the lessons being taught—that is, on the liberal nature of the stories being told." Mark Osiel, *Mass Atrocity, Collective Memory and the Law* (New Brunswick, NJ: Transaction Publishers, 1997), 65.

31. See, for example, Sharon Krause, "Desiring Justice: Motivation and Justification in Rawls and Habermas," *Contemporary Political Theory* 4, no. 4 (2005).

32. "The way to decide when an injustice is so evident as to require citizens and officials to interfere cannot, however, be found in the difference between publicly recognized injustices and merely subjective reactions. That distinction is, in fact, no more secure, and no less political, than that between nature and culture or between the objective and the subjective view. It is a question of who has the power to define the meaning of actions." Judith Shklar, *The Faces of Injustice* (New Haven, CT: Yale University Press, 1990), 7.

33. Ibid., 14.

34. Seyla Benhabib, *The Reluctant Modernism of Hannah Arendt* (Lanham, Md.: Rowman & Littlefield, 2003), 68.

35. Arendt, *Eichmann in Jerusalem*, 44.

36. ABC News Productions for PBS, "The Trial of Adolf Eichmann: A Companion to the Documentary" (1997).

37. Arendt, *Eichmann in Jerusalem*, 121.

38. For an excellent discussion of the significance of the trial for Israeli democracy and the ways in which political trials can assist in reconciliation, see Leora Bilsky, *Transformative Justice: Israeli Identity on Trial* (Ann Arbor: University of Michigan Press, 2004).

39. Arendt, *Eichmann in Jerusalem*, 260.

40. The univocal narrative of which Arendt is critical was facilitated by the state of Israel's acting as the sole prosecutor in the trial. In the Nuremberg trials, while the American presence was dominant, decisions about strategy had to be made with the consensus of justices from three other Allied nations.

41. Arendt, *Eichmann in Jerusalem*, 125.

42. With her criticism of Jewish cooperation with the Nazis, Arendt stumbled upon a highly controversial figure, Rudolf Kastner, the most prominent Jewish negotiator with the Nazis, whose contacts included Eichmann. After the war, Kastner was given a high position in the Israeli government, but when it was revealed that he had been a collaborator, Kastner said he was a victim of slander and pressed charges against Malchiel Gruenwald, the individual allegedly responsible for disseminating the information. He lost the case and resigned his government position. He was murdered in 1957, allegedly in retribution for his cooperation with the Nazis. In a 1963 letter to Karl Jaspers, Arendt wrote that it was rumored that the Israeli secret police were implicated in the murder. Han-

nah Arendt and Karl Jaspers, *Hannah Arendt – Karl Jaspers: Correspondence, 1926–1969* (New York: Harcourt Brace Jovanovich, 1992), 510.

43. On this controversy, see Elizabeth Young-Breuhl, *Hannah Arendt: For Love of the World* (New Haven, CT: Yale University Press, 1982), 339–47; Bilsky, *Transformative Justice*.

44. Arendt, *Eichmann in Jerusalem*, 132.

45. Ibid.; Young-Breuhl, *Hannah Arendt*, 361.

46. Arendt, *Eichmann in Jerusalem*, 9.

47. Ibid., 5.

48. Ibid., 8.

49. The distinction between public and private has been the subject of extensive scholarly debate. For an introduction, see Michael Warner, *Publics and Counterpublics* (New York: Zone Books, 2002); Jean Bethke Elshtain, *Public Man, Private Women: Women in Social and Political Thought* (Princeton, NJ: Princeton University Press, 1981); Nancy Fraser, "Rethinking the Public Sphere: A Contribution to the Critique of Actually Existing Democracy," in *Habermas and the Public Sphere*, ed. Craig Calhoun (Cambridge, MA: MIT Press, 1992); Susan Moller Okin, *Justice, Gender and the Family* (New York: Basic Books, 1989).

50. Arendt, *Eichmann in Jerusalem*, 121.

51. Ibid.

52. Douglas, *The Memory of Judgment*, 127.

53. Jürgen Habermas and Peter Dews, *Autonomy and Solidarity: Interviews* (London: Verso, 1986).

54. Douglas, *The Memory of Judgment*, 128.

55. See ibid., 138, for exchange with judges.

56. Oxford English Dictionary, online, www.oed.com (Accessed through Wesleyan University) July 26, 2011.

57. This is a topic that I address more fully in chap. 4 when looking at sympathy in the work of Adam Smith.

58. Douglas, *The Memory of Judgment*, 127.

59. I differ most starkly from Lawrence Douglas on the question of trials versus truth commissions, although I find many affinities with his orientation. He advocates for the "didactic trial": a criminal trial that can have broad pedagogic functions and serve ends other than criminal accountability. He envisions the courtroom as the location of contesting versions of history and collective memory and wants courts such as the ICTY (International Criminal Trial for the Former Yugoslavia) to embrace this function. To that end, he includes greater room for victim testimony in these "didactic trials," but I argue that a truth commission would be better able to connect the tone and content of victim testimony to the political questions that must be addressed as part of transitional justice.

Lawrence Douglas, "The Didactic Trial: Filtering History and Memory in the Courtroom," *European Review* 14, no. 4 (2006).

60. Benhabib, *The Reluctant Modernism of Hannah Arendt*, 65.

61. Ibid.

62. Arendt writes, "To a Jew this role of the Jewish leaders in the destruction of their own people is undoubtedly the darkest chapter of the whole dark story. It had been known about before, but it has now been exposed for the first time in all its pathetic and sordid detail." Arendt, *Eichmann in Jerusalem*, 117.

63. Related questions will be addressed in chap. 3.

64. Shoshana Felman, *The Juridical Unconscious: Trials and Traumas in the Twentieth Century* (Cambridge, MA: Harvard University Press, 2002).

65. Ibid., 124.

66. While Felman's analysis of trauma in the context of the Eichmann trial is insightful as a way to understand the tension between criminal trials and the memory of violence, it also reflects the limits of thinking about testimony from a psychoanalytically informed perspective. Scholarly interest in narratives about trauma and violence flourished in the 1990s as scholars such as Felman, Dori Laub, and Cathy Caruth ushered in the subfield of "trauma studies." Their work effectively introduced a new language with which to talk about the oral histories that emerged from war and other traumatic experiences, a language that ironically shows the limitations of language itself to adequately represent such experiences. Works such as Felman's *The Juridical Unconscious* reveal how the structure of testimonies regarding trauma are distinct from other types of recollections in their nonlinear patterns and mimetic repetition of the traumatic event. Many scholars in trauma studies have provided strong psychoanalytic interpretations of testimonies of trauma and focused on the unconscious workings of the mind suggesting a view of testimonies as closed systems that contain highly particular logics. Dori Laub, "Bearing Witness, or the Vicissitudes of Listening," in *Testimony*, ed. Shoshana Felman and Dori Laub (New York: Routledge, 1992); Shoshana Felman and Dori Laub, *Testimony: Crises of Witnessing in Literature, Psychoanalysis, and History* (New York: Routledge, 1992); Cathy Caruth, ed., *Trauma: Explorations in Memory* (Baltimore: Johns Hopkins University Press, 1995).

67. Felman, *The Juridical Unconscious*, 124.

68. In *Testimony after Catastrophe*, Stevan Weine suggests that the mimetic approach, often promoted by psychoanalysts, has been greatly hampered by its method and focus. He argues that a psychoanalytic approach to trauma that focuses on the manifestations of the unconscious precludes interpreting testimonies in specific historical and political contexts. Neither questions how understandings of the traumatic event may be shaped by current political circumstances or how the experience of trauma may have changed perceptions of the state, power, and politics—questions that are important in the aftermath of war.

Part of the reason for the focus on highly individual interpretations, including psychoanalytic ones, was that many of the people first interested in testimonies relating to trauma were mental-health professionals. Their primary concern was to address the victim as a patient and to use knowledge about the treatment of trauma, post-traumatic stress disorder, and other mental illnesses to respond to the testimonies. Stevan M. Weine, *Testimony after Catastrophe: Narrating the Traumas of Political Violence* (Evanston, IL: Northwestern University Press, 2006), 97.

69. Hayner, *Unspeakable Truths*, 14.

70. Truth commissions may use facts that they have gathered to criminally prosecute individuals at a later time, as was the case with Argentina's truth commission and the evidence in its final report on the government's crimes, *Nunca Más*. Given the different evidentiary and procedural rules in trials versus truth commissions, this practice presents complex legal questions.

71. Arendt and Jaspers, *Hannah Arendt – Karl Jaspers*, 413.

72. Although the reasons for victim impact statements (VIS in the American criminal justice system) may appear to parallel the arguments for the significance of victim testimony after war, this is a misleading comparison. I am not in favor of victim impact statements in the context of criminal trials because of the tendency for the sentencing entity—either the judge or the jury—to be more affected by the emotion-laden testimony of the victim than by the material evidence of the case. Given the reality of the biases in jury selection, it is more likely for jury members to put themselves in the position of a victim than that of a defendant and this introduces an unnecessary element of emotional affinity. The use of victim impact statements can also make it seem as if some victims are more worthy of empathy than others. See, for example, Peter Brooks, *Troubling Confessions: Speaking Guilt in Law and Literature* (Chicago: University of Chicago Press, 2000).

73. Hayner, *Unspeakable Truths*, chaps. 13 and 14.

74. Testimony is not the only significant aspect of truth commissions; material reparations and amnesty may also play a part in such commissions and are important to considerations of restorative justice. The relationship between anger and trust will be addressed in chap. 5.

75. Mark Sanders, *Ambiguities of Witnessing: Law and Literature in the Time of a Truth Commission* (Stanford, CA: Stanford University Press, 2007), 59.

76. Hayner, *Unspeakable Truths*.

77. The inherent drama of the TRC and its significance in South African history has been the subject of scholarly debate across disciplines. Among the works that have influenced my discussion in this section are the following: Tristan Anne Borer, ed., *Telling the Truths: Truth Telling and Peace Building in Post-Conflict Societies* (Notre Dame, IN: University of Notre Dame, 2006); Karin Chubb and Lutz van Dijk, *Between Anger and Hope: South Africa's Youth and*

the Truth and Reconciliation Commission (Johannesburg: Witwatersrand University Press, 2001); Alfred and Marietjie Allan, "The South African Truth and Reconciliation Commission as a Therapeutic Tool," *Behavioral Sciences and the Law* 18 (2000); Annie E. Coombes, *History after Apartheid: Visual Culture and Public Memory in a Democratic South Africa* (Durham, NC: Duke University Press, 2003); Jillian Edelstein, *Truth and Lies: Stories from the Truth and Reconciliation Commission in South Africa* (New York: New Press, 2001); James L. Gibson, *Overcoming Apartheid: Can Truth Reconcile a Divided Nation?* (New York: Russell Sage Foundation, 2004); Pumla Gobodo-Madikizela, *A Human Being Died That Night: A South African Story of Forgiveness* (Boston: Houghton Mifflin, 2003); Paul Gready, *The Era of Transitional Justice: The Aftermath of the Truth and Reconciliation Commission in South Africa and Beyong* (Oxon: Routledge, 2011).

78. Desmond Tutu, interviewed by Max Du Preez, *Truth Commission Special Report*, South African Broadcasting Corporation. Episode 31. From Yale University Law School. http://www.law.yale.edu/trc/index.htm (Accessed July 27, 2011).

79. Desmond Mpilo Tutu, *No Future without Forgiveness* (New York: Doubleday, 1999), 31.

80. I expand this argument in chap. 4.

81. Mahmood Mamdani, "Amnesty or Impunity? A Preliminary Critique of the Report of the Truth and Reconciliation Commission of South Africa (TRC)," *Diacritics* 32, no. 3–4 (2002).

82. Richard A. Wilson, *The Politics of Truth and Reconciliation in South Africa: Legitimizing the Post-Apartheid State* (Cambridge: Cambridge University Press, 2001), 10.

83. Wilson, an anthropologist, focuses his attention on evaluating the TRC and does not make larger normative claims about the potential of truth commissions. However, I find affinities in his work that support my argument. For example, in his critique of the TRC report, he writes, "An in-depth understanding of the social conditions (racism, class inequality, gender hierarchy, poverty) of wrongdoing is bypassed in favor of the moral category of 'evil' which resolves the problem of meaning: Why did people commit gross human rights violations? Because of the evil system of apartheid. End of story." (Ibid., 54.) Acknowledging and responding to victim testimony in a way that connects them to justice would assist with understanding the social conditions he mentions.

84. See, for example, Jacques Derrida, *On Cosmopolitanism and Forgiveness* (London: Routledge, 2001).

85. Testimony of Sepati Mlangeni, TRC Johannesburg, May 2, 1996., Case Number GO/0195.

86. Ibid.

Chapter Two

1. For more on the issue of what constituted a "gross human rights violation," see Mahmood Mamdani, "Amnesty or Impunity? A Preliminary Critique of the Report of the Truth and Reconciliation Commission of South Africa (TRC)," *Diacritics* 32, no. 3–4 (2002).

2. Richard Wilson describes this moment, "The narratives of victims and witnesses almost always began with the critical event itself—the phone call, the sound of an explosion. . . . After the critical moment, testimonies go in one direction or the other—either into the aftermath and consequences of the event, or they detail at length the events preceding the event. Many testifying at TRC hearings showed no regard for chronology at all, jumping from one episode to another." Richard A. Wilson, *The Politics of Truth and Reconciliation in South Africa: Legitimizing the Post-Apartheid State* (Cambridge: Cambridge University Press, 2001), 49.

3. Jillian Edelstein, *Truth and Lies: Stories from the Truth and Reconciliation Commission in South Africa* (New York: New Press, 2001), 20.

4. For an excellent discussion of how the TRC treated the testimonies of women, see Fiona C. Ross, *Bearing Witness: Women and the Truth and Reconciliation Commission in South Africa* (London: Pluto Press, 2003).

5. Charles Villa-Vicencio and Wilhelm Verwoerd, *Looking Back, Reaching Forward: Reflections on the Truth and Reconciliation Commission of South Africa* (Cape Town: University of Cape Town Press, 2000), 242. See also Mark Sanders, *Ambiguities of Witnessing: Law and Literature in the Time of a Truth Commission* (Stanford, CA: Stanford University Press, 2007).

6. The debate about reparations for slavery in the United States has inspired much academic debate on the topic of reparations. Thomas McCarthy, "Vergangenheitsbewältigung in the USA: On the Politics of the Memory of Slavery," *Political Theory* 30, no. 5 (2002); Martha Minow, *Between Vengeance and Forgiveness: Facing History after Genocide and Mass Violence* (Boston: Beacon, 1998).

7. Ernesto Verdeja, "A Normative Theory of Reparations in Transitional Democracies," *Metaphilosophy* 37, no. 3 (2006).

8. Minow notes that in 1996 only six of the five hundred women who were offered monetary compensation by the Japanese government for sexual crimes committed by the Japanese Army during World War II accepted the compensation. "Most others rejected it because the fund came from private sources rather than from the government itself. Even those who accepted the money, however, emphasized that no monetary payment could remedy the horrors and humiliations they experienced." Minow, *Between Vengeance and Forgiveness*, 105.

9. "Reparations can also have the effect of strengthening public trust in state institutions. In Latin America, where state security apparatuses committed most

of the recent violations, reparations highlight the state's commitment to principles of justice, the rule of law, and citizen welfare, as well as its rejection of past policies against perceived enemies." Verdeja, "A Normative Theory of Reparations," 493.

10. Promotion of National Unity and Reconciliation Act, 1995, Office of the President, South Africa.

11. For a discussion about how the South African legal community understood the mandate and role of the TRC, see David Dyzenhaus, *Judging the Judges: Truth, Reconciliation, and the Apartheid Legal Order* (Evanston, IL: Northwestern University Press, 1998).

12. Catherine M. Cole elucidates this tension in her discussion of the mothers of the Guguletu Seven, who expressed rage and sadness in a dramatic way during their testimonies at the TRC. She writes, "This incident from the Guguletu Seven hearings demonstrates that while only some truths could be contained within the commission's mandate and procedures, other truths constantly erupted in the live, embodied experience of public hearings. Yes, everyone had to perform, but the structure and format of live hearings also allowed room for those moments when individual agents took charge in unscripted and unexpected ways." Catherine M. Cole, "Performance, Transitional Justice, and the Law: South Africa's Truth and Reconciliation Commission," *Theatre Journal* 59, no. 2 (2007): 186.

13. In contrast, Gibson uses survey data and quantitative analysis to argue that reconciliation at the individual level, understood as trust and respect directed to those of other races (among other factors), was aided by the TRC process. James L. Gibson, *Overcoming Apartheid: Can Truth Reconcile a Divided Nation?* (New York: Russell Sage Foundation, 2004), 330; Wilson, *The Politics of Truth and Reconciliation*.

14. Wilson, *The Politics of Truth and Reconciliation*, xix.

15. See, for example, his discussion of the Sharpeville massacre and the communication of vengeance in local courts. Ibid., 199.

16. Ibid., 15.

17. Cornell is interested in both the philosophical and lived implications of *ubuntu* and this has led her to form the Ubuntu Project at the Stellenbosch Institute for Advanced Studies. The project seeks to explore how South Africans understand the significance of *ubuntu* in their lives, and building on this question, Cornell is interested in the feasibility of incorporating *ubuntu* more fully into legal frameworks. The project is also committed to engaging with critics who say that *ubuntu* is no longer relevant to the worldview of most South Africans.

18. Drucilla Cornell and Karin van Marle, "Exploring Ubuntu: Tentative Reflections," *African Human Rights Law Journal* 5, no. 2 (2005). For connections between *ubuntu* and restorative justice within a framework of legal pluralism,

see Drucilla Cornell, "uBuntu, Pluralism and the Responsibility of Legal Academics to the New South Africa," *Law and Critique* 20, no. 1 (2009).

19. Wilson, *The Politics of Truth and Reconciliation*, 45.

20. Madisha Mabotha Nurster, TRC Testimony, July 17, 1996. Pietersburg. Case Number 00513. Emphasis added.

21. See, for example, Miroslav Volf, *Exclusion and Embrace: A Theological Exploration of Identity, Otherness, and Reconciliation* (Nashville: Abingdon Press, 1996).

22. See Minow, *Between Vengeance and Forgiveness*.

23. Truth and Reconciliation Commission hearings, June 18, 1996.

24. For a quantitative assessment of how frequently forgiveness was articulated by witnesses, see Audrey R. Chapman and Hugo van de Merwe, eds., *Truth and Reconciliation in South Africa: Did the TRC Deliver?* (Philadelphia: University of Pennsylvania Press, 2008).

25. Gregory Edmund Beck, TRC testimony, April 29, 1996. Johannesburg. Case Number GO/0135. Emphasis added.

26. Villa-Vicencio and Verwoerd, *Looking Back, Reaching Forward*.

27. See Chapman and van de Merwe, *Truth and Reconciliation in South Africa*.

28. Heidi Grunebaum and Yazir Henri, *Re-membering Bodies, Producing Histories: Holocaust Survivor Narrative and Truth & Reconciliation Commission Testimony* (Cape Town: Direct Action Centre for Peace & Memory, 2005), 9.

29. "The core victims of the crime against humanity, of this 'system of enforced racial discrimination and separation,' could not have been individuals; they had to be *entire communities* marked out on grounds of race and ethnicity. Their injuries included forced relocation, forced disruption of community and family life, coerced labor through administrative and statutory regulation of movement and location, and so forth. To address their grievances required reparations for communities, not for individuals." Mamdani, "Amnesty or Impunity?" 54.

30. Although Chapman finds that the TRC actually initiated the subject of forgiveness in less than 5 percent of the cases, it still shaped the overall orientation of the commission. She writes, "Whether intentionally or not, commissioners frequently seemed to misinterpret comments of deponents. Not infrequently a deponent told the commissioners he would not forgive anyone, with the commissioner ignoring or misconstruing the statement in his summary remarks. Nor did commissioners seem inclined to probe, even when contradictory statements were made." Chapman and van de Merwe, *Truth and Reconciliation in South Africa*, 79.

31. Priscilla B. Hayner, *Unspeakable Truths: Facing the Challenge of Truth Commissions* (New York: Routledge, 2001), 156.

32. Testimony of Hester Grobelaar, TRC Johannesburg, May 2, 1996. Case Number GO/0121.

33. In his writings about the Amnesty Committee of the TRC, Allen Feldman focuses on the way that the *braai* form of torture (a form of burning alive) was deeply embedded in the political and economic cultures of apartheid life. The Amnesty Committee did not contextualize the violence in light of these realities and thus put forth its own form of a coercive narrative about how acts of violence could be remembered. He writes, "These interrogations, tortures, murders and body disposals, irrespective of their practical political goals and content, legitimized excessive disproportionate violence that sustained and fed the perpetrators of these atrocities at multiple levels of act, memory and meaning. These atrocities were re-enactments, material forms of anamnesis for the assailants that had only the most tenuous connection to anti-communist political or military strategies. . . . In neglecting the hegemonic contours of institutional memory, the TRC failed to develop a self-reflexive relationship to its own technologies of memory and failed to confront the human rights danger in not recalling the disproportionate character of so-called politically motivated institutional violence." Allen Feldman, "Strange Fruit: The South African Truth Commission and the Demonic Economies of Violence," *Social Analysis* 46, no. 3 (2002): 247, 60.

34. The topic will be addressed in chap. 4.

35. Testimony of Zimasile Joseph Bota, TRC Grahamstown, April 7, 1997. Case Number EC0509/96. Emphasis added.

36. Veena Das finds catharsis to be a misguided way to understand what is necessary in the wake of mass violence and instead calls for greater attention to mourning and to the ongoing task of acknowledging loss, tasks that state institutions are consistently unable to achieve. Veena Das, "Language and Body: Transactions in the Construction of Pain," *Daedalus* 125, no. 1 (1996). On the significance of mourning, see also Judith Butler, *Precarious Life: The Powers of Mourning and Violence* (London: Verso, 2004).

37. Michael Humphrey offers the argument that the suffering of victims, not victims themselves, is of utmost value to the state and testimony provides a conduit for this goal. If truth commissions continue to be administered as they have been to date, he suggests, "We will witness the recycling of empathy, trying once again to reassure ourselves that through the victims' revelation we can expel violence. Victimhood then becomes a mode of political containment based on the mobilization of shared feelings but without the necessary next step of engagement with the meaning of events for the future." Michael Humphrey, *The Politics of Atrocity and Reconciliation: From Terror to Trauma* (London: Routledge, 2002), 115.

38. See Mamphela Ramphele, "Political Widowhood in South Africa: The Embodiment of Ambiguity," *Daedalus* 125, no. 1 (1996).

39. Susan Sontag, *Regarding the Pain of Others* (New York: Farrar, Straus & Giroux, 2003), 113.

40. Testimony of Moganedi Ntoampe Stephen, TRC Pietersburg, July 19, 1996. Case Number 00581.

41. In their discourse analysis of the testimonies presented to the Human Rights Violations Committee, Hugo van de Merwe and Audrey Chapman of the Center for the Study of Violence and Reconciliation based in Johannesburg used a randomly stratified sample of 429 testimonies to identify patterns in the testimonies, particularly on the topics victims chose to include and how this might be correlated with their gender, race, and class identities. In his analysis, van der Merwe found that only 20 percent of victims chose to address the topic of justice explicitly in their testimonies. The class or race identity of the victim seemed to have a great impact on the willingness to bring up the topic of justice—van der Merwe found that white victims, high-status survivors, and massacre victims were the most likely to approach the subject. Van der Merwe's research suggests that better-educated and high-status victims are much more likely to articulate what they would like to see the government do in terms of justice, and although he did not use anger as an analytical category, connecting its expression to justice would have expanded the number of individuals who could have participated in the conversation. Chapman and van de Merwe, *Truth and Reconciliation in South Africa*, 28–30.

42. Testimony of Andries Koto, TRC Mmabatho, July 8, 1996. No case number. Emphasis added.

43. For another vivid example of this, see Brudholm's discussion of the testimony of Kalu and Villa-Vicencio's response. Thomas Brudholm, *Resentment's Virtue* (Philadelphia: Temple University Press, 2008), 37.

44. Employing a language of what is "normal" also served to bolster the criticism that the TRC failed to place the violence it was investigating in larger historical and social contexts. If they had taken these contexts into account, the possibility of "normal" may have appeared even more ill-suited as a point of reference. Mamdani and Feldman both make the argument that the TRC decontextualized the testimonies, and Fiona Ross suggests that a lack of cultural context had specific implications for women who testified before the commission. She writes, "Hidden within women's words are narratives of the destruction of kinship, of the alteration of time's expected flow, of the power of economies in shaping experience, of the intrusion of the state, and of women's determined attempts to create and maintain families. Read together, the accounts describe the penetration of violence into everyday life. The fact that the contexts of violence were so little elucidated—their taken-for-granted presence in testimonies—is evidence of the power of apartheid in shaping the quotidian world." Ross, *Bearing Witness*; Mamdani, "Amnesty or Impunity?"; Feldman, "Strange Fruit."

45. Cole, "Performance, Transitional Justice, and the Law," 186.

46. Testimony of Yazir Henry, TRC Cape Town, August 6, 1996. Case Number CT00405.

47. Yazir Henry, "A Space Where Healing Begins," in *Looking Back, Reaching Forward: Reflections on the Truth and Reconciliation Commission of South Africa*, ed. Charles Villa-Vicencio and Wilhelm Verwoerd (London: Zed Books, 2000).

48. Antjie Krog, *Country of My Skull: Guilt, Sorrow, and the Limits of Forgiveness in the New South Africa* (New York: Times Books, 1998).

Chapter Three

1. Elizabeth Young-Bruehl, *Hannah Arendt: For Love of the World* (New Haven, CT: Yale University Press, 1982), 337.

2. The *social*, discussed below, is Arendt's term for the realm of human activity that is distinct from both public and private life. It is defined neither by the expectations of generality and political universality required for public life nor by the norms of the private world of the household or intimate relationships. Arendt views the social as an amorphous and dangerous phenomenon, affected by the rise of a commodity-exchange economy and mass society, which threatens to dominate public life.

3. See Margaret Canovan's introduction in Hannah Arendt, *The Human Condition* (Chicago: University of Chicago Press, 1998).

4. Aristotle, *The Politics*, ed. Carnes Lord (Chicago: University of Chicago Press, 1984).

5. Benhabib writes, "The constitution of a public space always involves a claim to the generalizability of the demands, needs, and interests for which one is fighting. . . . Whichever class or social group enters the public realm, and no matter how class or group specific its demands may be in their genesis, the process of public-political struggle transforms the attitude of narrow self-interest into a more broadly shared public or common interest." Seyla Benhabib, *The Reluctant Modernism of Hannah Arendt* (Lanham, Md.: Rowman & Littlefield, 2003), 145.

6. Later historical developments led to categorizing the private as the realm of intimacy, in addition to the necessities of the household.

7. For a good overview of the scholarship, see Mary Dietz, "Feminist Receptions of Hannah Arendt," in *Feminist Interpretations of Hannah Arendt*, ed. Bonnie Honig (University Park: Pennsylvania State University Press, 1995).

8. Cf. "But what distinguishes the worst architect from the best of bees is this, that the architect raises his structure in imagination before he erects it in reality." Karl Marx and Friedrich Engels, "Capital," in *The Marx-Engels Reader*, ed. Robert C. Tucker (New York: W. W. Norton, 1978), 345.

9. For more on the role of storytelling in creating community, see Robert C. Pirro, *Hannah Arendt and the Politics of Tragedy* (Dekalb: Northern Illinois University Press, 2000).

10. Hannah Arendt, *The Human Condition* (Chicago: University of Chicago Press, 1958), 176.

11. Ibid., 179.

12. Kristeva elucidates the value of narrative over mere speech when she says, "If thought is a *sophia*, Arendt says in essence, political action accompanies it, but above all modifies it into a *phronesis* that is able to share in the plurality of living beings. It is through narrative, and not in language in and of itself (which nonetheless is the means and the vehicle in play here), that essentially political thought is realized." Julia Kristeva, *Hannah Arendt: Life Is a Narrative*, trans. Frank Collins (Toronto: University of Toronto Press, 2001), 26.

13. For an example of a scholarly perspective that celebrates the prominence of storytelling in Arendt's writings, see Lynn R. Wilkinson, "Hannah Arendt on Isak Dinesen: Between Storytelling and Theory," *Comparative Literature* 56, no. 1 (2004).

14. Dinesen is the author of her frequently quoted epigraph: "All sorrows can be borne if you put them into a story or tell a story about them." Arendt, *The Human Condition*.

15. Arendt quotes Dinesen (in Arendt's *Men in Dark Times*, 1st ed. [New York: Harcourt, 1968], 97).

16. Andrew Schaap suggests that testimony at truth commissions would also fulfill Arendt's understanding of the role of factual truth. She accepts that facts can be easily manipulated and are never free from interpretation, but they are still the common backdrop against which all action must take place, including new action. Thus, for Schaap: "Without a shared acknowledgement of the brute facts of state violence, a polity lacks a common starting point from which to initiate political reconciliation." Andrew Schaap, *Political Reconciliation* (London: Routledge, 2005), 136.

17. Arendt, *The Human Condition*, xx.

18. Bonnie Honig, "Toward an Agonistic Feminism: Hannah Arendt and the Politics of Identity," in *Feminist Interpretations of Hannah Arendt*, ed. Bonnie Honig (University Park: Pennsylvania State University Press, 1995).

19. While we share similar interests, Lara is more sanguine than I about the possibility of using Arendt to bolster the significance of testimony. She bases this upon the space it opens up for moral learning (the value of critical self-reflection) and writes, "Stories are always concrete. They can share similarities with other stories, but they are always original because they are immersed in finding the particular view of a storyteller." Maria Pia Lara, *Narrating Evil: A Postmetaphysical Theory of Reflective Judgment* (New York: Columbia University Press, 2007), 43.

20. The tension can be seen in two quotations taken from her *Truth and Politics* essay. She writes, "Factual evidence, moreover, is established through testimony by eyewitnesses—notoriously unreliable—and by records, documents, and monuments, all of which can be suspected as forgeries." At the same time, she values the power of narrative in the political realm under certain conditions: "The political function of the storyteller—historian or novelist—is to teach acceptance of things as they are." It is as if the unreliability of the witness must be controlled and harnessed by a gifted storyteller if it is to play an important political role. Hannah Arendt, *Between Past and Future: Eight Exercises in Political Thought* (New York. Penguin Books, 1977), 243, 62.

21. Arendt, *The Human Condition*, 50.

22. Arendt's criticism of the role of compassion in public life was profoundly shaped by her understanding of the writings of Jean-Jacques Rousseau and the way his emphasis on compassion was invoked during the French Revolution. For a discussion of the extent to which Rousseau's philosophy shaped the decisions by Robespierre and others during the French Revolution, see Carol Blum, *Rousseau and the Republic of Virtue: The Language of Politics in the French Revolution* (Ithaca, NY: Cornell University Press, 1986); François Furet, "Rousseau and the French Revolution," in *The Legacy of Rousseau*, ed. Clifford Owen and Nathan Tarcov (Chicago: University of Chicago Press, 1997).

23. "Poverty is more than deprivation, it is a state of constant want and acute misery whose ignominy consists in its dehumanizing force; poverty is abject because it put men under the absolute dictate of their bodies. . . . It was under the rule of this necessity that the multitude rushed to the assistance of the French Revolution, inspired it, drove it onward, and eventually sent it to its doom, for this was the multitude of the poor." Hannah Arendt, *On Revolution* (New York: Viking Press, 1963), 54.

24. See, also, Patrice Higonnet, "Terror, Trauma and the 'Young Marx' Explanation of Jacobin Politics," *Past and Present* 191, no. 1 (2006).

25. Arendt, *On Revolution*, 89.

26. Ibid., 81.

27. Ibid., 80.

28. Ibid., 82.

29. Ibid., 85.

30. As Elizabeth Spelman notes, Arendt's "use of *le peuple* . . . indicates that those who are the objects of the alleged feeling have had no say in the presentation of who they are and what they are going through." Elizabeth V. Spelman, *Fruits of Sorrow: Framing Our Attention to Suffering* (Boston: Beacon, 1997), 64.

31. Ibid., 84.

32. Hannah Arendt, "The Origins of Totalitarianism: A Reply," *Review of Politics* 15, no. 1 (1953): 79.

33. Arendt, *The Human Condition*, 50.

34. Elaine Scarry, *The Body in Pain: The Making and Unmaking of the World* (New York: Oxford University Press, 1985).

35. Ibid., 7.

36. Arendt, *The Human Condition*, 237.

37. Shoshana Felman suggests that, for Arendt, victim testimony causes "numbness" and thus cannot give rise to a radically new vision of the future. Felman does not use the language of the social to address this condition of numbness, but I find affinities with her argument that victim testimony poses a strong threat to Arendt's conservative jurisprudence. Shoshana Felman, *The Juridical Unconscious: Trials and Traumas in the Twentieth Century* (Cambridge, MA: Harvard University Press, 2002), 122.

38. Hanna Fenichel Pitkin, *The Attack of the Blob: Hannah Arendt's Concept of the Social* (Chicago: University of Chicago Press, 1998).

39. Arendt address two of the strongest forces that give rise to the social: "To have a society of laborers, it is of course not necessary that every member actually be a laborer or worker, not even the emancipation of the working class and the enormous political power which majority rule accords to it are decisive here—but only that all members consider whatever they do primarily as a way to sustain their own lives and those of their families. Society is the form in which the fact of mutual dependence for the sake of life and nothing else assumes public significance and where the activities connected with sheer survival are permitted to appear in public." Arendt, *The Human Condition*, 46.

40. Pitkin, *The Attack of the Blob*, 4.

41. Arendt, *The Human Condition*, 47.

42. In her writings on Arendt's *Rahel Varnhagen: The Life of a Jewish Woman*, Benhabib suggests that the social may be seen in an alternative light. Instead of understanding the social as an undesirable alternative to the public sphere, Benhabib portrays the space of the *salon* and the types of friendships it engenders as favorable consequences of modernity. While the more agonistic portrayal of the public sphere found in *The Human Condition* works to exclude women and places constraints on the types of speech that can be considered political, the language of the salons encourages intimacy based on the disclosure of both private and public aspects of the self. Benhabib's construction of the social in Arendt's writing on Rahel Varnhagen serves as a necessary reminder that Arendt's distinction between public and private may be more beholden to context than is usually believed. Yet, for the purposes of my argument, I engage with the dominant conception of the social found in *The Human Condition*. Seyla Benhabib, "The Pariah and Her Shadow: Hannah Arendt's Biography of Rahel Varnhagen," in *Feminist Interpretations of Hannah Arendt*, ed. Bonnie Honig (University Park: Pennsylvania State University Press, 1995), 94.

43. Arendt, *The Human Condition*, 50.

44. I am not suggesting that there be no boundary between public and private, but that, in the period after mass violence, it must be reconsidered because so much of what was supposed to be protected in private life (the body, sexuality, family relationships, etc.) were affected by the violence.

45. Richard Sennett, *The Conscience of the Eye: The Design and Social Life of Cities* (New York: Knopf, 1990).

46. For an exploration of Arendt's relationship to psychoanalysis, see Young-Bruehl, *Hannah Arendt*.

47. Benhabib cites an excerpt about romantic inwardness from Arendt's writing that aptly describes this phenomenon: "Introspection accomplishes two feats: it annihilates the actual existing situation by dissolving it in mood, and at the same time it lends everything subjective an aura of objectivity, publicity, and extreme interest. In mood, the boundaries between what is intimate and what is public become blurred; intimacies are made public, and public matters can be experienced and expressed only in the realm of the intimate—ultimately, in gossip." Benhabib, "The Pariah and Her Shadow," 91.

48. Cf. Bonnie Honig, ed., *Feminist Interpretations of Hannah Arendt* (University Park: Pennsylvania State University Press, 1995).

49. Manqué (adj.): "as a post-modifier. That might have been but is not, that has missed being." Oxford English Dictionary online, www.oed.com. Accessed through Wesleyan University, February 1, 2011; Pitkin, *The Attack of the Blob*, 182.

50. Pitkin, *The Attack of the Blob*, 182.

51. Benhabib, *The Reluctant Modernism of Hannah Arendt*, 194.

52. Hannah Arendt, *Lectures on Kant's Political Philosophy*, ed. Ronald Beiner (Chicago: University of Chicago Press, 1982), 43.

53. Arendt, *Between Past and Future*, 220. Emphasis added.

54. "To think with an enlarged mentality means that one trains one's imagination to go visiting. I must warn you here of a very common and easy misunderstanding. The trick of critical thinking does not consist in an enormously enlarged empathy through which one can know what actually goes on in the mind of all others." Arendt, *Lectures on Kant's Political Philosophy*, 43.

55. Ibid.

56. Benhabib, *The Reluctant Modernism of Hannah Arendt*, 191.

57. Leora Bilsky uses the lens of reflective judgment to examine Arendt's coverage of the Eichmann trial and writes, "Arendt's report on the trial can be read as an exercise in enlarged mentality. Arendt reacted to Eichmann's manifest lack of judgment by attempting to 'enter his shoes' in order to understand the cause of this failure before rendering her judgment. . . . However, Arendt herself failed in two respects. First, she failed to practice enlarged mentality in relation to the Jewish victims. On guard against the flood of emotion that their testimonies might produce in the spectators, she failed to understand the importance

of oral testimonies in general and victims' narratives in particular to the process of enlarged mentality. Second, anxious to render an 'objective' judgment, she seemed to forget her own role as an actor in the Jewish community." Leora Bilsky, *Transformative Justice: Israeli Identity on Trial* (Ann Arbor: University of Michigan Press, 2004), 139.

58. Although Arendt does not address how a lack of an affective connection (e.g., a lack of solidarity) may undermine the ability of an individual to make a judgment as a member of that community, Beiner elaborates on this tension: "The condition of detached judgment is critical distance; thus it may come about that judgment can only be bought at the price of severe alienation of the judging spectator from the community which he judges. . . . Consequently a tragic conflict can arise between political membership and political judgment. Perhaps judgment in such situations inevitably opens the judging subject to the charge of betrayal, perhaps even the very act of judging amounts to an act of betrayal." Beiner's suggestion that judging may be seen as an act of betrayal has interesting implications for thinking about political responses to victim testimony. In some respects, his formulation of betrayal is similar to the frustration voiced by witnesses who felt they had been betrayed by the TRC. They thought that the TRC had "used" their testimonies and offered nothing back in return; their particular stories had become part of a larger judgment that the nation and the international media made about the apartheid era, but it not did help them in their everyday lives. At the same time, the premise that betrayal is a *precondition* of political judgment is overdetermined and it closes off possibilities for thinking about an intermediate level of particularity that allows for the inclusion of emotional insight. There are ways to practice judgment that are attuned to patterns of emotional reflection and do not necessarily alienate the spectator from the community. Ronald Beiner, *Political Judgment* (Chicago: University of Chicago Press, 1983), 115.

59. Arendt, *Lectures on Kant's Political Philosophy.*

60. Ibid., 71.

61. In the following passage Arendt elaborates on the sensus communis as a rational and linguistic mode of communication—one that is distinctly superior to the "gestures" and raw volatility of the emotions: "The *sensus communis* is the specifically human sense because communication, i.e., speech, depends on it. To make our needs known, to *express* fear, joy, etc., we would not need speech. Gestures would be enough, and sounds would be a good enough substitute for gestures if one needed to bridge long distances." Ibid., 70.

62. Ibid.

63. In another line of critique, Bryan Garsten notes that while Arendt's interpretation of the sensus communis serves her desire to make interpersonal communication a central feature of judgment, it denies the singular authority of reason that Kant maintains as foundational. Sensus communis is not so much an

appreciation of the intuitive or experiential responses of citizens as it is a way to subject all ideas to the rigors of critical thinking and the rational autonomy which are the mark of the mature subject. While Arendt may want to include an egalitarian component in which the perspective of "ordinary" citizens can be considered as part of political discourse (as long as it adheres to the requisite separation of particular emotions from generalizable goals), Garsten is adamant that this is not supported by the text in which Kant attributes authority only to "professional reasoners or scholars." Bryan Garsten, *Saving Persuasion: A Defense of Rhetoric and Judgment* (Cambridge, MA: Harvard University Press, 2006), 86.

64. Ronald Beiner, "Hannah Arendt on Judging," in *Lectures on Kant's Political Philosophy* (Chicago: University of Chicago Press, 1982), 107–8.

65. Arendt, *Lectures on Kant's Political Philosophy*, 77.

66. Cf. Aletta J. Norval, "A Democratic Politics of Acknowledgement: Political Judgment, Imagination, and Exemplarity," *Diacritics* 38, no. 4 (2010); Linda Zerilli, "Truth and Politics," *Theory & Event* 9, no. 4 (2006); April Flakne, "Through Thick and Thin: Validity and Reflective Judgment," *Hypatia* 20, no. 3 (2005).

67. Flakne, "Through Thick and Thin," 119.

68. Maurizio D'Entrèves suggests that the concept of exemplary validity is the best way to frame Arendt's discussions of important historical events, such as the American and French Revolutions, as well as the Hungarian uprising of 1956. He writes, "All these events possess the kind of exemplary validity that makes them of universal significance. Thus, by attending to these events in their particularity the historian or judging spectator is able to illuminate their universal import and thereby preserves them as 'examples' for posterity." Maurizio Passerin D'Entrèves, "Arendt's Theory of Judgment," in *The Cambridge Companion to Hannah Arendt*, ed. Dana Villa (Cambridge: Cambridge University Press, 2000), 251.

69. Arendt's sentence "Courage is like Achilles" points to metaphor as a way to bridge the gap between the particular and the universal, a method that Mark Johnson takes up in his book *Moral Imagination*, where he argues that metaphors provide the best way for moving beyond prototypical cases to new ones in the process of moral deliberation. Mark Johnson, *Moral Imagination: Implications of Cognitive Science for Ethics* (Chicago: University of Chicago Press, 1993).

70. Michael Warner's work on *counterpublics*, drawing on work in queer theory, offers a promising way of thinking about the role of the emotions in public life. He writes, "Counterpublics of sex and gender are teaching us to recognize in newer and deeper ways how privacy is publicly constructed. They are testing our understanding of how private life can be made publicly relevant. . . . It is of-

ten thought, especially by outsiders, that the public display of private matters is a debased narcissism, a collapse of decorum, expressivity gone amok, the erosion of any distinction between public and private. But in a counterpublic setting, such display often has the aim of transformation." Arendt would likely have agreed that victim testimony represents "debased narcissism, a collapse of decorum, expressivity gone amok" and she preferred to maintain the standing division between public and private content. In doing so, she would have missed the possibility of transformation that comes not merely from expressing emotion or displaying a private identity but also from letting emotional expression provide clues for political communities to address the needs of citizens after war. Michael Warner, *Publics and Counterpublics* (New York: Zone Books, 2002), 62.

Chapter Four

1. Boltanski evocatively calls the impartial spectator the "spectator of the spectator." Luc Boltanski, *Distant Suffering: Morality, Media, and Politics* (Cambridge: Cambridge University Press, 1999), 49.

2. The distinction between anger and resentment for Smith is based on the legitimacy of the cause; a justifiable injury causes resentment, and anger is the excessive variant of it. I disagree with the distinction and will use only anger when discussing my own typology.

3. As Griswold writes, "Smith seeks to understand and justify the passions as a basis for decent ethical life." Charles Griswold, *Adam Smith and the Virtues of the Enlightenment* (Cambridge: Cambridge University Press, 1999), 14.

4. For more on how integral social interaction is to identity for Smith, see Knud Haakonssen, *Natural Law and Moral Philosophy: From Grotius to the Scottish Enlightenment* (Cambridge: Cambridge University Press 1996).

5. Adam Smith, *The Theory of Moral Sentiments* (Oxford: Clarendon, 1976), I.i.1.1.

6. Ibid., I.i.4.6.

7. Ibid., I.i.1.3.

8. Ibid., I.ii.1.9.

9. Smith is willing to go so far with his assessment of psychological over physical pain that he makes this suggestion, one that seems somewhat off the mark when considered in relation to the physical pain of war: "A disappointment in love, or ambition, will, upon this account call forth more sympathy than the greatest bodily evil." The use of this example may be more revealing as a sign that Smith was not considering actors who had experienced the type of bodily harm with which truth commissions are concerned. Ibid., I.ii.1.6.

10. Ibid., I.i.i.7. Griswold highlights the third category of emotions, the selfish

ones, which include grief and joy and occupy a middle place between the other two. He also notes that the passions may overlap. Griswold, *Adam Smith and the Virtues of the Enlightenment*, 117–18.

11. Ibid., I.ii.intro.1.

12. Ibid., I.ii.3.1.

13. Ibid., I.i.1.4.

14. Ibid., I.i.1.12.

15. In his biography of Smith, Phillipson notes that the death of Smith's own mother prompted an uncharacteristically heartfelt expression of his love. Nicholas Phillipson, *Adam Smith: An Enlightened Life* (New Haven, CT: Yale University Press, 2010).

16. Boltanski makes a similar point when he says that the spectator's sentiment "depends essentially on how the description of the actor we have called the agent is filled out, that is, as either helper full of pity or as cruel prosecutor." Boltanski, *Distant Suffering*, 47.

17. Forman-Barzilai goes so far as to say that the maintenance of social order, not moral perfection, was Smith's primary concern. Fonna Forman-Barzilai, *Adam Smith and the Circles of Sympathy: Cosmpolitanism and Moral Theory* (Cambridge: Cambridge University Press, 2010), 13.

18. D. D. Raphael's reading of Smith's impartial spectator as a mechanism of self-regulation continues to be the dominant one in the scholarship. Raphael identifies this aspect as one of Smith's major contributions to the literature, especially in distinction to Hutcheson and Hume. D. D. Raphael, "The Impartial Spectator," in *Essays on Adam Smith*, ed. Andrew S. Skinner and Thomas Wilson (Oxford: Clarendon, 1975), 85.

19. See Martha Craven Nussbaum, *Upheavals of Thought: The Intelligence of Emotions* (Cambridge: Cambridge University Press, 2001).

20. Ibid., 22.

21. I draw on Nussbaum's chapter entitled "The Stoics and the Extirpation of the Passions." Ibid.

22. Sherman nicely describes the need for "correction" of the emotions in Stoic thought, even though they may have been cognitively revealing in their uncorrected state. "For if passions are through and through reason-based states, then they should be reformable through a method that works specifically on beliefs. If they are no more than aberrant forms of judgment, then persuasion and argument can grab hold without remainder . . . at the heart of such therapy is constant self-watchfulness and comprehensive belief reform." Nancy Sherman, *Making a Necessity of Virtue: Aristotle and Kant on Virtue* (Cambridge: Cambridge University Press, 1997), 105.

23. Forman-Barzilai, *Adam Smith and the Circles of Sympathy*, 79.

24. Smith, *The Theory of Moral Sentiments*, II.i.5.6.

25. For an interesting discussion of Hume's conception of sympathy and its influence on Adam Smith, as well as the medical understanding of sympathy during the Scottish Enlightenment, see Alexander Broadie, "Sympathy and the Impartial Spectator," in *Cambridge Companion to Adam Smith*, ed. Knud Haakonssen (Cambridge: Cambridge University Press, 2006).

26. Eisikovits draws a connection between the sympathy advocated by Smith and the legitimacy of the TRC. He argues that through the details provided by the testimonies, audience members were able to understand the circumstances of fellow citizens and were thus primed to complete the formal tasks of political reconciliation. My theory is skeptical about the substance of the sympathetic connection between victim and audience and places more emphasis on the practice of sharing risk through an engagement with anger. Nir Eisikovits, "Rethinking the Legacy of Truth Commissions: I Am the Enemy You Killed, My Friend," *Metaphilosophybos* 37, no. 3–4 (2006).

27. In Marshall's reading the trope of the actor and spectator is not only a theoretical tool to understanding the nature of sympathy and learn self-command; it provides a unique type of motivation. For all of Smith's Stoic affinities, the spectator model is one that invites most people to be exhibitionists, though philosophers can transcend these concerns through the internalization of the impartial spectator. He writes, "In Smith's view, our state is the theatre, and an intense concern with theatricality governs both our acts and our reaction. According to Smith, we either dread or desire this theatricality, depending upon the point of view of the spectators who represent the eyes of world." David Marshall, "Adam Smith and the Theatricality of Moral Sentiments," *Critical Inquiry* 10, no. 4 (1984): 606.

28. Smith, *The Theory of Moral Sentiments*, I.i.5.1.

29. Ibid., I.i.1.7.

30. Smith writes that resentment is "the safeguard of justice and the security of innocence. It prompts us to beat off the mischief which is attempted to be done to us, and to retaliate that which is already done; that the offender may be made to repent of his injustice, and that others, through fear of the like punishment, may be terrified from being guilty of the like offence." Ibid., I.ii.1.4.

31. In McLachlan's analysis of resentment in Smith, she decouples it from his understanding of sympathy. Rather she shows how the "moralized" version of resentment in Part II of the *Theory of Moral Sentiments* draws upon the more instinctive version of the emotion in Part I. Thus, resentment becomes a sophisticated cognitive tool that includes a social engagement with the perpetrator. While I appreciate her analysis of the internal logic of resentment, the influence of the impartial spectator and the move to self-command play a greater role than she suggests in which types of resentment can be moralized. Alice McLachlan, "Resentment and Moral Judgment in Smith and Butler," in *The Philosophy of*

Adam Smith: Essays Commemorating the 250th Anniversary of the Theory of Moral Sentiments, ed. Vivienne Brown and Samuel Fleishacker (New York: Routledge, 2010).

32. Smith, *The Theory of Moral Sentiments*, II.i.5.6.

33. Ibid., II.i.5.5.

34. "Whether the person who has received the benefit conceives gratitude or not, cannot, it is evident, in any degree alter our sentiments with regard to the merit of him who has bestowed it. No actual correspondence of sentiments, therefore, is here required." Ibid., II.i.5.11.

35. Ibid., III.ii.3.3.

36. The justice advocated by Smith is always negative and implies an infringe ment of one's person or property in a straightforward sense. To emphasize the limits to his negative conception of justice, Smith gives the case of assaulting one's neighbor. Here he makes it clear that his conception of justice should not be confused with benevolence and is only evident once a transgression has occurred: "Mere justice is, upon most occasions, but a negative virtue, and only hinders us from hurting our neighbor. The man who barely abstains from violating either the person or the estate or the reputation of his neighbors has surely very little positive merit. He fulfills, however, all the rules of what is peculiarly called justice, and does every thing which his equals can with propriety force him to do, or which they can punish him for not doing." Ibid., II.ii.1.10.

37. Ibid., I.i.5.5.

38. Ibid.

39. Valihora sees an analogy between Smith's judgments about virtue and aesthetic judgments about taste. Both eschew the absolutes of moral judgments, and while tied to the opinions of others, they are directed toward a higher ideal. In Smith's case, she suggests that this ideal is one of magnanimity and honorable conduct. Karen Valihora, "The Judgement of Judgement: Adam Smith's Theory of Moral Sentiments," *British Journal of Aesthetics* 41, no. 2 (2001): 151.

40. "It is interesting that at one place edition 2 dropped a paragraph which had appeared in edition 1 about the unreliability of the imagination as a 'moral-looking glass'. After speaking of the function of the imagination as the mirror in which we see our own character, Smith had added that, while ordinary mirrors can conceal deformities, 'there is not in the world such a smoother of wrinkles as is every man's imagination, with regard to the blemishes of his own character.'" As potent as the mirror metaphor is for him, Smith realizes that the potential for self-deception is particularly high when it comes to assessing one's own virtues. Raphael, "The Impartial Spectator," 92.

41. Smith, *The Theory of Moral Sentiments*, I.i.4.8.

42. Broadie notes that even though Smith articulates the ideal for the impartial spectator, he is always aware that this best version is "constrained by limited information admixed with error and by an affective nature that can yield to pres-

sure from outside forces and, in yielding, distort the agent's moral judgments. Broadie, "Sympathy and the Impartial Spectator," 184.

43. Smith, *The Theory of Moral Sentiments*, I.i.5.4.

44. "The ancient stoics were of opinion, that as the world was governed by the all-ruling providence of a wise, powerful, and good God, every single event ought to be regarded as making a necessary part of the plan of the universe. . . . No speculation of this kind, however, how deeply soever it might be rooted in the mind, could diminish our natural abhorrence for vice, whose immediate effects are so destructive." These vices, for Smith, include anger, and his fear at its excesses was strong enough to warrant a clear critique of Stoic thought. Ibid.I.ii.3.4.

45. Ibid., I.ii.3.8.

46. Ibid., I.ii.5.3.

47. Raphael notes that in lectures that preceded the publication of *The Theory of Moral Sentiments*, Smith included greater uncertainty about finding a consensus around punishment. Perhaps these exceptions are remnants of this earlier perspective. Raphael, "The Impartial Spectator," 88.

48. Ryan Patrick Hanley, *Adam Smith and the Character of Virtue* (New York: Cambridge University Press, 2009), 187.

49. Smith, *The Theory of Moral Sentiments*, I.i.5.8. Emphasis added.

50. Ibid., I.ii.5.4., 43. Emphasis added.

51. "But if your misfortune is not of this dreadful kind, if you have only been a little baulked in your ambition, if you have only been jilted by your mistress, or are only hen-pecked by your wife, lay your account with the raillery of all your acquaintance." Smith, *The Theory of Moral Sentiments*, I.ii.5.4.

52. My critique of the impartial spectator stands in contrast to the much more positive reading found in Amartya Sen's article "Open and Closed Impartiality." Sen suggests that Smith puts forward a valuable model of what he calls "open impartiality," impartiality that is not confined to the experiences of one's own polity or conventional identity group. Sen's particular interest is in the ability of individuals to make ethical comparisons between cultures, and Smith's open impartiality is much more radical than Rawls's veil of ignorance because it values the evaluation of the spectator who stands at a distance from the situation. This is the spectator from whom we are least likely to *expect* sympathy. Sen applauds the fact that being a cultural or political insider is a burden, not a benefit, for the task of the impartial spectator in Smith's model. I do not see such robust support for sympathy across lines of nation, race, and religion because I question the extent to which Smith's impartial spectator is truly oriented to the actor, able to acknowledge the unsocial emotions, and respond in a politically meaningful way. Amartya Sen, "Open and Closed Impartiality," *Journal of Philosophy* 99, no. 9 (2002).

53. See Smith, *The Theory of Moral Sentiments*, I.ii.3.4.

54. Forman-Barzilai, *Adam Smith and the Circles of Sympathy*, 8.

55. Smith, *The Theory of Moral Sentiments*, III.3.23.

56. Ibid., I.ii.3.5.

57. Ibid., I.ii.3.6.

58. George E. Marcus, *The Sentimental Citizen: Emotion in Democratic Politics* (University Park: Pennsylvania State University Press, 2002).

59. Erin Halperin et al., "Anger, Hatred, and the Quest for Peace: Anger Can Be Constructive in the Absence of Hatred," *Journal of Conflict Resolution* 55, no. 2 (2011).

60. Charles Hirschkind, *The Ethical Soundscape: Cassette Sermons and Islamic Counterpublics* (New York: Columbia University Press, 2006).

61. Ibid., 106.

62. Susan Bickford, *The Dissonance of Democracy: Listening, Conflict, Citizenship* (Ithaca, NY: Cornell University Press, 1996).

63. Ibid., 22.

64. Ibid., 24.

65. Ibid.

66. Smith, *The Theory of Moral Sentiments*, I.i.2.5.

67. Forman-Barzilai's article describes the different types of spaces—proximate, affective, and historical—within Smith's framework and serves to further highlight the potential embodied by the unusual political space of a truth commission beyond ordinary life. Her work also emphasizes the need to cultivate the practices of sympathy within the constraints of each type of space. Fonna Forman-Barzilai, "Sympathy in Space(s): Adam Smith on Proximity," *Political Theory* 13, no. 2 (2005).

68. The distancing of one's own perspective and the setting aside of defensiveness that is required to listen to anger in the way I suggest find affinities with some aspects of impartiality celebrated by Smith (but without the same aspirations to universality). Both models are trying to break the preoccupation with one's own experiences that makes communication between actor and spectator impossible. I thank Don Moon for pointing out this connection.

Chapter Five

1. Audre Lorde, *Sister Outsider* (Trumansburg, NY: Crossing Press, 1984). For an overview of five approaches to understanding the emotions (sensational, behavioral, evolutionary, evaluative, and cognitive), see Cheshire Calhoun and Robert C. Solomon, eds., *What Is an Emotion? Classic Readings in Philosophical Psychology* (New York: Oxford University Press, 1984); Martha Craven Nussbaum, *Upheavals of Thought: The Intelligence of Emotions* (New York: Cam-

bridge University Press, 2001); Antonio R. Damasio, *Descartes' Error: Emotion, Reason, and the Human Brain* (New York: G. P. Putnam's Sons, 1994).

2. Remy Debes, "Neither Here Nor There: The Cognitive Nature of Emotion," *Philosophical Studies: An International Journal for Philosophy in the Analytic Tradition* 146, no. 1 (2009).

3. Jaggar notes that the interplay between the intentional and unintentional aspects of the emotions must be valued in a cognitive-evaluative approach. Emotions "have both 'mental' and 'physical' aspects, each of which conditions the other; in some respects, they are chosen, but in others they are involuntary; they presuppose language and a social order. Thus, they can be attributed only to what are sometimes called 'whole persons,' engaged in the ongoing activity of social life." Alison M. Jaggar, "Love and Knowledge: Emotion in Feminist Epistemology," in *Women, Knowledge, and Reality: Explorations in Feminist Philosophy*, ed. Ann Garry and Marilyn Pearsall (New York: Routledge, 1996), 173.

4. There are affinities between the way I situate the value of anger for political life and Tarnopolsky's work on shame. She writes, "I argue that shame points simultaneously inwards to what the individual desires and believes, and outward to the world of other individuals and groups, as well as to the laws and practices within which he moves and lives. This bipolar or two-directional character of shame is reflected in the fact that it involves the cognitive-affective gaze of an other that reveals a certain inadequacy in the self." Christina H. Tarnopolsky, *Prudes, Perverts, and Tyrants: Plato's Gorgias and the Politics of Shame* (Princeton, NJ: Princeton University Press, 2010), 17.

5. See Damon Linker, "The Uses of Anger," *First Things* 121 (2002); Jen McWeeny, "Liberating Anger, Embodying Knowledge: A Comparative Study of Maria Lugones and Zen Master Hakuin," *Hypatia* 25, no. 2 (2010); Elizabeth V. Spelman, "Anger and Insubordination," in *Women, Knowledge, and Reality: Explorations in Feminist Philosophy*, ed. Ann Garry and Marilyn Pearsall (New York: Routledge, 1996); Gabriele Taylor, *Deadly Vices* (New York: Oxford University Press, 2006); Kenneth S. Zagacki and Patrick A. Boleyn-Fitzgerald, "Rhetoric and Anger," *Philosophy and Rhetoric* 39, no. 4 (2006); Peter F. Strawson, *Freedom and Resentment, and Other Essays* (London: Methuen, 1974).

6. I agree with Lisa Tessman that although the types of social justice concerns that motivated King and Mandela are impossible to contextualize within Aristotle's understanding of slavery, his concept of eudaimonia can still be useful in thinking about the practices of what she calls "liberatory movements." Lisa Tessman, *Burdened Virtues: Virtue Ethics for Liberatory Struggles* (New York: Oxford University Press, 2005).

7. My own perspective has been shaped by the significant work done within black feminist thought that has considered anger as a response to both racism and sexism. See Lorde, *Sister Outsider*; bell hooks, *Killing Rage, Ending Rac-*

ism (New York: Henry Holt, 1995); and Patricia Hill Collins, *Fighting Words: Black Women and the Search for Justice* (Minneapolis: University of Minnesota, 1998).

8. The three dimensions of anger I describe here are frames by which to understand the significance of anger. I am not suggesting that victims necessarily realize or plan for their testimonies to be interpreted in these ways, but there may be a value to making these dimensions explicit at the beginning of a truth commission, especially for the listening public.

9. Calhoun and Solomon, *What Is an Emotion?* 318.

10. Ibid.

11. Ibid., 324.

12. Jon Elster, *Alchemies of the Mind: Rationality and the Emotions* (Cambridge: Cambridge University Press, 1999), 271. (Emphasis added.)

13. Tarnopolsky, *Prudes, Perverts, and Tyrants.*

14. See Aristotle, *The Nicomachean Ethics* (Oxford: Oxford University Press, 1998), and *On Rhetoric*, trans. George A. Kennedy (New York: Oxford University Press, 2007).

15. By using Aristotle as a way to investigate the cognitive significance of anger and its application to testimonies, I do not mean to suggest that the Greek definition is universal or that other languages parallel the emphasis on slight in their definitions of anger. For discussion of the cultural variations of anger, see Catherine Lutz, "Emotion, Thought, and Estrangement: Emotion as a Cultural Category," *Cultural Anthropology* 1, no. 3 (1986); Anna Wierzbicka, *Emotions across Language and Cultures: Diversity and Universals* (Cambridge: Cambridge University Press, 1999); James R. Averill, *Anger and Aggression: An Essay on Emotion* (New York: Springer-Verlag, 1982); Carol Zisowitz Stearns and Peter N. Stearns, *Anger* (Chicago: University of Chicago Press, 1986).

16. Aristotle, *On Rhetoric*, 116.

17. "It is evident that the causes of anger, in Aristotle's view, are far more limited than is the case in English. Anger is not a response to harm as such, even when the harm is intentional. It is not that one is indifferent to deliberate injury, of course, but one reacts to it, if I understand Aristotle correctly, not with anger but with hatred or hostility." David Konstan, *The Emotions of the Ancient Greeks* (Toronto: University of Toronto Press, 2006). The anger contained within testimony at a truth commission does not necessarily fit into the narrow definition, but I consider Aristotle's insights to be valuable more broadly.

18. Fisher evocatively describes anger as a warning about the potential for future violence: "Anger within an ongoing series of actions does two things. It looks backward to put a frame around what has just occurred, and announces that a diminution of the perimeter of the self, of what I think I deserve, has just taken place. But then it also looks forward, putting the other on notice that any next action will be costly, and for that reason, just as in the strategy of tit-for-

tat, anger imagines a future made up of escalating acts that might have taken place if this one had not been protested. Anger insists they not take place and attempts to make them unthinkable. In anger, the first injury is regarded as a test." Philip Fisher, *Vehement Passions* (Princeton, NJ: Princeton University Press, 2002), 187.

19. It is interesting to note that, in his analysis of Aristotle's language and politics, Konstan sees anger, rather than hatred, as the basis for genocide in Greek accounts. David Konstan, "Anger, Hatred, and Genocide in Ancient Greece," *Common Knowledge* 13, no. 1 (2007).

20. Barbara Koziak, *Retrieving Political Emotion: Thumos, Aristotle, and Gender* (University Park: Pennsylvania State University Press, 2000).

21. Plato, Richard W. Sterling, and William C. Scott, *The Republic*, 1st ed. (New York: Norton, 1985).

22. Koziak, *Retrieving Political Emotion*, 96–97.

23. See William V. Harris, *Restraining Rage: The Ideology of Anger Control in Classical Antiquity* (Cambridge, MA: Harvard University Press, 2001).

24. Ibid., 275.

25. See Simon Kemp and K. T. Strongman, "Anger Theory and Management: A Historical Analysis," *American Journal of Psychology* 108, no. 3 (1995); Averill, *Anger and Aggression*.

26. "Outlaw emotions are 'inappropriate' emotions, that is, emotions that are considered disproportionate to the circumstances or that are occasioned by stimuli that do not normally elicit those responses. A woman might be humiliated, saddened, or infuriated, not flattered, by leers and whistles on the street. Her boss's or clients' bawdy jokes might prompt her to retreat into her shell or arouse her indignation instead of the laughter and camaraderie that these humorists expect. The prevailing norms and values that govern interpretations of subjective experience classify these ostensibly misdirected or overblown emotions as aberrations and make it impossible to see them for what they are." Diana Tietjen Meyers, "Emotion and Heterodox Moral Perception: An Essay in Moral Social Psychology," in *Feminists Rethink the Self* (Boulder, CO: Westview Press, 1997), 145.

27. Spelman, "Anger and Insubordination," 267.

28. Spelman's writing can nicely be applied to the case of truth commissions emphasized here: "The censorship of anger is a way of short-circuiting, of censoring, judgments about wrong-doing . . . to silence anger may be to repress political speech." Ibid., 272.

29. Testimony of Lendiso Richard Ndumo Galela, South African Truth and Reconciliation Commission, Grahamstown, South Africa, April 8, 1997. No case number. Emphasis added.

30. In actuality, the Reparation and Rehabilitation Committee of the TRC was widely criticized for not providing more material reparations to the victims.

In 2003, President Thabo Mbeki announced that families of victims would receive a payment of $3,900, amounting to a total far less than the TRC had recommended. Ginger Thompson, "South Africa Will Pay $3900 to Apartheid Victims' Families," *New York Times*, April 16, 2003.

31. Testimony of Ellen Kuzwayo, South African Truth and Reconciliation Commission. Soweto. July 22, 1996. No case number. Kuzwayo was a well-known activist, and her death was covered in the international press. Donald J. McNeil Jr., "Ellen Kuzwayo, Anti-Apartheid Crusader, Dies at 91," *New York Times*, April 22, 2006.

32. Testimony of Ellen Kuzwayo, TRC Soweto. July 22, 1996. No case number. Emphasis added.

33. Both the Galela and Kuzwayo testimonies focus on how black manhood has been affected by the violence and the transition. This attention to gender is part of what could be revealed in a cognitive-evaluative account and later connected to the work of restorative justice.

34. Testimony of Johannes Frederik Van Eck, TRC Nelspruit, September 3, 1996. Case Number 0707. Emphasis added.

35. Brudholm's concept of nested or compounded resentments is useful here. He writes, "To the degree that the victim's response to various post-atrocity policies or attitudes is seen as related only to the 'darker' complex of original atrocities and their related emotional responses (outrage, horror, consternation, fear) and remainders (shame, guilt, distrust, and the like), this narrow focus leads in turn to a truncated understanding." Thomas Brudholm, *Resentment's Virtue: Jean Amery and the Refusal to Forgive* (Philadelphia: Temple University Press, 2008), 58.

36. Brudholm cites Améry, ibid., 104.

37. Maria Lugones, "Hard-to-Handle Anger," in *Overcoming Racism and Sexism*, ed. Linda A. Bell and David Blumenfeld (Lanham, MD: Rowman & Littlefield, 1996), 210.

38. Antjie Krog, Nosisi Mpolweni, and Kopano Ratele, *There Was This Goat: Investigating the Truth Commission Testimony of Notrose Nobomvu Konile* (Scottsville: University of KwaZulu-Natal Press, 2009).

39. The hearings of the Guguletu Seven at the Amnesty Committee were the scene of the shoe-throwing incident, described in chap. 2. Konile was not the woman who threw the shoe.

40. Krog, Mpolweni, and Ratele, *There Was This Goat*, 54.

41. Ibid., 184.

42. Testimony of Nomakula Evelyn Zweni, TRC Cape Town, August 22, 1996. Case Number CT/00104.

43. Ibid.

44. The confrontational value of anger is similar to the prominence of upheaval within agonistic theory as a way to show the limitations of politics, justice,

and the possibility of consensus. Davide Panagia takes the concept of upheaval further, and his understanding of the possibilities of sensation as a political category bridges the confrontational and kinetic dimensions. He writes, "The limits posed by sensation's unrepresentability thus interrupt our conventional ways of perceiving the world and giving it value. I argue that such moments of interruption (or what I will variously call disarticulation or disfiguration) are political moments because they invite occasions and actions for reconfiguring our associational lives." Davide Panagia, *The Political Life of Sensation* (Durham, NC: Duke University Press, 2009), 3.

45. Capturing the crux of this position, Thurman writes, "Anger when bound up with hate overwhelms the reasonable person with a painful vice-grip and uses him or her as a slave or tool to injure or destroy the target of that hateful anger, regardless of whether this action destroys the tool in the process. It is never useful, never justifiable, always harmful to self as well as others." Robert A. F. Thurman, *Anger: The Seven Deadly Sins* (Oxford: Oxford University Press, 2005), 8.

46. See McWeeny, "Liberating Anger"; Peter Vernezze, "Moderation or the Middle Way: Two Approaches to Anger," *Philosophy East and West* 58, no. 1 (2008).

47. Thurman, *Anger*, 124.

48. Catherine M. Cole, *Performing South Africa's Truth Commission: Stages of Transition* (Bloomington: Indiana University Press, 2010), 11.

49. "That which each voice as voice signifies—namely, the uniqueness and the relationality that the vocal manifests—does not even get proposed as a matter for reflection. Stripped of a voice that then gets reduces to a secondary role as the vocalization of signifieds, logos is thus taken over by sight and gravitates increasingly toward the universal." Adriana Cavarero, *For More than One Voice: Toward a Philosophy of Vocal Expression* (Stanford, CA: Stanford University Press, 2005), 42.

50. Ibid.

51. Bonnie Honig, "Antigone's Two Laws: Greek Tragedy and the Politics of Humanism," *New Literary History* 41, no. 1 (2010): 18.

52. Jean-Paul Sartre, *Sketch for a Theory of Emotions* (London: Routledge, 2003).

Chapter Six

1. Danielle S. Allen, *Talking to Strangers: Anxieties of Citizenship after Brown v. Board of Education* (Chicago: University of Chicago Press, 2004), 4.

2. Walker's formulation presents another way to think about the initial conditions for an engagement with anger: "What is essential in meeting the resentment of victims of injustice is that there be clear practices of communal acknowledge-

ment that assert the victims' deservingness of repair and the wrongdoer's obligation to make amends, as well as communal determination to see that meaningful
repair is done." Margaret Urban Walker, *Moral Repair* (Cambridge: Cambridge
University Press, 2006), 144.

3. In light of the debate about what reconciliation and justice mean in the
transitional period, the question of what the goals of a truth commission should
be is still active. I agree with Doxtader's reading of the rhetorical force of reconciliation but think that the goal of trust can and should be more explicit than
that. It can have both substantive and procedural markers. Erik Doxtader, "Reconciliation—A Rhetorical Concept/ion," *Quarterly Journal of Speech* 89, no. 4
(2003).

4. See Philip Pettit, "The Cunning of Trust," *Philosophy & Public Affairs* 24,
no. 3 (1995): 218.

5. For more on the relationship between hope and trust, see Victoria McGeer,
"Trust, Hope, and Empowerment," *Australasian Journal of Philosophy* 86, no. 2
(2008).

6. For an excellent discussion of the costs of pity, see Elizabeth V. Spelman,
Fruits of Sorrow: Framing Our Attention to Suffering (Boston: Beacon, 1997).

7. It is interesting to note that Aristotle writes that in his distinction between atechnic (nonartistic) and entechnic (artistic) "witnesses, testimony of
slaves taken under torture, contracts and the like" are all considered atechnic (bk. 1, chap. 2). Testimony, particularly that of persons who do not have the
status of citizens, is not seen to require the same attention as artistic types of
speech which include persuasion and interpretation on the part of the listener.
For my purposes, testimony should be placed in the category of artistic speech.
For entechnic speech, Aristotle indicates that the success of persuasion relies on
trust between the speaker and listener and the process for gaining this trust lies
with establishing a shared sense of what is honorable or noble (bk. 1, chap. 9).
Through a common idea of the good, the one who listens comes to believe that
the ultimate goals of the speaker are in agreement with his own and is better able
to consider more complex claims. This insight can be brought to bear in an interesting way on testimonies of anger in truth commissions. It seems to be that
testimonies marked by anger have difficulty gaining the trust of listeners in this
way. Aristotle, *On Rhetoric*, tran. George A. Kennedy (New York: Oxford University Press, 2007).

8. Karen Jones, "Trust as an Affective Attitude," *Ethics* 7, no. 1 (1996).

9. William Connolly, *Pluralism* (Durham, NC: Duke University Press, 2005),
125.

10. Stephen K. White, "'Critical Responsiveness' and Justice," *Philosophy &
Social Criticism* 24, no. 1 (1998): 76.

11. "The term 'restorative justice' is usually attributed to Albert Eglash

(1977), who sought to differentiate between what he saw as three distinct forms of criminal justice [retributive, distributive, and restorative]." James Dignan, *Understanding Victims and Restorative Justice* (Berkshire: Open University Press, 2005). Braithwaite has used empirical evidence to show that restorative justice satisfies victims, offenders, and communities better than existing criminal justice practices. See John Braithwaite, *Restorative Justice and Responsive Regulation* (New York: Oxford University Press, 2002).

12. See Adam Crawford and Todd R. Clear, "Community Justice: Transforming Communities through Restorative Justice?" in *Restorative Justice: Critical Issues*, ed. Eugene McLaughlin et al. (London: Sage, 2003); Chris Cunnen, "Reparations and Restorative Justice: Responding to the Gross Violation of Human Rights," in *Restorative Justice and Civil Society*, ed. John Braithwaite and Heather Strange (Cambridge: Cambridge University Press, 2001).

13. Bell and O'Rourke argue that restorative justice may not be advantageous for women during the transitional justice period; see Christine Bell and Catherine O'Rourke, "Does Feminism Need a Theory of Transitional Justice? An Introductory Essay," *International Journal of Transitional Justice* 1, no. 1 (2007).

14. Annalise Acorn, *Compulsory Compassion: A Critique of Restorative Justice* (Vancouver: UBC Press, 2004).

15. "Every year they drove two undesirable members of the community out of the city in rituals resembling stonings to deal with the problem of the city's guilt and implication in violence. Such a scapegoat is called *pharmakos*. The word *pharmakos* is the human equivalent of *pharmakon*, which means both medicine and poison. . . . The festival was an admission that a system of punishment founded on the principle of retribution requires explicit acknowledgement of the mutual implication of citizens with one another." Danielle S. Allen, "Democratic Dis-ease: Of Anger and the Troubling Nature of Punishment," in *The Passions of the Law*, ed. Susan Bandes (New York: New York University Press, 1999), 198.

16. Ibid.

17. I thank Philip Pettit for bringing this point to my attention.

18. Allen, *Talking to Strangers*, 25.

19. Annette Baier, "Trust and Antitrust," *Ethics* 96 (1986): 259. Emphasis added.

20. Walker, *Moral Repair*, 210.

21. Allen, *Talking to Strangers*; ibid.

22. Pettit's standards for institutions are relevant for truth commissions and provide another way to understand the conditions for active listening mentioned in the previous chapter. Pettit, "The Cunning of Trust," 224.

23. Russell Hardin, *Trust and Trustworthiness* (New York: Russell Sage Foundation, 2002).

24. Bernard Williams, "Formal Structures and Social Reality," in *Trust: Making and Breaking Cooperative Relations*, ed. Diego Gambetta (New York: Blackwell, 1988), 10.

25. Thomas Dumm, *Loneliness as a Way of Life* (Cambridge, MA: Harvard University Press, 2008).

26. Ibid., 120.

27. The parable could also be read as an ethical issue that demands making an exception to an accepted and legitimate rule because of fidelity to a higher ideal.

28. Jones, "Trust as an Affective Attitude," 7–8.

29. Ibid., 7.

Epilogue

1. Lisa Tessman, *Burdened Virtues: Virtue Ethics for Liberatory Struggles* (New York: Oxford University Press, 2005), 107.

2. She writes, for example, "Politically resistant anger, then, will have trouble hitting the right target: those responsible for perpetrating injustice. Nevertheless, as hard as it may be to target anger well, anger that fails in its targeting is not to be praised; there is no temptation to praise it, though, because it is not even helpful as an oppositional force in the service of liberatory politics." Ibid., 122.

3. I take Gürsözlü's point that trying too hard to reconcile agonistic and deliberative approaches does a disservice to the core ideas of both, yet the framework here seeks both to intensify the agonistic aspects of discussion through including a space for anger and to seek to achieve trust, a value embedded within the liberal deliberative approach. The juxtaposition of these two concepts is meant to alter conventional understandings of both approaches. Fuat Gürsözlü, "Debate: Agonism and Deliberation—Recognizing the Difference," *Journal of Political Philosophy* 17, no. 3 (2009).

4. Harvey M. Weinstein, "The Myth of Closure, the Illusion of Reconciliation: Final Thoughts on Five Years as Co-Editor-in-Chief," *International Journal of Transitional Justice* 5, no. 1 (2011).

Bibliography

Acorn, Annalise. *Compulsory Compassion: A Critique of Restorative Justice.* Vancouver: UBC Press, 2004.

Allan, Alfred and Marietjie. "The South African Truth and Reconciliation Commission as a Therapeutic Tool." *Behavioral Sciences and the Law* 18 (2000): 459–77.

Allen, Danielle S. "Democratic Dis-Ease: Of Anger and the Troubling Nature of Punishment." In *The Passions of the Law*, edited by Susan Bandes. New York: New York University Press, 1999.

———. *Talking to Strangers: Anxieties of Citizenship after Brown v. Board of Education.* Chicago: University of Chicago Press, 2004.

———. *The World of Prometheus: The Politics of Punishing in Democratic Athens.* Princeton, NJ: Princeton University Press, 2000.

Arendt, Hannah. *Between Past and Future: Eight Exercises in Political Thought.* New York: Penguin Books, 1977.

———. *Eichmann in Jerusalem: A Report on the Banality of Evil.* New York: Penguin, 1994.

———. *The Human Condition.* Chicago: University of Chicago Press, 1998.

———. *Lectures on Kant's Political Philosophy.* Edited by Ronald Beiner. Chicago: University of Chicago Press, 1982.

———. *Men in Dark Times.* [1st ed.] New York: Harcourt, 1968.

———. *On Revolution.* New York: Viking Press, 1963.

Arendt, Hannah, and Karl Jaspers. *Hannah Arendt–Karl Jaspers: Correspondence, 1926–1969.* New York: Harcourt Brace Jovanovich, 1992.

Aristotle. *The Nicomachean Ethics.* Oxford: Oxford University Press, 1998.

———. *On Rhetoric.* Translated by George A. Kennedy. New York: Oxford University Press, 2007.

———. *The Politics.* Edited by Carnes Lord. Chicago: University of Chicago Press, 1984.

Averill, James R. *Anger and Aggression: An Essay on Emotion.* New York: Springer-Verlag, 1982.

Baier, Annette. "Trust and Antitrust." *Ethics* 96 (1986): 231–60.

Ball, Howard. *Prosecuting War Crimes and Genocide.* Lawrence: University Press of Kansas, 1999.

Bass, Gary Jonathan. *Stay the Hand of Vengeance: The Politics of War Crimes Tribunals.* Princeton, NJ: Princeton University Press, 2000.

Beiner, Ronald. "Hannah Arendt on Judging." In Hannah Arendt, *Lectures on Kant's Political Philosophy.* Chicago: University of Chicago Press, 1982.

———. *Political Judgment.* Chicago: University of Chicago Press, 1983.

Bell, Christine, and Catherine O'Rourke. "Does Feminism Need a Theory of Transitional Justice? An Introductory Essay." *International Journal of Transitional Justice* 1, no. 1 (2007): 23–44.

Bell, Macalester. "Anger, Virtue, and Oppression." In *Feminist Ethics and Social and Political Philosophy: Theorizing the Non-Ideal*, edited by Lisa Tessman. New York: Springer, 2009.

Beltrán, Cristina. *The Trouble with Unity.* Oxford: Oxford University Press, 2010.

Benhabib, Seyla. "The Pariah and Her Shadow: Hannah Arendt's Biography of Rahel Varnhagen." In *Feminist Interpretations of Hannah Arendt*, edited by Bonnie Honig. University Park: Pennsylvania State University Press, 1995.

———. *The Reluctant Modernism of Hannah Arendt.* Lanham, MD: Rowman & Littlefield, 2003.

Bickford, Susan. *The Dissonance of Democracy: Listening, Conflict, Citizenship.* Ithaca, NY: Cornell University Press, 1996.

Bilsky, Leora. *Transformative Justice: Israeli Identity on Trial.* Ann Arbor: University of Michigan Press, 2004.

Bisset, Alison. *Truth Commissions and Criminal Courts.* Cambridge: Cambridge University Press, 2012.

Blum, Carol. *Rousseau and the Republic of Virtue: The Language of Politics in the French Revolution.* Ithaca, NY: Cornell University Press, 1986.

Boltanski, Luc. *Distant Suffering: Morality, Media and Politics.* Cambridge: Cambridge University Press, 1999.

Borer, Tristan Anne, ed. *Telling the Truths: Truth Telling and Peace Building in Post-Conflict Societies.* Notre Dame, IN: University of Notre Dame, 2006.

Bowlby, John. *Attachment and Loss, Vol. 2: Separation.* New York: Basic Books, 1973.

Braithwaite, John. *Restorative Justice and Responsive Regulation.* New York: Oxford University Press, 2002.

Broadie, Alexander. "Sympathy and the Impartial Spectator." In *Cambridge*

Companion to Adam Smith, edited by Knud Haakonssen. Cambridge: Cambridge University Press, 2006.

Bronwyn, Anne Leebaw. "Legitimation or Judgment? South Africa's Restorative Approach to Transitional Justice." *Polity* 34, no. 1 (2003): 23–51.

Brooks, Peter. *Troubling Confessions: Speaking Guilt in Law and Literature.* Chicago: University of Chicago Press, 2000.

Brown, Wendy. "Wounded Attachments." *Political Theory* 21, no. 3 (1993): 390–410.

Brudholm, Thomas. *Resentment's Virtue: Jean Amery and the Refusal to Forgive.* Philadelphia: Temple University Press, 2008.

Burack, Cynthia. *The Problem of the Passions: Feminism, Psychoanalysis, and Social Theory.* New York: New York University Press, 1994.

Butler, Judith. *Precarious Life: The Powers of Mourning and Violence.* London: Verso, 2004.

Calhoun, Cheshire, and Robert C. Solomon, eds. *What Is an Emotion? Classic Readings in Philosophical Psychology.* New York: Oxford University Press, 1984.

Card, Claudia. *The Atrocity Paradigm: A Theory of Evil.* Oxford: Oxford University Press, 2002.

Caruth, Cathy, ed. *Trauma: Explorations in Memory.* Baltimore: Johns Hopkins University Press, 1995.

Cavarero, Adriana. *For More than One Voice: Toward a Philosophy of Vocal Expression.* Stanford, CA: Stanford University Press, 2005.

Chapman, Audrey R., and Hugo van de Merwe, eds. *Truth and Reconciliation in South Africa: Did the TRC Deliver?* Philadelphia: University of Pennsylvania Press, 2008.

Christodoulidis, Emilios. "'Truth and Reconciliation' as Risks." *Social and Legal Studies* 9, no. 2 (2000): 179–204.

Chubb, Karin, and Lutz van Dijk. *Between Anger and Hope: South Africa's Youth and the Truth and Reconciliation Commission.* Johannesburg: Witwatersrand University Press, 2001.

Ci, Jiwei. *The Two Faces of Justice.* Cambridge, MA: Harvard University Press, 2006.

Cole, Alyson. *Cult of True Victimhood: From the War on Welfare to the War on Terror.* Palo Alto, CA: Stanford University Press, 2006.

Cole, Catherine M. "Performance, Transitional Justice, and the Law: South Africa's Truth and Reconciliation Commission." *Theatre Journal* 59, no. 2 (2007): 167–87.

———. *Performing South Africa's Truth Commission: Stages of Transition.* Bloomington: Indiana University Press, 2010.

Collins, Patricia Hill. *Fighting Words: Black Women and the Search for Justice.* Minneapolis: University of Minnesota, 1998.

Connolly, William. *Pluralism*. Durham, NC: Duke University Press, 2005.

Connolly, William E. *Identity/Difference: Democratic Negotiations of Political Paradox*. Ithaca, NY: Cornell University Press, 1991.

Coombes, Annie E. *History after Apartheid: Visual Culture and Public Memory in a Democratic South Africa*. Durham, NC: Duke University Press, 2003.

Cornell, Drucilla. "Ubuntu, Pluralism and the Responsibility of Legal Academics to the New South Africa." *Law and Critique* 20, no. 1 (2009): 43–58.

Cornell, Drucilla, and Karin van Marle. "Exploring Ubuntu: Tentative Reflections." *African Human Rights Law Journal* 5, no. 2 (2005): 195–220.

Crawford, Adam, and Todd R. Clear. "Community Justice: Transforming Communities through Restorative Justice?" In *Restorative Justice: Critical Issues*, edited by Eugene McLaughlin, Ross Fergusson, Gordon Hughes, and Louise Westmarland. London: Sage, 2003.

Cunnen, Chris. "Reparations and Restorative Justice: Responding to the Gross Violation of Human Rights." In *Restorative Justice and Civil Society*, edited by John Braithwaite and Heather Strange. Cambridge: Cambridge University Press, 2001.

Dahl, Robert A. *A Preface to Democratic Theory*. Chicago: University of Chicago Press, 1956.

Damasio, Antonio R. *Descartes' Error: Emotion, Reason, and the Human Brain*. New York: G. P. Putnam's Sons, 1994.

———. *The Feeling of What Happens: Body and Emotion in the Making of Consciousness*. San Diego: Harcourt, 1999.

Das, Veena. "Language and Body: Transactions in the Construction of Pain." *Daedalus* 125, no. 1 (1996): 67–92.

Debes, Remy. "Neither Here nor There: The Cognitive Nature of Emotion." *Philosophical Studies: An International Journal for Philosophy in the Analytic Tradition* 146, no. 1 (2009): 1–27.

D'Entrèves, Maurizio Passerin. "Arendt's Theory of Judgment." In *The Cambridge Companion to Hannah Arendt*, edited by Dana Villa. Cambridge: Cambridge University Press, 2000.

Derrida, Jacques. *On Cosmopolitanism and Forgiveness*. London: Routledge, 2001.

Dietz, Mary. "Feminist Receptions of Hannah Arendt." In *Feminist Interpretations of Hannah Arendt*, edited by Bonnie Honig. University Park: Pennsylvania State University Press, 1995.

Dignan, James. *Understanding Victims and Restorative Justice*. Berkshire: Open University Press, 2005.

Douglas, Lawrence. "The Didactic Trial: Filtering History and Memory in the Courtroom." *European Review* 14, no. 4 (2006): 513–22.

———. *The Memory of Judgment: Making Law and History in the Trials of the Holocaust*. New Haven, CT: Yale University Press, 2001.

Doxtader, Erik. "Reconciliation—a Rhetorical Concept/Ion." *Quarterly Journal of Speech* 89, no. 4 (2003): 267–92.

Dumm, Thomas. *Loneliness as a Way of Life*. Cambridge, MA: Harvard University Press, 2008.

Dyzenhaus, David. *Judging the Judges: Truth, Reconciliation, and the Apartheid Legal Order*. Evanston, IL: Northwestern University Press, 1998.

Edelstein, Jillian. *Truth and Lies: Stories from the Truth and Reconciliation Commission in South Africa*. New York: New Press, 2001.

Eisikovits, Nir. "Rethinking the Legacy of Truth Commissions: I Am the Enemy You Killed, My Friend." *Metaphilosophy* 37, no. 3–4 (2006): 489–514.

———. *Sympathizing with the Enemy: Reconciliation, Transitional Justice, Negotiation*. Dordrecht: Republic of Letters, 2009.

Elshtain, Jean Bethke. *Public Man, Private Women: Women in Social and Political Thought*. Princeton, NJ: Princeton University Press, 1981.

Elster, Jon. *Alchemies of the Mind: Rationality and the Emotions*. Cambridge: Cambridge University Press, 1999.

Feldman, Allen. "Strange Fruit: The South African Truth Commission and the Demonic Economies of Violence." *Social Analysis* 46, no. 3 (2002): 235–65.

Felman, Shoshana. *The Juridical Unconscious: Trials and Traumas in the Twentieth Century*. Cambridge, MA: Harvard University Press, 2002.

Felman, Shoshana, and Dori Laub. *Testimony: Crises of Witnessing in Literature, Psychoanalysis, and History*. New York: Routledge, 1992.

Fisher, Philip. *Vehement Passions*. Princeton, NJ: Princeton University Press, 2002.

Flakne, April. "Through Thick and Thin: Validity and Reflective Judgment." *Hypatia* 20, no. 3 (2005): 115–26.

Forman-Barzilai, Fonna. *Adam Smith and the Circles of Sympathy: Cosmopolitanism and Moral Theory*. Cambridge: Cambridge University Press, 2010.

———. "Sympathy in Space(S): Adam Smith on Proximity." *Political Theory* 13, no. 2 (2005): 189–217.

Fraser, Nancy. "Rethinking the Public Sphere: A Contribution to the Critique of Actually Existing Democracy." In *Habermas and the Public Sphere*, edited by Craig Calhoun. Cambridge, MA: MIT Press, 1992.

Frazer, Michael L. *The Enlightenment of Sympathy: Justice and Moral Sentiments in the Eighteenth Century and Today*. New York: Oxford University Press, 2010.

Frye, Marilyn. "A Note on Anger." In *Politics of Reality*. Trumansburg, New York: Crossing Press, 1983.

Furet, François. "Rousseau and the French Revolution." In *The Legacy of Rousseau*, edited by Clifford Owen and Nathan Tarcov. Chicago: University of Chicago Press, 1997.

Garsten, Bryan. *Saving Persuasion: A Defense of Rhetoric and Judgment.* Cambridge, MA: Harvard University Press, 2006.

Gibson, James L. *Overcoming Apartheid: Can Truth Reconcile a Divided Nation?* New York: Russell Sage Foundation, 2004.

Gobodo-Madikizela, Pumla. *A Human Being Died That Night: A South African Story of Forgiveness.* Boston: Houghton Mifflin, 2003.

Gready, Paul. *The Era of Transitional Justice: The Aftermath of the Truth and Reconciliation Commission in South Africa and Beyond.* Oxon: Routledge, 2011.

Grunebaum, Heidi, and Yazir Henri. *Re-Membering Bodies, Producing Histories: Holocaust Survivor Narrative and Truth & Reconciliation Commission Testimony.* Cape Town: Direct Action Centre for Peace & Memory, 2005.

Gürsözlü, Fuat. "Debate: Agonism and Deliberation—Recognizing the Difference." *Journal of Political Philosophy* 17, no. 3 (2009): 356–68.

Haakonssen, Knud. *Natural Law and Moral Philosophy: From Grotius to the Scottish Enlightenment.* Cambridge: Cambridge University Press, 1996.

Habermas, Jürgen. *The Theory of Communicative Action.* Boston: Beacon, 1985.

Habermas, Jürgen, and Peter Dews. *Autonomy and Solidarity: Interviews.* London: Verso, 1986.

Halperin, Erin, Alexandra G. Russell, Carol S. Dweck, and James J. Gross. "Anger, Hatred, and the Quest for Peace: Anger Can Be Constructive in the Absence of Hatred." *Journal of Conflict Resolution* 55, no. 2 (2011).

Halpern, Jodi, and Harvey M. Weinstein. "Rehumanizing the Other: Empathy and Reconciliation." *Human Rights Quarterly* 26, no. 3 (2004): 561–83.

Hanley, Ryan Patrick. *Adam Smith and the Character of Virtue.* New York: Cambridge University Press, 2009.

Hardin, Russell. *Trust and Trustworthiness.* New York: Russell Sage Foundation, 2002.

Harris, William V. *Restraining Rage: The Ideology of Anger Control in Classical Antiquity.* Cambridge, MA: Harvard University Press, 2001.

Hayner, Priscilla B. *Unspeakable Truths: Facing the Challenge of Truth Commissions.* New York: Routledge, 2001.

Henry, Yazir. "A Space Where Healing Begins." In *Looking Back, Reaching Forward: Reflections on the Truth and Reconciliation Commission of South Africa*, edited by Charles Villa-Vicencio and Wilhelm Verwoerd. London: Zed Books, 2000.

Herman, Barbara. "Contingency in Obligation." In *Moral Universalism and Pluralism Nomos XLIX*, edited by Henry Richardson and Melissa S. Williams. New York: New York University Press, 2009.

Higonnet, Patrice. "Terror, Trauma and the 'Young Marx' Explanation of Jacobin Politics." *Past and Present* 191, no. 1 (2006): 121–64.

Hirschkind, Charles. *The Ethical Soundscape: Cassette Sermons and Islamic Counterpublics*. New York: Columbia University Press, 2006.

Hobbes, Thomas. *Leviathan*. Edited by Herbert W. Schneider. New York: Macmillan, 1958.

Honig, Bonnie. "Antigone's Laments, Creon's Grief: Mourning, Membership, and the Politics of Exception." *Political Theory* 37, no. 1 (2009): 5–43.

———. "Antigone's Two Laws: Greek Tragedy and the Politics of Humanism." *New Literary History* 41, no. 1 (2010).

———, ed. *Feminist Interpretations of Hannah Arendt*. University Park: Pennsylvania State University Press, 1995.

———. *Political Theory and the Displacement of Politics*. Ithaca, NY: Cornell University Press, 1993.

———. "Toward an Agonistic Feminism: Hannah Arendt and the Politics of Identity." In *Feminist Interpretations of Hannah Arendt*, edited by Bonnie Honig. University Park: Pennsylvania State University Press, 1995.

hooks, bell. *Killing Rage, Ending Racism*. New York: Henry Holt, 1995.

Humphrey, Michael. *The Politics of Atrocity and Reconciliation: From Terror to Trauma*. London: Routledge, 2002.

International Military Tribunal. *The Trial of German Major War Criminals: Opening Speeches of the Chief Prosecutors*. London: Under the Authority of H.M. Attorney-General by His Majesty's Stationery Office, 1946.

Jackson, Robert H. *The Nürnberg Case*. New York: Knopf, 1947.

Jaggar, Alison M. "Love and Knowledge: Emotion in Feminist Epistemology." In *Women, Knowledge, and Reality: Explorations in Feminist Philosophy*, edited by Ann Garry and Marilyn Pearsall. New York: Routledge, 1996.

Johnson, Mark. *Moral Imagination: Implications of Cognitive Science for Ethics*. Chicago, IL: University of Chicago Press, 1993.

Jones, Karen. "Trust as an Affective Attitude." *Ethics* 7, no. 1 (1996): 4–25.

Kemp, Simon, and K. T. Strongman. "Anger Theory and Management: A Historical Analysis." *American Journal of Pyschology* 108, no. 3 (1995): 397–417.

Kochin, Michael S. *Five Chapters on Rhetoric: Character, Action, Things, Nothing, and Art*. University Park: Pennsylvania State University Press, 2009.

Konstan, David. "Anger, Hatred, and Genocide in Ancient Greece." *Common Knowledge* 13, no. 1 (2007): 170–87.

———. "Aristotle on Anger and the Emotions: The Strategies of Status." In *Ancient Anger: Perspectives from Homer to Galen*, edited by Susanna Braund and Glenn W. Most. Cambridge: Cambridge University Press, 2003.

———. *The Emotions of the Ancient Greeks*. Toronto: University of Toronto Press, 2006.

Koziak, Barbara. *Retrieving Political Emotion: Thumos, Aristotle, and Gender*. University Park: Pennsylvania State University Press, 2000.

Krause, Sharon. *Civil Passions: Moral Sentiment and Democratic Deliberation.* Princeton, NJ: Princeton University Press, 2008.

——. "Desiring Justice: Motivation and Justification in Rawls and Habermas." *Contemporary Political Theory* 4, no. 4 (2005): 363–85.

Kristeva, Julia. *Hannah Arendt: Life Is a Narrative.* Translated by Frank Collins. Toronto: University of Toronto Press, 2001.

Krog, Antjie. *Country of My Skull: Guilt, Sorrow, and the Limits of Forgiveness in the New South Africa.* New York: Times Books, 1998.

Krog, Antjie, Nosisi Mpolweni, and Kopano Ratele. *There Was This Goat: Investigating the Truth Commission Testimony of Notrose Nobomvu Konile.* Scottsville: University of KwaZulu-Natal Press, 2009.

Lara, Maria Pia. *Narrating Evil: A Postmetaphysical Theory of Reflective Judgment.* New York: Columbia University Press, 2007.

Laub, Dori. "Bearing Witness, or the Vicissitudes of Listening." In *Testimony,* edited by Shoshana Felman and Dori Laub. New York: Routledge, 1992.

Leonard, Eric K. *The Onset of Global Governance: International Relations Theory and the International Criminal Court.* Hampshire: Ashgate, 2005.

Leys, Ruth. "The Turn to Affect: A Critique." *Critical Inquiry* 37, no. 3 (2011): 434–72.

Linker, Damon. "The Uses of Anger." *First Things* 121 (2002): 9–10.

Loraux, Nicole. *Mothers in Mourning.* Ithaca, NY: Cornell University Press, 1998.

Lorde, Audre. *Sister Outsider.* Trumansburg, NY: Crossing Press, 1984.

Lugones, Maria. "Hard-to-Handle Anger." In *Overcoming Racism and Sexism,* edited by Linda A. Bell and David Blumenfeld. Lanham, MD: Rowman & Littlefield, 1996.

Lutz, Catherine. "Emotion, Thought, and Estrangement: Emotion as a Cultural Category." *Cultural Anthropology* 1, no. 3 (1986): 287–309.

Mamdani, Mahmood. "Amnesty or Impunity? A Preliminary Critique of the Report of the Truth and Reconciliation Commission of South Africa (TRC)." *Diacritics* 32, no. 3–4 (2002): 33–59.

Marcus, George E. *The Sentimental Citizen: Emotion in Democratic Politics.* University Park: Pennsylvania State University Press, 2002.

Marshall, David. "Adam Smith and the Theatricality of Moral Sentiments." *Critical Inquiry* 10, no. 4 (1984): 592–613.

Marx, Karl, and Friedrich Engels. "Capital." In *The Marx-Engels Reader,* edited by Robert C. Tucker. New York: W. W. Norton, 1978.

Massumi, Brian. *Parables for the Virtual: Movement, Affect, Sensation.* Durham, NC: Duke University Press, 2002.

McCarthy, Thomas. "Practical Discourse: On the Relation of Morality to Politics." In *Habermas and the Public Sphere,* edited by Craig Calhoun. Cambridge, MA: M.I.T. Press, 1992.

———. "Vergangenheitsbewältigung in the USA: On the Politics of the Memory of Slavery." *Political Theory* 30, no. 5 (2002): 623–48.

McGeer, Victoria. "Trust, Hope, and Empowerment." *Australasian Journal of Philosophy* 86, no. 2 (2008): 237–54.

McLachlan, Alice. "Resentment and Moral Judgment in Smith and Butler." In *The Philosophy of Adam Smith: Essays Commemorating the 250th Anniversary of the Theory of Moral Sentiments*, edited by Vivienne Brown and Samuel Fleishacker. New York: Routledge, 2010.

McWeeny, Jen. "Liberating Anger, Embodying Knowledge: A Comparative Study of Maria Lugones and Zen Master Hakuin." *Hypatia* 25, no. 2 (2010): 295–315.

Meyers, Diana Tietjen. "Emotion and Heterodox Moral Perception: An Essay in Moral Social Psychology." In *Feminists Rethink the Self*. Boulder, CO: Westview, 1997.

———. "Narrative Structures, Narratives of Abuse, and Human Rights." In *Feminist Ethics and Social and Political Philosophy: Theorizing the Non-Ideal*, edited by Lisa Tessman. New York: Springer, 2009.

Minow, Martha. *Between Vengeance and Forgiveness: Facing History after Genocide and Mass Violence*. Boston: Beacon, 1998.

Mouffe, Chantal. *The Democratic Paradox*. London: Verso, 2000.

Muldoon, Paul. "The Moral Legitimacy of Anger." *European Journal of Social Theory* 11, no. 3 (2008): 299–314.

Murphy, Jeffrie G., and Jean H. Hampton. *Forgiveness and Mercy*. Cambridge: Cambridge University Press, 1988.

Nancy, Jean-Luc. *Listening*. New York: Fordham University Press, 2007.

Nietzsche, Friedrich Wilhelm. *On the Genealogy of Morals*. Translated by Walter Kaufmann. New York: Vintage, 1967.

Norval, Aletta J. "A Democratic Politics of Acknowledgement: Political Judgment, Imagination, and Exemplarity." *Diacritics* 38, no. 4 (2010): 5–76.

Nussbaum, Martha. *Hiding from Humanity: Disgust, Shame, and the Law*. Princeton, NJ: Princeton University Press, 2004.

Nussbaum, Martha Craven. *Upheavals of Thought: The Intelligence of Emotions*. Cambridge: Cambridge University Press, 2001.

Okin, Susan Moller. *Justice, Gender and the Family*. New York: Basic Books, 1989.

Osiel, Mark. *Mass Atrocity, Collective Memory and the Law*. New Brunswick, NJ: Transaction Publishers, 1997.

Panagia, Davide. *The Political Life of Sensation*. Durham, NC: Duke University Press, 2009.

Pettit, Philip. "The Cunning of Trust." *Philosophy & Public Affairs* 24, no. 3 (1995): 202–25.

Phillipson, Nicholas. *Adam Smith: An Enlightened Life*. New Haven, CT: Yale University Press, 2010.

Pirro, Robert C. *Hannah Arendt and the Politics of Tragedy*. Dekalb: Northern Illinois University Press, 2000.

Pitkin, Hanna Fenichel. *The Attack of the Blob: Hannah Arendt's Concept of the Social*. Chicago: University of Chicago Press, 1998.

Plato. *The Republic*. Trans. Richard W. Sterling and William C. Scott. 1st ed. New York: Norton, 1985.

Ptacek, James. "Resisting Co-Optation: Three Feminist Challenges to Antiviolence Work." In *Restorative Justice and Violence against Women*, edited by James Ptacek. Oxford: Oxford University Press, 2010.

Ramphele, Mamphela. "Political Widowhood in South Africa: The Embodiment of Ambiguity." *Daedalus* 125, no. 1 (1996): 99–118.

Raphael, D. D. "The Impartial Spectator." In *Essays on Adam Smith*, edited by Andrew S. Skinner and Thomas Wilson. Oxford: Clarendon, 1975.

Rawls, John. *A Theory of Justice*. Cambridge, MA: Belknap Press, 1999.

Ross, Fiona C. *Bearing Witness: Women and the Truth and Reconciliation Commission in South Africa*. London: Pluto Press, 2003.

Sanders, Mark. *Ambiguities of Witnessing: Law and Literature in the Time of a Truth Commission*. Stanford, CA: Stanford University Press, 2007.

Sartre, Jean-Paul. *Sketch for a Theory of Emotions*. London: Routledge, 2003.

Scarry, Elaine. *The Body in Pain: The Making and Unmaking of the World*. New York: Oxford University Press, 1985.

Schaap, Andrew. *Political Reconciliation*. London: Routledge, 2005.

Scheler, Max. *Ressentiment*. New York: Free Press of Glencoe, 1961.

Schmidt, Leigh Eric. *Hearing Things: Religion, Illusion, and the American Enlightenment*. Cambridge, MA: Harvard University Press, 2000.

Segal, Charles. "Spectator and Listener." In *The Greeks*, edited by Jean-Pierre Vernant. Chicago: University of Chicago Press, 1995.

Sen, Amartya. "Open and Closed Impartiality." *Journal of Philosophy* 99, no. 9 (2002): 445–69.

Seneca. "On Anger." In *Moral and Political Essays*, edited by John M. Cooper and J. F. Procope. Cambridge: Cambridge University Press, 1995.

Sennett, Richard. *The Conscience of the Eye: The Design and Social Life of Cities*. New York: Knopf, 1990.

Sherman, Nancy. *Making a Necessity of Virtue: Aristotle and Kant on Virtue*. Cambridge: Cambridge University Press, 1997.

Shklar, Judith. *The Faces of Injustice*. New Haven, CT: Yale University Press, 1990.

Shklar, Judith N. *Legalism: Law, Morals, and Political Trials*. Cambridge, MA: Harvard University Press, 1986.

Smith, Adam. *The Theory of Moral Sentiments*. Oxford: Clarendon, 1976.

Solomon, Robert C. *A Passion for Justice: Emotions and the Origins of the Social Contract*. Reading, MA: Addison-Wesley, 1990.

Sontag, Susan. *Regarding the Pain of Others*. New York: Farrar, Straus & Giroux, 2003.

Spelman, Elizabeth V. "Anger and Insubordination." In *Women, Knowledge, Reality: Explorations in Feminist Philosophy*, edited by Ann Garry and Marilyn Pearsall. Boston: Unwin Hyman, 1989.

——. "Anger: The Diary." In *Wicked Pleasures: Meditations on the Seven 'Deadly Sins*, edited by Robert C. Solomon. Lanham, MD: Rowman & Littlefield, 1999.

——. *Fruits of Sorrow: Framing Our Attention to Suffering*. Boston: Beacon, 1997.

Stearns, Carol Zisowitz, and Peter N. Stearns. *Anger*. Chicago: University of Chicago Press, 1986.

Stover, Eric, and Rachel Shigekane. "Exhumation of Mass Graves: Balancing Legal and Humanitarian Needs." In *My Neighbor, My Enemy: Justice and Community in the Aftermath of Mass Atrocity*, edited by Eric Stover and Harvey M. Weinstein. Cambridge: Cambridge University Press, 2004.

Strawson, Peter F. *Freedom and Resentment, and Other Essays*. London: Methuen, 1974.

Strejilevich, Nora. "Testimony: Beyond the Language of Truth." *Human Rights Quarterly* 28, no. 3 (2006): 701–13.

Tarnopolsky, Christina. "Prudes, Perverts, and Tyrants: Plato and the Contemporary Politics of Shame." *Political Theory* 32, no. 4 (2004): 468–94.

Tarnopolsky, Christina H. *Prudes, Perverts, and Tyrants: Plato's Gorgias and the Politics of Shame*. Princeton, NJ: Princeton University Press, 2010.

Taylor, Gabriele. *Deadly Vices*. New York: Oxford University Press, 2006.

Tessman, Lisa. *Burdened Virtues: Virtue Ethics for Liberatory Struggles*. New York: Oxford University Press, 2005.

Thurman, Robert A. F. *Anger: The Seven Deadly Sins*. Oxford: Oxford University Press, 2005.

Tully, James. "The Agonic Freedom of Citizens." *Economy and Society* 28, no. 2 (1999): 161–82.

Tutu, Desmond Mpilo. *No Future without Forgiveness*. New York: Doubleday, 1999.

Valihora, Karen. "The Judgement of Judgement: Adam Smith's Theory of Moral Sentiments." *British Journal of Aesthetics* 41, no. 2 (2001): 138–61.

Verdeja, Ernesto. "A Normative Theory of Reparations in Transitional Democracies." *Metaphilosophy* 37, no. 3 (2006): 449–68.

Vernezze, Peter. "Moderaton or the Middle Way: Two Approaches to Anger." *Philosophy East and West* 58, no. 1 (2008): 2–16.

Villa-Vicencio, Charles, and Wilhelm Verwoerd. *Looking Back, Reaching For-*

ward: Reflections on the Truth and Reconciliation Commission of South Africa. Cape Town: University of Cape Town Press, 2000.

Volf, Miroslav. *Exclusion and Embrace: A Theological Exploration of Identity, Otherness, and Reconciliation.* Nashville: Abingdon, 1996.

Walker, Margaret Urban. *Moral Repair.* Cambridge: Cambridge University Press, 2006.

Warner, Michael. *Publics and Counterpublics.* New York: Zone Books, 2002.

Weine, Stevan M. *Testimony after Catastrophe: Narrating the Traumas of Political Violence.* Evanston, IL: Northwestern University Press, 2006.

White, Stephen K. "'Critical Responsiveness' and Justice." *Philosophy & Social Criticism* 24, no. 1 (1998): 73–81.

Wierzbicka, Anna. *Emotions across Language and Cultures: Diversity and Universals.* Cambridge: Cambridge University Press, 1999.

Wilkinson, Lynn R. "Hannah Arendt on Isak Dineson: Between Storytelling and Theory." *Comparative Literature* 56, no. 1 (2004): 77–98.

Williams, Bernard. "Formal Structures and Social Reality." In *Trust: Making and Breaking Cooperative Relations*, edited by Diego Gambetta. New York: Blackwell, 1988.

Wilson, Richard A. *The Politics of Truth and Reconciliation in South Africa: Legitimizing the Post-Apartheid State.* Cambridge: Cambridge University Press, 2001.

Young-Breuhl, Elizabeth. *Hannah Arendt: For Love of the World.* New Haven, CT: Yale University Press, 1982.

Zagacki, Kenneth S., and Patrick A. Boleyn-Fitzgerald. "Rhetoric and Anger." *Philosophy and Rhetoric* 39, no. 4 (2006): 290–309.

Zerilli, Linda. "Truth and Politics." *Theory & Event* 9, no. 4 (2006).

Index